FORESTRY COMMISSION

DECORATIVE TREES
FOR COUNTRY, TOWN AND GARDEN

Alan Mitchell and John Jobling

HER MAJESTY'S STATIONERY OFFICE

ISBN 0 11 710038 2

Designed by HMSO Graphic Design

HER MAJESTY'S STATIONERY OFFICE

Government Bookshops

49 High Holborn, London WC1V 6HB
13a Castle Street, Edinburgh EH2 3AR
Brazennose Street, Manchester M60 8AS
Southey House, Wine Street, Bristol BS1 2BQ
258 Broad Street, Birmingham B1 2HE
80 Chichester Street, Belfast BT1 4JY

*Government publications are also available
through booksellers*

Printed in the UK for HMSO
Dd 718456 C800 3/84

Contents

Foreword   7

Introduction   9

Visual aid to tree selection   11

Broadleaves   23

Conifers   101

Index to common names   143

ACKNOWLEDGEMENTS

All photographs are by Alan Mitchell with the following exceptions.
Front cover: Douglas Green, Forestry Commission, Photographic
Library, Edinburgh. Back cover: Jarrold Colour Publications.
Pages 25 and 70 (top): Roy Lancaster. Pages 28, 42, 62, 67, 68,
77, 86, 122 (bottom), 123, 131, 142: A–Z Collection.

Foreword

Trees are the natural vegetative climax of the land of Britain, but in present conditions there are less and less opportunities for tree seedlings to survive and reach maturity without protection. As almost all our primal forests have been destroyed over the centuries for cultivation and grazing or as fuel for industry, we are fortunate to have the legacy of trees planted by landowners and perceptive farmers in the 18th and early 19th centuries. What we may not all realise is that these plantings are all reaching the end of their lives at a similar time, and that many field trees have been, and are, being lost through disease, pests, urban spread, hedgerow removal for larger fields, and the other depredations of man.

It is timely therefore to consider the value of trees to our human well-being, and to promote replantings on the scale that our ancestors accomplished. It is my firm view that man needs for his full happiness, a direct contact with the natural rhythms of living things, such as climatic changes, the migration of birds, the breeding cycles of animals, and the growth and seasonal changes of plants. Perhaps nothing gives us such daily contact with seasonal change so well as trees which exhibit their characteristics of leaf, bark, flower, berry, and changing colour even in dense urban surroundings.

It is, of course, important to consider the *scale* of things. As buildings get taller and gardens smaller there is a tendency to grow lesser plants in place of trees, or to plant only the small flowering trees. This policy can lead to a dull monotony of scale and deprive us of the grandeur that is found in forest trees, in large avenues, in beech clumps and in ascending conifers.

In this book the Forestry Commission – which may previously have been thought of as only concerned with a few species of timber producing softwoods – has done a service to the landscape by making available a mass of data on amenity trees. These facts are based on accurate research and the authors consider, with reliable judgement, the merits and disadvantages of each species and variety as well as their form, their features, and their cultural requirements. Such information makes it possible to select exactly the tree which is needed and which is suitable for its location and purpose. It is particularly beneficial that each tree is illustrated – not by a detailed photograph of its best feature – but by a sketch showing the habit, size and form to which it will develop.

While it is tempting to choose on the basis of personal likes and dislikes, and on the attractive features – as one would choose a bunch of cut flowers – these criteria are inadequate in the selection of a tree which is going to stand as a part of its environment for a hundred years. Ecological conditions (no longer an unfamiliar piece of scientific jargon) are essential considerations in landscape design, and trees must not only look well individually but need to be part of the living community in which they stand. They must suit soil, climate, and water levels; they can be a refuge for local wildlife; they should be in scale with their surroundings and they should not be incongruous in the pattern of other vegetation around them, nor in the local and regional character of the part of Britain in which they are to be planted.

These principles may lead one to think that only locally indigenous species should be planted, but this may be unnecessarily restricting. Few of our 'native' trees are wholly indigenous; most of them were introduced at some time in the past. It is true however that a good artist needs only a small palette, and a landscape designer may use but a comparatively small number of species at any one time. However the reasons put forward by the authors for including many unfamiliar and even rare species in the expectation that they will come to be produced commercially, are unassailable and this wide-ranging list is to be welcomed. From it one can easily make a select list for each project of trees which suit the conditions obtaining.

It is to be hoped that this book will contribute to a greater awareness of the individuality of trees; stimulate the nursery trade into a more adventurous stocking of the large, vigorous, but lesser-known tree species; and encourage government bodies, local authorities, landowners, and private individuals in planting more and more trees to maintain our national heritage.

Clifford R V Tandy OBE PPILA RIBA

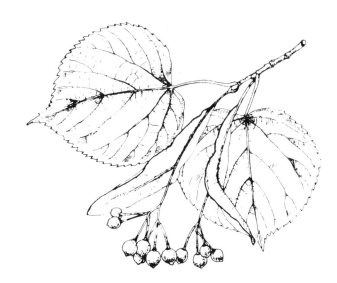

Introduction

This work has been written for those who have decided to plant trees and know where they are proposing to plant them. There is no need therefore to repeat the necessity and value of trees. The need is to make the potential tree planter aware of the wide range of trees from which he can select and to help the selection and make it a less formidable task. The aim is to do this by listing the main features of the trees and their requirements and limitations. The site to be planted will have some inherent features of size, soil, exposure and geographical region which will usually limit the choice. The wish for some aspect like flowers, autumn colour or fruit will narrow the possibilities further.

The inclusion of species which are not readily obtainable may be questioned. It is annoying to decide that a certain tree is just what is needed and then to find it cannot be acquired. The decision to include a number of trees in which this is all too likely to happen is deliberate and is necessary before the position can be improved. Large nurseries tend to concentrate on the well-known and therefore quick-selling species and these have reached this position largely because they are easy to produce and rapidly make saleable plants. The nurseries cannot be expected to produce the less-known trees unless or until they find there is a demand for them. That demand can come only from publications like this one making the trees known. This does work although it sounds rather a forlorn hope. Within a few years of the widely made recommendation to plant Small-leaved lime and Italian alder for example, to replace elms, the trade began strenuous efforts to have these trees for sale. To recommend only the already available tree is to limit drastically the variety in current plantings and to make any future improvement less likely.

Planting is the most critical break in the life of a tree from seed to senility, and the longer it is delayed the bigger the disruption in the growth. Ideally a tree should be planted out when only two or three years old when the root system is small enough to be moved intact and the crown area is small and in the new more exposed conditions make little extra demand on the roots. Juvenile vigour also greatly aids establishment and rapid growth. Trees planted in public places, however, are usually much older and very much bigger than is culturally desirable. Ceremonially planted trees are expected to be big plants, several metres tall because the planter wishes to be seen to have marked the occasion with a tree, and the public expect a tree to be planted when of considerable size. In many places a big, substantial tree is necessary to withstand probable vandalism. Again, many of the species chosen are grown as grafted standards starting life two metres tall. It is therefore frequently unavoidable that a big tree is planted, and there are now quantities of trees well-prepared for this sort of planting. It should be borne in mind that the big crown will, despite a reduction in shoot-growth and size of leaf from the shock of moving, make extra demands on the root-system at a time when that is first establishing its hold on the new soil and the tree will need plenty of water even in a damp season.

The kind of tree which is grown for planting as a large tree is restricted to those able to surmount the problems inherent in the operation. Some desirable trees either will not survive sufficiently frequently to be worthwhile or, if they survive, their subsequent growth pattern is disrupted and their crown and form are spoiled. Magnolias, Tulip-trees and hickories are poorly adapted for moving when large. Eucalypts should never be checked at the roots and they grow at their proper rate of two metres a year only when planted out about eight weeks from seed and 25 cm tall. Larches, Silver firs (*Abies*) and spruces (*Picea*) grow annual whorls of branches and these are about a metre apart at good rapid growth proper to the trees when 2–3 m tall. If moved when about this size the resultant check is severe, the whorls of many years' growth are crowded into the top 30 cm upsetting the balance of the tree and growth is permanently retarded.

When planted small no trees, except sometimes a *Eucalyptus*, should need a stake. They grow sturdily and well-branched from the start. In dry seasons they should be watered well (but the small root-area needs but a tiny fraction of the water that a big transplant must receive) and perennial weeds and grass must be kept clear for a metre radius. Where possible this is best achieved by a deep mulch in a ring round the tree. Groups of trees intended as a windbreak, screen or background, can be established behind a temporary fence by using small transplants which will give, at very little expense and with simple planting and no stakes or ties, far more rapid and effective results than big, staked individual trees.

The limitations of each tree are an important aspect of the selection. Many problems arise in later years due to insufficient attention to these. The most frequent trouble is a tree too large for the available space. In the text here, it is given as a limitation when a tree either takes up a lot of space by its growth or requires to be seen more or less in isolation to show its character. Figures for spread are not given because these increase with age and are variable within species so that a single stated figure can be misleading. As a general working rule most conifers will eventually spread to between a third and a half of their ultimate height whereas most broadleafed trees will extend to at least as great a width as they are tall. Fastigiate cultivars are usually around a quarter as broad as they are high.

A small 'silhouette' appears in most entries to show what shape the mature tree will assume. These 'silhouettes' have not been reproduced at a constant scale due to the large variation in size of the trees listed (2 m to over 40 m high). Instead they are grouped in three sizes: small (2 m to 10 m); medium (11 m to 20 m); and large (over 20 m) and coded with a small capital letter S, M or L respectively.

Descriptions in the text of foliage, bark and so on are detailed only where the character concerned is a feature of the plant for which it may be selected. Otherwise only a brief description is spread through the sections, 'Features' and 'Merits', since this is not a descriptive handbook and fuller details may be found elsewhere.

It will be seen that many of the trees which rank high for decorative value are described as unusual, rare or very rare. In almost all cases stocks could be rapidly built up and amenity plantings would be much enriched. It is hoped that by making trees of this kind more widely known and appreciated a step may be taken in this direction.

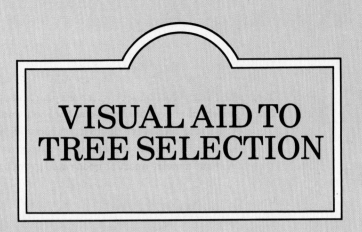

VISUAL AID TO TREE SELECTION

KEY TO SYMBOLS USED IN TABLE

No mark   Not recommended. Unsuitable for conditions; features not significant.

●   Not recommended. Tolerates conditions but not well suited; features slightly developed.

●   Recommended. Grows adequately; suitable for conditions and site; notable features.

●   Strongly recommended. Thrives; amongst best for site; outstanding features.

A   Notable for autumn colours

D   Deciduous (conifers)

E   Evergreen (broadleaves)

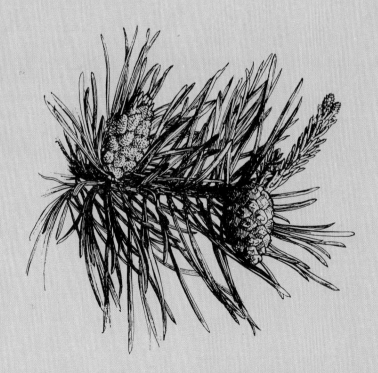

BROADLEAVES

SPECIES/CULTIVAR	SOIL					SITE					SHELTER			FEATURES				
	Wet soils	Clay soils	Chalk soils	Dry sandy soils	Industrial spoils	Seaside	Exposed sites	Smoke and fumes	Small spaces	Roads and streets	Hedges	Screens	Shelter belts	Flowers	Fruit	Bark	Leaves	
Acacia dealbata		●	●	●		●		●						●		●	●	E
Acer campestre	●	●	●	●	●	●	●	●			●		●				●	A
A. davidii	●	●	●	●			●	●								●		A
A. hersii	●	●	●	●		●	●	●							●	●		A
A. lobelii		●	●			●	●	●	●	●								
A. macrophyllum	●	●	●	●		●	●	●									●	
A. negundo 'Variegatum'	●	●	●	●		●	●	●	●	●							●	
'Auratum'	●	●	●	●		●		●		●							●	
A. nikoense		●	●	●				●						●	●		●	A
A. platanoides	●	●	●	●	●	●	●	●	●			●	●	●			●	A
'Schwedleri'	●	●	●	●			●	●	●					●			●	A
'Drummondii'	●	●	●				●	●	●								●	
A. pseudoplatanus	●	●	●	●	●	●	●	●	●			●	●					
'Worleei'	●	●	●	●													●	
A. rubrum	●	●		●				●		●			●	●			●	A
A. saccharinum	●	●	●	●	●			●		●	●	●					●	A
'Laciniatum'	●	●	●	●				●		●							●	
A. saccharum	●	●	●	●				●		●							●	A
A. velutinum																		
var. *vanvolxemii*	●	●	●	●		●	●	●									●	
Aesculus × carnea	●	●	●	●		●	●	●	●					●				
'Briotii'	●	●	●	●		●	●	●		●				●				
A. flava	●	●	●	●		●	●	●									●	A
A. hippocastanum	●	●	●	●	●			●		●				●	●			
A. indica	●	●	●	●				●		●				●	●	●		
'Sydney Pearce'	●	●	●	●				●		●				●	●	●		
A. turbinata	●	●	●	●		●	●	●						●	●		●	A
Ailanthus altissima		●	●	●	●	●		●		●		●			●		●	
Alnus cordata	●	●	●	●	●	●	●	●		●	●	●		●	●			
A. glutinosa	●	●	●	●	●	●	●	●	●		●	●		●				
A. incana	●	●	●	●	●		●	●	●	●	●	●		●				
'Aurea'	●	●	●	●	●		●	●									●	

● STRONGLY RECOMMENDED   ● RECOMMENDED   ● NOT RECOMMENDED

SPECIES/CULTIVAR	SOIL					SITE					SHELTER			FEATURES			
	Wet soils	Clay soils	Chalk soils	Dry sandy soils	Industrial spoils	Seaside	Exposed sites	Smoke and fumes	Small spaces	Roads and streets	Hedges	Screens	Shelter belts	Flowers	Fruit	Bark	Leaves
'Pendula'	○	○	○	●	●		●	○	○								
'Ramulis-Coccineis'	○	○	○	●	●		●									○	
A. rubra	◎	○	●		●	○		○	●				●				
A. subcordata	●	○	●								●	●					
Betula jacquemontii	○	○	●	○		●	○	○	●							○	
B. lutea	●	●		○			○									●	A
B. maximowicziana	●	○		○			○									●	●
B. nigra	●	○		●						●						●	
B. papyrifera		●		○			○	○		●						●	
B. pendula	●	○	●	●	●	○	●	○	○	○			●			●	A
'Dalecarlica'	○	○	●	○		○	○	●	○							○	● A
'Youngii'	○	○	●	○		○	○									●	
B. pubescens	●	○	●	○	●		○	○	○	●			●				
B. utilis	○	○		○		●	○	○								○	○ A
Buxus sempervirens		○	●	○		●		●	●		●	○	○				E
Carpinus betulus	○	●	○	○	●	●	○	○		●	●	●	●	●			A
'Fastigiata'	○	○	○	○	●	○	○	○	●	○		○	○				A
Carya cordiformis	●	○	●	●			●	○								●	A
C. ovata		○	●	●			●									●	A
C. tomentosa		○					●	○								●	A
Castanea sativa	●	○		●		○	●	○						●	●	●	A
Catalpa bignonioides		○	●	●	●	●		●	○					●	●	●	
'Aurea'		○	●	●	●			○									○
C. × erubescens	○	○	●	○	●	●		●	○					●	●	●	
Cercidiphyllum japonicum	●	●	●													●	A
Cercis siliquastrum		●	○	○		○		●	●					●	●		
Corylus colurna	○	○	○	○			●	○		●						●	
Crataegus crus-galli	○	○	○		●	●	○	○		○	●				●		A
C. × grignonensis	○	●	○			●	○	○			●				○		
C. × lavallei	○	○	○	○	●	●	○	○		○	●			●	●		A
C. monogyna	○	○	○	●	●	●	○	○		●	●		●	●	●		
C. oxyacantha	●	●	○			●	●	○		●				●			
C. × prunifolia	○	○	○	○		●	○	○		●	●				●		● A

Legend: ● strongly recommended · ○ recommended

SPECIES/CULTIVAR	SOIL					SITE					SHELTER			FEATURES			
	Wet soils	Clay soils	Chalk soils	Dry sandy soils	Industrial spoils	Seaside	Exposed sites	Smoke and fumes	Small spaces	Roads and streets	Hedges	Screens	Shelter belts	Flowers	Fruit	Bark	Leaves
Davidia involucrata	○	○	●					○		○				○	●		
var. *vilmoriniana*	○	○	●					○		○				○	●		
Eucalyptus gunnii	●	○	●	○		●	●	○					●	●		●	● E
E. niphophila	●	○		●		●	●	○					●			○	● E
E. nitens	●	○		●		●		●					●			●	● *E*
Euodia hupehensis		○	●	●		○	○			●				○	○		●
Fagus sylvatica		●	●	●	●	○	●	●			●	●	●				● A
'Dawyck'		○	●	●	●	○	●	●	●	○	●						● A
'Asplenifolia'		○	○			●	●	○									
'Pendula'		○	○			●											
'Purpurea'	●	○	○	○	●	○	●	●									●
'Zlatia'		○	●	●	●		●	●		●							● A
Fraxinus americana	○	○		○			○	●					●				● A
F. angustifolia		○	○			●	○	●		●			●				
F. excelsior	●	○	●			○	●	●					●				
F. ornus	●	○	○	●		●	●	○		●				●			
F. oxycarpa	○	○	○	●		○	○	○		○					●	●	
'Raywood'	○	●	○	●		○	○	○		●					●		● A
Gleditsia triacanthos		○	○	●	●		●	●				●			●		● A
'Inermis'		●	○	●	●		●	●		●		●			●		● A
'Sunburst'		●	○	○	●		●	●		●					●		●
Griselinia littoralis	○	○				●	○										● E
Ilex × *altaclarensis* 'Camellifolia'	○	○	○	○		○	○	●			●	●		●			● E
'Golden King'	○	○		○		●	●	●			●	●		●			● E
'Hendersonii'	○	○		○		●	●	●			●	●		●			● E
'Hodginsii'	○	●		○		●	●	●			●	●					● E
I. aquifolium	○	●	●	●		●	●	●			○	●		●			E
'Bacciflava'	○	●	●	●		●	●	●			○			●			E
'Ferox'	○	●	●	○		●	●	●				●					● E
'Handsworth New Silver'	○	●	●			○	●										● E
'Perry's Weeping Holly'	○	●	●	○		●	●	●				●					● E
Juglans nigra	○	○	●				○									●	○

● STRONGLY RECOMMENDED   ○ RECOMMENDED   ● NOT RECOMMENDED

SPECIES/CULTIVAR	SOIL					SITE					SHELTER			FEATURES			
	Wet soils	Clay soils	Chalk soils	Dry sandy soils	Industrial spoils	Seaside	Exposed sites	Smoke and fumes	Small spaces	Roads and streets	Hedges	Screens	Shelter belts	Flowers	Fruit	Bark	Leaves
J. regia	○	○	○	○		○	○	○						○			
Koelreuteria paniculata		○	●	○		●		●		●			●	●			●
Laurus nobilis		○	○	●		●	●	○			●	●	●			●	● E
Ligustrum lucidum		○	○			●	●	●		○	●	●		○			● E
Liquidambar formosana var. *monticola*	○	●	●	●		●	●	●									● A
L. styraciflua	●	●	●	●		○	○	○		●							● A
Liriodendron chinense	●	●	○	○		●		●		●				○			● A
L. tulipifera	○	●	●	●		●		●		●				●			● A
'Aureomarginatum'	○	●	○	●													●
'Fastigiatum'	○	●	○	○		●		●	●	●							● A
Magnolia campbellii	○	●		○		●	●	○						○			
'Charles Raffill'	○			○		●	●	○						○			
M. denudata	○	●	●	○		●	●	○						●			
M. grandiflora 'Goliath'	○	○	●	●		○		●	●					○			● E
M. salicifolia	○		●											○			
Malus × *atrosanguinea*	●	●	○	○		●	○	○		●				○			
M. floribunda		●	○		●	●	○	○		●				○			
M. 'Golden Hornet'	●	●	○	○	●	○	○	○						●	○		
M. hupehensis	●	●	○	○	●	●	●	●		●		●		●	●		
M. 'John Downie'	●	●	○	○		○	○	●		●				○	○		
M. × *purpurea*	●	●	○	○	●	○	○	○		●				○	●		
M. tschonoskii	●	●	●	●	●	●			○		●						● A
Nothofagus dombeyi	●	○		●				●			●						○ E
N. obliqua	○	●	○	○			●	●				●					● A
N. procera		●	●	●			●	●				●					● A
Nyssa sylvatica	○	●															○ A
Paulownia tomentosa		○	○	○		○	●	○		●				●			●
Platanus × *acerifolia*	○	●	○	○	○	●	●	●		●						●	●
'Suttneri'	○	●	○	○		●	●	●		●						●	○
P. orientalis	○	○	○	○		●	●	○		○						●	● A
Populus alba	●	●	●	●	○	●	●	○			●	●				●	○
'Racket'	●	●	●	○	●	○	○	○	●	●							○
'Richardii'	●	●	●	○		○	○	●		○							○

SPECIES/CULTIVAR	SOIL					SITE					SHELTER			FEATURES			
	Wet soils	Clay soils	Chalk soils	Dry sandy soils	Industrial spoils	Seaside	Exposed sites	Smoke and fumes	Small spaces	Roads and streets	Hedges	Screens	Shelter belts	Flowers	Fruit	Bark	Leaves
P. candicans 'Aurora'	●	○	●	●	●	○	●	○									○
P. canescens	●	●	●	○	○	●	●	○				●				●	○
P. × euramericana 'Eugenei'	●	●	○	●	●		●				●						
'Robusta'	●	●	●	●	●	○	○	○			●			○			
'Serotina'	●	●	●	●	○	○	○	○			●						
'Serotina Aurea'	●	●	●	●		○		○									●
P. nigra var. betulifolia	●	●	○	●	○	●	○	●			●						
'Gigantea'	●	●	○	●					●		●						
'Italica'	●	●	○	●		○	○	○	●		●						
'Vereecken'	●	●	○	●		○	○	○	○		●						
P. trichocarpa and cultivars	●	○		●	●	○	○	○			●	●					●
'Balsam Spire'	●	○		●	●		●	○	●		●						
Prunus avium		●	○	○		○	●	○		○		●		○	●		A
'Plena'		●	○	○		○	○	○		○				○			A
P. dulcis	○	○	○	○		○	●	●		●				○			
P. maackii	○	●	○	○		●	●	○								●	
P. padus	○	○	○	○			●	○						●			
'Watereri'	○	○	○	○		○	○	○						●			
P. sargentii[1]	○	○	○	○		○	●	●		●				○			A
'Kursar'	●	○	○	●		●	○	●	●	●				○			
'Shosar'		○	○	●		●	○	●	●	●				●			
P. serrula	○	○	○	○		●	●	○						●		●	
P. 'Amanogawa'	●	○	○	●		●		●	●	○				●			A
P. 'Fugenzo'	●	○	○	●		●		●						●			
P. 'Hokusai'	●	○	○	●		●	●	●		●				●			A
P. 'Horinji'	●	○	○	●		●		●						●			
P. 'Kanzan'	●	○	○	○		○	●	●		○				●			A
P. 'Kiku-shidare'	●	○	○	●		○	●	●	●					○			
P. 'Okiku'	●	○	○	●		●		●		●				●			
P. 'Pink Perfection'	●	○	○	●		●	●	●		○				●			
P. 'Shimidsu'	●	○	○	●		○	○	●						●			

[1] Ornamental cherries normally on *P. avium* rootstock; affected by soils in same manner.

● STRONGLY RECOMMENDED   ○ RECOMMENDED   ● NOT RECOMMENDED

Species/Cultivar	Wet soils	Clay soils	Chalk soils	Dry sandy soils	Industrial spoils	Seaside	Exposed sites	Smoke and fumes	Small spaces	Roads and streets	Hedges	Screens	Shelter belts	Flowers	Fruit	Bark	Leaves
P. 'Shirofugen'	●	○	○	●		○	○	●						●			
P. 'Shirotae'	●	●	○	●		○	●	●						●			
P. 'Tai-haku'	●	○	●	○		●	●	●	○					●			● A
P. 'Ukon'	●	○	●	○		●	●	●	●					●			
P. subhirtella 'Autumnalis'	○	○	○	○		○	○	●						○			
'Pendula'	●	○	○	○		○		○									
P. × *yedoensis*	○	○	○	○		●	●	○		●				●			
Pterocarya fraxinifolia	●	○	○	●			●	○							●		● A
P. × *rehderana*	●	●	●	●			●	○							●		● A
Pyrus calleryana 'Bradford'	○	●	●	●		●	●	●	○	●	●	●					
'Chanticleer'	●	●	●	●		●	○	●	○	●				○			● A
P. salicifolia		●	○	●		○	○	○	○					●			●
Quercus acutissima	●	●		●		●		●		●							●
Q. canariensis	○	○	○	○		○											●
Q. castaneifolia		●	○	○		○		○									●
Q. cerris	○	●	○	○		●	●	●			●	●					●
Q. coccinea	○	●		○				●				●					● A
Q. frainetto	○	●	●	●		○	●	●									●
Q. × *hispanica* 'Lucombeana'	○	●	○	○		●	●	○			●	●					● E
Q. ilex	●	●	●	○		●	●	●			●	●	●				E
Q. macranthera	○	●		○		○	○	○			●	●					●
Q. palustris	○	●		○				○	○		●	●					● A
Q. petraea	●	○	●	●	●	●	●	●									●
Q. phellos	○	●		○		○	●	●		○							●
Q. robur	○	●	●	○	●	○	●	○			●	●					● A
'Concordia'	●	●	●	○													● A
'Fastigiata'	○	●	●	●	●	○		○	●		●						○ A
Q. rubra	○	●	●	○		●	●	●		●							○ A
Robinia pseudoacacia		○	○	●	●	○	●	●		●				●			
'Frisia'		○	○	●	●			●	○	●				●			○
Salix alba	●	●	●	●	●	○	○	●			●					●	●
'Chermesina'	●	●	●	●	●	●	○	●			●	●				●	

17

SPECIES/CULTIVAR	SOIL					SITE					SHELTER			FEATURES			
	Wet soils	Clay soils	Chalk soils	Dry sandy soils	Industrial spoils	Seaside	Exposed sites	Smoke and fumes	Small spaces	Roads and streets	Hedges	Screens	Shelter belts	Flowers	Fruit	Bark	Leaves
'Coerulea'	●	●	●	●	●	●	○	○			●						
'Tristis'	●	●	●	○		○	○	●									
S. caprea	●	●		○	●	○	●				●			●			
S. daphnoides	●	●	○	●	●	○	○	●			●					●	●
S. fragilis	●	●	●		○	●	○	●			●						
S. matsudana 'Tortuosa'	●	○	●	○		●	●	●									
S. pentandra	●	●		●		●	○	●				●					●
Sorbus aria		●	○	○	●	○	○	●		●		●		●	●		● A
'Chrysophylla'		●	●	●		○	○										
'Decaisneana'		●	○	○		●		○		●	●	●		○	○		● A
'Lutescens'		●	●	○		●		○	●	●	●	●		○	○		● A
S. aucuparia	●	○	○	○	●	●	●	●		○	●	●		○	○	○	●
'Beissneri'	○	○	○	○		○	○	○		●						●	● A
'Xanthocarpa'	○	○	○	○		○	○	○		○		●		○	●		
S. cashmiriana	●	●	●	●		○	○	○	○					●	○		
S. cuspidata	●	○	○	○		●	●	○						○	○		○
S. domestica		○		○				○		●				●	●		
S. commixta 'Embley'	○	○	○	○		○	○	●		●				○	○		● A
S. hupehensis	○	○	○	○		○	○	○		●				○	●		●
S. intermedia		●	○	○	○	●	●	●		●				●	●		●
S. 'Joseph Rock'		●	●	○		○	○	●	●	○				●	●		● A
S. sargentiana		●	○	○		●	●	○		○				●	○		● A
S. thibetica 'John Mitchell'	○	●	○	○			○	○		○				○	○		●
S. torminalis	○	●	○	○			○			●							● A
S. 'Wilfrid Fox'		●	○	○		○	●	●		●				●	○		●
Tilia cordata	○	○	○	○	●		●	●		○		○	○	○			
T. euchlora		●	○	○	●	○	○	○		○	●	●					●
T. mongolica		●	●	●		○	○	●		○							●
T. petiolaris		●	●	●		○	○	●		●							●
T. platyphyllos	○	●	○	○	●	○	●	●		●							
'Rubra'	○	○	○	○	●	○	○	○		●						●	
T. tomentosa	○	●	○	○		○	○	●		○			●	●			●
Ulmus carpinifolia		○	●		●	●	●	●		●							A

18   ● STRONGLY RECOMMENDED   ○ RECOMMENDED   ● NOT RECOMMENDED

SPECIES/CULTIVAR	SOIL					SITE					SHELTER			FEATURES			
	Wet soils	Clay soils	Chalk soils	Dry sandy soils	Industrial spoils	Seaside	Exposed sites	Smoke and fumes	Small spaces	Roads and streets	Hedges	Screens	Shelter belts	Flowers	Fruit	Bark	Leaves
var. *cornubiensis*		○	○			○	●	●	●	●	●						A
var. *sarniensis*		○	○	●	●	○	●	●	●	●	●						A
U. glabra	○	●	○			●	○	●			●	●					
'Camperdown'	○	●	○			●		●	●								
'Lutescens'	○	●	○			●		●		●							
U. × hollandica 'Vegeta'		●	●	●		●		●		●	●	●		○			
U. parvifolia	●	○	○			○	●	●		●						●	●
U. pumila	●	●	○			○	●	●									●
Zelkova carpinifolia		●	○	○		●	○										A
Z. serrata		●	●	●		●	●			●	●	●				●	● A
Z. sinica		●	●	●		●	○			●							

CONIFERS

Abies alba	●	○		●		○	○										
A. bracteata		●		○													
A. cephalonica	○	○	○	●			○	○									
A. concolor	○	●															
var. *lowiana*	○	●		○			○	●									
'Violacea'	●	○		●				○									
A. grandis	○	○					●	●									
A. homolepis	○	○		○			○	○									
A. nordmanniana	○	●					○										
A. numidica	○	○		●		○	○	●									
A. procera	○	○		○			●										●
A. veitchii	○	○		●			●										
Araucaria araucana	●	○	●	●		○	○										
Cedrus atlantica	○	○	○	●		○	○	○									
var. *glauca*	○	●	○	●		○	○	○									○
C. deodara	○	●	○	○		○	○										
C. libani	○	●	○	●		●	●	○									
Chamaecyparis lawsoniana	●	●	●	●	●	●	●	●	○		●	●	●				
'Allumii'	●	●	●	○	●	○	●	●	●		●	●	●				●

SPECIES/CULTIVAR	SOIL					SITE					SHELTER			FEATURES			
	Wet soils	Clay soils	Chalk soils	Dry sandy soils	Industrial spoils	Seaside	Exposed sites	Smoke and fumes	Small spaces	Roads and streets	Hedges	Screens	Shelter belts	Flowers	Fruit	Bark	Leaves
'Columnaris'	●	●	●	◐		●	◐	●	●								●
'Ellwoodii'	●	●	●	◐		●	●	●	◐		●						
'Fletcheri'	●	●	●	◐		●	◐	◐		●	●	●					●
'Green Pillar'	●	●	●	◐		●	●	●		●	●	●					●
'Green Spire'	●	●	●	◐		●	●	●		●		●					●
'Hillieri'	●	●	●	◐		●	◐	●	●								
'Lutea'	●	●	●	◐	●	●	●	◐	◐			●	●				●
'Lanei'	●	●	●	◐		●	●	●		●							●
'Pottenii'	●	●	●	◐		●	●	●		●							
'Stewartii'	●	●	●	◐		●	●	◐		●		●	●				●
'Triomphe de Boskoop'	●	●	●	◐		●	●	◐				●	●				●
'Winston Churchill'	●	●	●	◐		●	◐	◐		●							●
'Wisselii'	●	●	●	◐		●	●	●		●							●
C. nootkatensis	◐	●	◐	◐		◐	●	●	●								
C. obtusa	◐	●															
'Crippsii'	◐	●	◐	●		◐	●	◐					●				●
C. pisifera	◐	●		◐		●	●	◐									●
'Aurea'	◐	◐		◐		●											●
'Filifera Aurea'		●		●		◐			●								●
'Plumosa'		●	◐	●		◐		◐									
'Plumosa Aurea'		●	◐	◐		◐		◐									●
'Squarrosa'		●	◐	◐		●	●										
Cryptomeria japonica	●	●	●	◐		◐		◐	◐		●						
'Elegans'	◐	●	●	◐		●											
'Lobbii'	●	●	●	◐		●	◐	●									
× Cupressocyparis leylandii	◐	●	◐	◐	◐	●	●	◐			●	●	●				
'Castlewellan Gold'	◐	●	◐	◐	●	●	●	◐				◐	◐				◐
'Haggerston Grey'	◐	●	◐	◐	◐	●	●	◐			●	◐					
'Leighton Green'	◐	●	◐	◐	◐	●	●	◐			●	●	●				
'Naylor's Blue'	◐	●	◐	◐		◐	●	●	●		●	●					●
'Robinson's Gold'		●	◐	◐		◐	◐	◐									◐
'Stapehill 20'	●	●	◐			●	●	●									

20 ● STRONGLY RECOMMENDED ◐ RECOMMENDED ● NOT RECOMMENDED

SPECIES/CULTIVAR	SOIL					SITE					SHELTER			FEATURES			
	Wet soils	Clay soils	Chalk soils	Dry sandy soils	Industrial spoils	Seaside	Exposed sites	Smoke and fumes	Small spaces	Roads and streets	Hedges	Screens	Shelter belts	Flowers	Fruit	Bark	Leaves
'Stapehill 21'	○	●	○	○	●		○	○			●	●	●				
Cupressus glabra	●	●	●	●		●	○	●	●		○	○	○				●
'Pyramidalis'		●	●	●		○	○	●				○	●				●
C. lusitanica	○		○			●											
var. *benthamii*	●	○		●													
'Glauca'	●	○		●													●
C. macrocarpa	○	●	○	○		●	○	●				○	○				
'Donard Gold'	●	●	○	○		●											●
'Lutea'	●	●	○	○		●	●	●									●
C. torulosa	●	○						●									
Ginkgo biloba	○	●	○	○	●	●	○	○	○	●							● AD
'Fastigiata'	○	○	○	○	●	●	○	●	●	●							● AD
Juniperus drupacea		●	●	○					○								
Larix decidua	○	○	●	○	○	●	●	●				●	●				● AD
L. × eurolepis	○	○	●	○	○	○	●	○				●	●				● AD
L. kaempferi	○	○	●	●	○	○	●	○				●	●				● AD
Metasequoia glyptostroboides	●	●	○	○				○	●							●	● AD
Picea abies	○	●	○		●		○				●						
P. brewerana	○	○	○					●									
P. omorika	○	○	○				○	○	○			●					
P. orientalis	○	●	○	○			●										
'Aurea'	○	●	○	○													
P. pungens var. *glauca*	○	●		●		●	●	○									●
P. sitchensis	●	●			●	○	●	●				●					
Pinus ayacahuite		○		○		●	●	●							○		
P. cembra	●	●	○	●		○	○	○	●								
P. contorta var. *contorta*	●	○		●	●	○	○	○				●					
P. jeffreyi		○		●			○								●		
P. leucodermis	●	●	●	●		○	○	○	●						●		
P. muricata	○	○		●		●	●	●				●					
P. nigra var. *maritima*	○	○	○	●	●	●	○	○				●					
var. *nigra*		○	○	●	●	●	○	○				○					

21

SPECIES/CULTIVAR	SOIL — Wet soils	Clay soils	Chalk soils	Dry sandy soils	Industrial spoils	SITE — Seaside	Exposed sites	Smoke and fumes	Small spaces	Roads and streets	SHELTER — Hedges	Screens	Shelter belts	FEATURES — Flowers	Fruit	Bark	Leaves
P. peuce	●	○	○	○	○	○	○	●									
P. pinaster				●		●	○	●				●			●	●	
P. ponderosa		●		●		●	○									●	
P. radiata	●	○		●	●	●	○					●	●	●			
P. sylvestris		●		●	○		○	●			●		●			●	
P. wallichiana	●	●	●	○				●							○		●
Podocarpus andinus	●	●		○		●	●	●			○						
Pseudotsuga menziesii	○	○		●		●											
var. glauca	●	○		○													
Sequoia sempervirens	●	○		●							●					●	
Sequoiadendron giganteum	○	○	●	◑		○	●	●					●				
Taxodium distichum	●	●	●			●	●	○		●							● AD
Taxus baccata	○	○	○	○		○	●	○			●	●	●				
'Adpressa'	○	○	○	○		○	○	●	●								
'Dovastoniana'	○	○	○	○		●											
'Fastigiata'	○	○	○	○		○	●	○	●								
Thuja occidentalis	●	●	○	●		●	●	○			●	●	●				
'Lutea'	●	●	○	●		●	●										●
'Spiralis'	●	●	○	●		●		○									
T. orientalis	○	●				●	●	●			●						
'Elegantissima'	○	●	○			●		○									●
T. plicata	●	○	○	○		●	○				○	●	●				
'Semperaurescens'	●	○	○	●		●	●										●
'Zebrina'	○	○	○	●		○	●				●	●					●
Thujopsis dolabrata	●	●	●	●		●							●				●
Tsuga canadensis	●	●		○		●	○				●	●	●				
T. caroliniana	○	○															●
T. heterophylla	●	●		●		○	●				●	●	●				
T. mertensiana	○	●		●		○	●	●									●

● STRONGLY RECOMMENDED   ○ RECOMMENDED   ● NOT RECOMMENDED

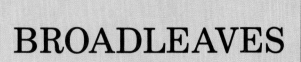
BROADLEAVES

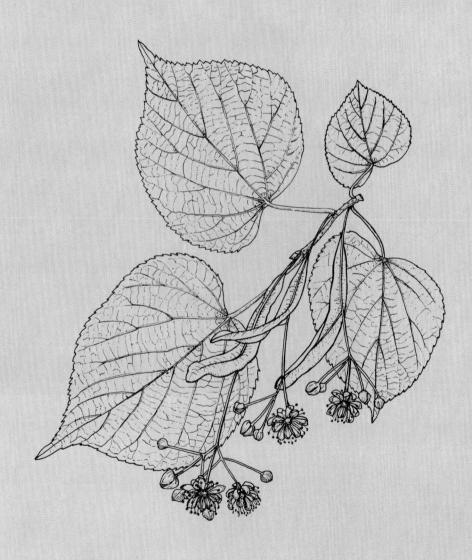

Acacia dealbata
Mimosa

FEATURES: A small tree with chocolate-brown bark and blue-grey shoots which can be 6 m tall in five or six years and carries a fairly dense crown of doubly pinnate leaves with tiny leaflets and a mass of small yellow flowers very early in the year.

MERITS: Rapid growth; much divided bright blue-green foliage; prolific flowers January (Devon) to March (Surrey); very unusual in Britain.

LIMITATIONS: Not hardy as a free-standing tree north and east of the Isle of Wight except in London; against a wall survives in most southern counties but is cut to the ground by severe winters.

ORIGIN: South-east Australia; Tasmania. Introduced 1820.

Acer campestre
Field maple

FEATURES: A sturdy tree of moderate growth, often 15 m tall and known in Kent and in Angus to 25 m. The crown of straight shoots, upswept towards their tips is a fairly dense dome. The small leaves are deeply lobed with a few blunt teeth on the biggest lobes and emerge bright-green a little before the small yellow flowers, but become dark-green. New leaves during the summer emerge dark-red. The winged fruit is stained crimson during the summer. The shoots and branches in a hedge especially often have a deeply flanged corky bark.

MERITS: Reliable good gold, sometimes crimson, in middle to late autumn. Good growth on shallow soil over chalk. Good resistance to exposure. A native, countryside tree.

LIMITATIONS: Grows poorly without some lime in the soil. Can be shrubby and broad. Somewhat dull in summer.

ORIGIN AND OCCURRENCE: Native to England, locally abundant on chalk in the South, North to the Midlands, often as a hedge; planted but locally and uncommon in Wales, Scotland and Ireland.

Acer davidii
Père David's maple

FEATURES: Several very distinct forms of this maple are in cultivation. The most frequent is 'George Forrest' which has an open crown, arching branches and large leaves, shallowly three-lobed on long scarlet petioles. Another from frequently seen tends to have several stems and more dense foliage, with oblong-lanceolate leaves unlobed. This one colours well in autumn. All forms have striped bark and copious flowering.

MERITS: The bark is handsomely striped blue-white on smooth green. Good foliage; in most forms, large leaves with scarlet stalks and shoots. Prolific and precocious in flower and fruit, the long racemes from each short shoot adding interest to the crown, whether as yellow-green flowers or strings of small winged fruit. Some forms colour well in autumn, pale- or dark-orange, red and crimson.

LIMITATIONS: Young trees apt to die back seriously for some years and need pruning to shape. A spreading tree in most forms, requiring room. Requires shelter and prefers a rich soil.

ORIGIN AND OCCURRENCE: Central China. One form was introduced in 1879; another in 1902 and 'George Forrest' probably after 1910. This maple is found in collections; many large and a few small gardens, and occasionally in public parks.

Acer hersii
Hers's maple

FEATURES: A very olive-green tree, this colour being dominant in the bark, new and mature leaves, shoots, flowers and fruit. The crown is dense and partly pendulous as long, unbranched shoots arch over.

MERITS: An exceedingly attractive tree with bright striped bark, elegantly arching branches closely clothed in rich olive-green leaves, copious flowers and fruit and spectacular orange, red and crimson autumn colours.

LIMITATIONS: Good growth requires shelter, a good soil and plenty of room. Not suitable in smoky atmospheres but can be planted in cities with clean air.

ORIGIN AND OCCURRENCE: China. Introduced in 1924 and now much planted in large gardens and in some parks.

Acer lobelii
Lobel's maple

FEATURES: This tree, with nearly vertical long branches, bears few side-shoots and has long one-year growth which is well bloomed whitish or violet. The leaves are broad, light-green and five-lobed, the three main lobes with waved or obscurely toothed margin. Autumn colour is a fleeting yellow at best.

MERITS: An upright tree narrow until very old, holding its branches clear of street furniture. Vigorous in growth, hardy and not particular as to soil, this tree is often 6 m tall within six years of planting but slows thereafter. The leaves are decorative as they are held generally level and the tips of the lobes rise from them.

LIMITATIONS: Tall-growing, and somewhat gaunt in winter.

ORIGIN AND OCCURRENCE: Southern Italy, introduced in 1838. The few big old trees are in the major collections (Westonbirt, Gloucestershire; Smeaton House, East Lothian) but young trees are in a few parks and occasionally beside roads.

Acer macrophyllum
Oregon maple

FEATURES: A sturdy, big-boled tree with orange and brown, fissured bark, and long branches which arch over at the top of a high-domed crown. The leaves, which may be 25 × 25 cm or more, are deeply divided into three main lobes each with a few big blunt teeth. The flowers are on long, thick racemes expanding during flowering to 25 cm long and the fruit have wings 5 cm long at a narrow angle from big, white-bristled nuts. Autumn colour is dull-brown.

MERITS: A fine tree of good vigour, big stature, very large foliage and unusual flowers, and one that can grow in city air if not too smoky. A good tree in London parks.

LIMITATIONS: Very few; probably best in slight shelter and good soils, but needs room.

ORIGIN AND OCCURRENCE: Coastal British Columbia south to mid, and sparsely to south, California. Introduced by David Douglas in 1827 but known and perhaps in cultivation in America in 1812, the Oregon maple is nowhere in Britain more than a rare tree. It is found in a few of the largest gardens north to Roxburghshire and in Ireland west to Co. Tipperary and since the tallest known is in the former and that with the largest bole is in the latter, these cannot be the range-limits in those directions.

Acer negundo
'Variegatum'
Variegated ash-leafed maple

FEATURES: A broad-headed tree seldom 9 m tall with level branching. This is a female form and the flower racemes hang from shoot-ends in March before the leaves unfold. The shoots are smooth and dark-green, becoming bloomed violet in their second year. The leaves have five or seven large acuminate leaflets with a few coarse teeth and fall early without giving noticeable autumn colours.

MERITS: A good tree in towns, withstanding a paved root-run and tolerant as to soil. The heavily variegated foliage makes a splash of bright-white where this can be unexpected and pleasing; the curved wings of abundant fruit are white, green and pink and, hanging in bunches, make objects of interest at close quarters.

LIMITATIONS: Constant attention (inspection every two to three years) is necessary to maintain the variegated foliage which is weaker than the green-leafed shoots that sprout regularly. A short-lived tree and apt to lean with age.

ORIGIN AND OCCURRENCE: This cultivar was raised in Toulouse in 1845. The species ranges across North America with distinct varieties in the far west. The ordinary eastern form was first sent in 1688 to Bishop Compton at Fulham Palace. There are several variegated forms and these are commonly planted in suburban streets, front gardens, parks and car-parks, but in the absence of attention the variegated foliage is lost. The type, green-leafed tree is common but is very rarely planted as it has little to recommend it, and occurs so often only because the variegated forms will revert unless the green foliage is pruned out.

'Auratum'

This is a similar tree but the foliage is a bright golden colour, greening somewhat in late summer. It arose in Berlin in 1891 and whilst quite frequent in suburban south London and in big gardens in the south, it is reputed to be less hardy than other forms. Highly decorative and desirable where it can be grown.

Acer nikoense
Nikko maple

FEATURES: This unusual tree has smooth, grey bark and a broad crown with level or slightly ascending branches. The flowers are quite big for a maple, two bunches of three hanging from each node, pale-yellow and cup-shaped, and are followed rapidly by big fruit densely pubescent with broad wings.

MERITS: A maple giving splendid autumn colouring, tolerant of lime in the soil, and making a neat, rather broad, small tree.

LIMITATION: Not good in an exposed position.

ORIGIN AND OCCURRENCE: This tree is from the mountains of Japan and was introduced in 1881. It is unusual in small gardens or public plantings but good specimens are in many of the biggest gardens.

Acer platanoides
Norway maple

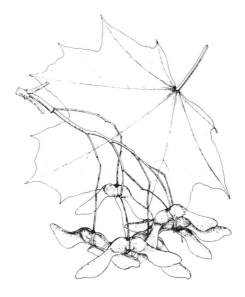

FEATURES: A fine, big tree with pale grey bark finely folded rather than fissured, on a short bole. The crown is a large hemisphere, densely leafed in summer. The flowers are in clusters and have bright-yellow petals, opening before the leaves emerge, usually at the end of March, and remain prominent until the leaves unfold. The leaves are broad, thinly textured and generally five-lobed, the lobe tips and those of the few large teeth on the lobes, drawn out into fine points.

MERITS: A strong-growing tree, decorative from the March flowering until late October's autumn colours, fitting well in rural landscapes and thriving on chalk or acid sands. Mostly bright-gold turning orange in autumn, but a few are bright-red.

LIMITATION: Soon becomes a big, spreading tree, casting a dense shade.

ORIGIN AND OCCURRENCE: Ranging widely from the Caucasus Mountains through central Europe and north to southern Sweden and Norway, this species was being grown in Edinburgh Royal Botanic Garden before 1683. It is now common in parks, large gardens, even in the suburbs of towns and in shelter belts, particularly on and near the chalklands.

'SCHWEDLERI'

CULTIVARS: 'Schwedleri' arose in Germany in 1870 and is distinguished by the dark-red calyx and by smaller petals giving the flowers a largely red appearance. The emerging leaves are red-brown and in summer they are tinged purple. It is really the autumn colour that gives this tree a place, for the leaves turn early and are orange, scarlet and crimson.

'DRUMMONDII'

'Drummondii' arose in Stirling 1903 with a dense crown of leaves held rather level and heavily spotted and margined pale-cream or white. This is a highly effective tree on its own.

Acer pseudoplatanus
Sycamore

FEATURES: A very robust tree with grey, smooth bark in young trees. On big boles the bark is pale orange-brown or pinkish-orange, broken into long scales which come away. The crown is a huge dome, often broader than tall but in the regions of best growth (see below) it may be very tall and less broad. Leafing out occurs early, especially in shade, and late growth in July may emerge bright pink. Flowering occurs when the leaves are newly expanded, slender catkins of flowers without visible petals hanging some 10 cm long and attracting hordes of bumblebees. The leaves are soon very dark on red petioles in young trees but may be yellowish on pink petioles in old trees. There is rarely any worthwhile colour in the autumn, but occasionally they turn a good, bright-yellow.

MERITS: An extremely tough and adaptable tree. This is the only tree to attain tree-stature in some areas much exposed to sea winds and often the only one on shallow limestone rocks. It is also excellent in polluted air.

LIMITATIONS: A vigorous coarse tree needing much room and invading the neighbourhood through seedlings; has little attraction to wildlife except aphids and bees. In a park or garden the crown is dull and casts a heavy shade. It is also far from easy to grow on from seedlings that are moved.

ORIGIN AND OCCURRENCE: The species spreads across central and southern Europe from the Caucasus Mountains to Corsica and to near Paris. It may have been brought here by the Romans but is more likely to have been introduced to Scotland some time before 1600. It is locally abundant on good damp soils over limestone or chalk and is common in all parks and gardens. Even small suburban gardens in inner London frequently have trees growing rapidly where the owner is slow with his saw. The best trees, tall with good boles, are curiously confined largely to Kent, the Yorkshire Pennines, Cumbria, Dumfriesshire and Perthshire.

CULTIVARS: **'Worleei'** is a strong-growing form with golden leaves on scarlet petioles and useful for a splash of colour on a fairly severe site.

L

Acer rubrum
Red maple

FEATURES: This useful and decorative tree has smooth, pale-grey bark, darkening and cracking into long flakes with age. Long boles are rare, most trees dividing fairly low into several ascending or vertical stems. Leaves vary in size and shape among trees, there being great variation in the wide natural range, but they are always distinguishable by the sightly silvered underside, predominant three-lobing and rounded base. Fruit appear early, and are shed very early during May, but are irregular in occurrence.

MERITS: A tree of strong growth and neat crown when young, this is an attractive tree with a long season. In March, well before the leaves unfold, the shoots are wreathed in bright, deep-red, little flowers. The leaves are fairly small, predominantly three-lobed and somewhat silvered beneath, on scarlet petioles. In autumn young trees turn through yellow to bright-scarlet then deep-red, although some old trees show deep-red only on some parts of the crown. In America, autumn colours range from bright pale-yellow to deep-purple.

LIMITATIONS: A vigorous tree of reasonably large ultimate size and rather untidy crown, this tree is reputed not to thrive or colour well on chalky soils. Unattractive in winter.

ORIGIN AND OCCURRENCE: Is exceedingly common on mountainsides and in lowland swamps throughout the Appalachian Mountains from Newfoundland south and beyond to Texas. Among the first to be introduced from this area, as early as 1656, the tree has never become more than distinctly infrequent, verging on the rare.

Acer saccharinum
Silver maple

FEATURES: This tall-growing vigorous tree has flowers which are bunched against the slender, straight shoots and open green and red in February or March. These are an interesting change in aspect rather than a spectacle. The leaves unfold brownish-red at first, and are silvered beneath. The five lobes are deeply divided by acute sinuses and bear many sharp teeth. Fruit are soon shed and seldom borne in this country.

MERITS: This tree is among the fastest of all in early growth and very soon makes an attractive specimen on any but the driest sites. When established it can tolerate considerable encroachment on its rooting area by paving or tarmac, and a great variety of soils. It grows very well over chalk or limestone and the biggest trees tend to be on damp clay-loams overlying limestone. The deeply lobed and sharply toothed leaves are decorative and their silvery undersides and pale upper side, together with their moderate size and the open pendulous habit give the tree a light, delicate appearance despite its great size. Autumn colours, yellows and pinks, are restrained but good; rarely bright with scarlet and crimson.

LIMITATIONS: A tree of very vigorous early growth often making shoots 1.5 m long; this demands plenty of space as the tall, domed crown bears increasingly spreading, arched branches. These crowns are liable to breakage in high winds, so the tree cannot be recommended for sites which are more than moderately exposed. The bole, with bark more shaggy with increasing age, can bear dense growths of sprouts. A short-lived tree.

ORIGIN AND OCCURRENCE: A common tree in the Appalachian Mountain system, extending north to the Great Lakes and Quebec, this was

introduced in 1725. It is fairly frequent in large gardens and parks, around towns especially, and has been used beside some main roads. The cultivar 'Laciniatum' has been planted in and around pedestrian precincts and car-parks recently, by some Local Authorities.

CULTIVARS: 'Laciniatum' is much planted and decidedly more decorative. It has a more pendulous crown developed in early youth; leaves more deeply lobed and jaggedly toothed, their upper surface a shiny deep-green, are borne on red petioles.

Acer saccharum
Sugar maple

FEATURES: The Sugar maple is not so rare as is often thought. It makes a big tree with an open crown of handsome leaves, each with three main lobes acutely pointed and with a few acute large teeth. In general this tree resembles the Norway maple but differs in the bark breaking into slightly shaggy plates; in the teeth of the leaves being finely rounded at the tips and the lobes more deeply cut, and there is usually a purple band across the shoot by each pair of leaves.

MERITS: This tree seems able to grow strongly on a variety of soils and in climates as varied as Kent, Perthshire and eastern Ireland. It is a tree of attractive foliage and of good autumn colours. In New England, the fiery scarlet and subtle flame-orange colours are the best of all the fall displays but in the cool summer areas in Britain these cannot be expected. Some trees turn good scarlet and gold but the leaves tend to be shed early.

LIMITATIONS: The Sugar maple requires full light and plenty of room. Where the leaves are shed early it spends rather a lot of the year as a somewhat gaunt tree.

ORIGIN AND OCCURRENCE: The Sugar maple ranges in the wild from Newfoundland to Texas and is an abundant countryside tree in New England and a street and town square tree throughout the south-eastern States where it is infrequent in the wild. It was introduced in 1735 but has never been much planted. Large gardens in Scotland and Ireland tend to have a specimen or two but fewer are seen in England.

Acer velutinum
var. *vanvolxemii*
Van Volxem's maple

FEATURES: An unusual, sturdy tree with the bark on the stout bole unusually smooth grey, except for concentric rings around branch scars. Flowers open amongst the new leaves on erect, domed inflorescences but are themselves rather insignificant and yellowish-green. Grown amongst other trees, this species makes a fine, smooth-barked, long bole, and bears handsome, large foliage.

MERITS: A fine tree of good growth and no particular requirements. The foliage is always large and often huge, very like a giant and very green sycamore.

LIMITATIONS: A vigorous tree with level branches and a widely spreading crown if open grown, this tree needs plenty of room to develop unless grown among others for its fine bole. The big, substantial leaves will block drains and gutters and make roads slippery. This foliage rarely shows any autumn colour beyond brief and vague yellows.

ORIGIN AND OCCURRENCE: A Caucasian tree, this was introduced in 1877. Fine specimens exist in a few big collections (Westonbirt; Tortworth Court; Royal Botanic Garden, Edinburgh) but it is decidedly rare.

Aesculus × carnea
Red horse-chestnut

M

FEATURES: This tree is often grafted on Common horse-chestnut although it comes true from seed and this is therefore unnecessary. The change in bark is apparent at the union for this tree has a warm red-brown bark, smooth over large areas between blisters and wide fissures. The leaves are big with very short petioles on the coarsely toothed leaflets. The flowers open later than those of the Common horse-chestnut and are a dull, slightly purpled-red, tubular at base. The fruit is smooth-skinned enclosing a dull-brown conker or several small ones.

MERITS: This tree seems to be popular with the public although it has no real merits and is altogether inferior to *Aesculus flava*.

LIMITATIONS: A spreading tree casting a deep shade from a broad crown, this is also of unreliable health over long periods, being prone to a canker in the branches. Except to some extent in the cultivar 'Briotii', the foliage is dark and the flowers are not a pure colour, so the tree should be used for occasional variation and not for massed effect.

ORIGIN AND OCCURRENCE: A hybrid between the

Common horse-chestnut and the American Red buck-eye (*A. pavia*), of European origin in around 1800, this tree is very common on village greens and in parks and gardens. It is unusual among hybrids in breeding true.

CULTIVAR: **'Briotii'** is a superior form selected in France in 1858. It has shiny leaves of greater substance and lighter colour, while the flowers are a clear, bright-red. It is much to be preferred at all times.

Aesculus flava
(syn. *A. octandra*)
Yellow buck-eye

FEATURES: This most desirable, decorative tree bears shoots which are shiny, fawn-grey with pink-brown buds with the margins of the scales brighter-pink. The crown is domed and old trees are relatively tall, narrow and slightly pendulous. A most desirable tree and an excellent alternative to the Red horse-chestnut in most situations.

MERITS: A tree of exceedingly handsome foliage, this has fine slender leaflets of bright, glossy-green and finely toothed on slender petioles. The flowers are clear yellow, tubular, on small panicles in good numbers. In early autumn the foliage begins to turn orange and by mid-October it is orange and scarlet, then crimson, often a spectacular display.

LIMITATIONS: A large, fairly spreading tree, this is all too frequently seen as a graft with an obvious and ugly union with the Common horse-chestnut rootstock at 1.5 m. Seedlings should be available and should be planted exclusively.

ORIGIN AND OCCURRENCE: This tree is frequent on the upper slopes of the Allegheny Mountains to 1,500 m and in some places it is a remarkably fine tree to 43 m tall with a straight bole for 30 m. It was introduced in 1764 but has never become as common as it deserves and is seldom seen outside the largest gardens, collections, and London parks.

Aesculus hippocastanum
Common horse-chestnut

FEATURES: A familiar tree, taken for granted but outstanding as a flowering tree. The bark of old trees becomes red-brown in large, vertical plates which lift away from the bole. The buds are very resinous, rich shiny red-brown. The leaflets are sessile as in *A. turbinata* but differ in this from other Asiatic species and those from America.

MERITS: As a flowering tree this has, in some respects, no equal. It unfailingly yields vast quantities of big panicles of flowers all over the crown, which may be 37 m tall, every year. The fruit are much in demand by schoolboys, although this can lead to dangers (see below), and are highly attractive. It is a remarkably tough tree, especially considering its origin, and withstands with impunity both city air and pavements over its roots. In autumn the leaves of some trees turn early scarlet but the majority turn a good golden colour at the normal time and some then go on to a russet-brown.

LIMITATIONS: A tree growing to a very large size (35–37 m × 2 m diameter). This not only requires room but it should not be planted where the public are likely to spend long periods beneath it, as in school playgrounds or the open grass areas of public parks. This is because after it is about 100-years-old it is liable to shed suddenly a very heavy branch. The gathering of conkers from roadside or public trees can also lead to dangers from the missiles which may be used to dislodge the fruit.

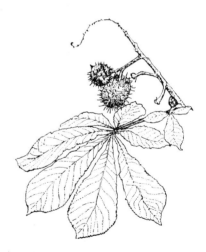

ORIGIN AND OCCURRENCE: This tree is found wild only in a small area of mountains in Albania and Greece. It was first described in 1596 and introduced here probably in 1616 but has long behaved like a native tree. Very common in parks, streets and gardens, it is almost traditional to have a big specimen in the rectory garden and on the village green, and is widely planted in city parks, often in avenues.

CULTIVAR: **'Baumannii'** is a double-flowered form arising at Geneva in 1820. Having double flowers it retains its flowers longer and does not yield any conkers, so it has been planted fairly widely by public authorities.

Aesculus indica
Indian horse-chestnut

FEATURES: A handsome tree on which the foliage is usually rather pendulous with slender leaflets on a red petiole. The flowers are on tall, narrow cylindric panicles and have their stamens prominent in a downward curve with an upward sweep at the anthers.

MERITS: The leaves emerge from the bud a bright orange-brown, an attractive colour. The flowers open late, in July, several weeks after those of the Common horse-chestnut have faded, and in many trees appear a soft-pink at a distance due to red blotches. The conkers are rather fun, coal-black, but are unlikely to be sought in the traditional manner. The foliage is attractive with the usually red petioles and the slender, crinkled leaflets on petiolules, and the tree withstands city conditions.

LIMITATIONS: This can become a reasonably large tree. Some specimens have grown with many stems radiating from a short bole, so care may be needed to ensure a shapely tree.

ORIGIN AND OCCURRENCE: Introduced from the western Himalaya in 1851, this tree has been planted more frequently in recent years and older trees are found only in some of the larger gardens.

CULTIVAR: **'Sydney Pearce'** was selected as a seedling at Kew in 1928 and is a very sturdy tree with large leaves on green petioles and reliable in its very numerous long panicles of flowers.

Aesculus turbinata
Japanese horse-chestnut

FEATURES: A splendid foliage tree which deserves greater recognition. On young trees the bark is pale-fawn and flaky with systems of white streaks, but on old trees the smooth bark is a feature. The seven leaflets are sessile, as in the Common horse-chestnut, and differ from those only in size and in being much more tapered to the tip. The bud is rather less resinous but a similar glossy red-brown.

MERITS: The attraction of this species, compared with the Common horse-chestnut, resides in the massive leaves which, on young trees in particular (5–10 years old), are impressive, some being 65 cm across on a stout petiole over 40 cm long. Further, these leaves turn a good orange then brown in the autumn.

LIMITATIONS: A broad-crowned tree of fairly rapid growth, this should not be planted where the shedding of big leaflets will interfere with gutters or make roads slippery. The flower-heads are relatively small and sparsely borne.

ORIGIN AND OCCURRENCE: Introduced in about 1880 from Japan, this tree is fairly rare but makes a tree over 20 m tall in some of the larger gardens and collections.

Ailanthus altissima
(syn. *A. glandulosa)*
Tree of Heaven

FEATURES: This tree should be familiar to Londoners but is seldom recognised. The smooth pale-brown or dark-grey bark is streaked with white on a good, cylindric bole, which is usually 3–6 m long. The crown is of large upswept branches. The leaves emerge bright-red in mid-June and may be over 60 cm long (90 cm on young trees) with 11–43 leaflets each with one to four small lobes around the base. The male flowers are clusters of cream colour opening in July.

MERITS: The very vigorous growth where summers are warm can be an advantage. The big pinnate leaves are handsome and the female trees bear innumerable bunches of winged seeds which are scarlet in late summer. This tree will tolerate very trying conditions of atmosphere and soil.

LIMITATIONS: A tree of exceedingly great vigour, above and below ground, this should not be grown in a confined space nor where strong root suckers arising at 10 or 15 m from the tree are undesirable. In cities of slightly warmer climate than ours, like Washington DC, this species takes over spare plots, untidy gardens and roadsides and is ineradicable. Late into leaf and early to shed, it has limitations as a shade or screen tree. It has a rather short life, in the region of 150 years and towards the end becomes unsafe. It shows no autumn colour. Growth in cooler northern areas is slow and uncertain.

ORIGIN AND OCCURRENCE: This tree is native to north China and was sent to France by d'Incarville in 1751 and to Britain in 1754. It is now most commonly seen in London squares, parks and gardens and in large gardens, parks and churchyards in the suburbs and in the towns of East Anglia and southern England.

Alnus cordata
Italian alder

FEATURES: This splendid, vigorous tree should be planted more widely. The dark-grey bark is smooth until the rapid increase in size causes a few wide fissures to open. The crown is ovoid-conic, maintaining a good dominant leading shoot.

MERITS: A handsome tree of robust growth and excellent shape. Like all alders, its ability to fix nitrogen through bacteria in the root nodules makes it a valuable pioneer and it enriches the soil. Early in the year, often in February, the long, stout, male catkins are bright-yellow. The leaves are glossy, rich-green and heart-shaped, while the fruit are twice the size of those of the Common alder. It will grow well on shallow loam over chalk.

LIMITATIONS: A vigorous tree rapidly attaining a large size and capable of exceeding 27 m in height. It lacks, like all alders, any autumn show of colour, the leaves falling late but green. Needs a moist soil.

ORIGIN AND OCCURRENCE: This tree is native to southern Italy and Corsica and was introduced in 1820. There are moderately old and relatively very big trees in a few old gardens and parks but it was little known or planted until the last 20 years. A few were planted beside by-passes a little before this, and more recently it has been used in small plots on chalk downland forests and in parks and gardens.

Alnus glutinosa
Common alder

FEATURES: A tree with dull, grey bark which becomes fissured with age into small square plates, very like the Common oak. The male catkins are small, dull brownish-yellow and shed pollen variously from February to April. Young leaves remain tinged copper after emerging on coppice shoots and sprouts.

MERITS: A useful tree for watersides and very moist places, even where winter flooding is frequent. Single trees can be reasonably shapely and may achieve 20 m but soon lose the conic form of the young plant. Ten years after planting they may be 10 m tall but only on favourable soils.

LIMITATIONS: A tree of rapid early growth, this needs a retentive or very moist soil to grow well. As a coppiced tree or in thickets it has an untidy crown and is generally dull. Boles are apt to bear many sprouts.

ORIGIN AND OCCURRENCE: A native tree in all parts, found to 500 m above sea-level by streams, this tree is rarely planted but is common in parks and gardens which include open water. It is abundant by lowland streams and marshes.

Alnus incana
Grey alder

FEATURES: This tree, useful on a number of difficult sites, has the shoots covered in short, grey pubescence for some years, reddish-brown beneath the hairs, later smooth and pale-grey. The leaves are large, to 10 × 10 cm ovate with small lobules from the middle to the tip, and remain very late on the tree, dark-green.

MERITS: For an alder, this tree is tolerant of a wide range of soils, extending to drier sites than other alders although not at home on very dry sands. It grows vigorously and has attractive foliage, large catkins and fruit and the bark can be an interesting feature, smooth and grey.

LIMITATIONS: A tree of rapid growth, this alder requires room and light. It is apparently short-lived since no old or big trees can be found.

ORIGIN AND OCCURRENCE: Widely distributed across Europe to the Caucasus Mountains this species was introduced in 1780 but is very infrequent, a few small stands were made around 1900 but have now been felled and a few younger plots remain. Few gardens have a specimen, but it is now found in car-parks at beauty spots.

CULTIVARS: 'Aurea' is a low, domed tree with smaller leaves an excellent golden colour, and the shoots are, in winter, bright-red.

'Ramulis-Coccineis' is similar to 'Aurea' but the buds of leaves and of catkins are brighter-red in spring and the leaves less golden.

'Pendula' makes a good weeping mound-shaped tree.

Alnus rubra
(syn. *A. oregona*)
Red alder

FEATURES: The Red alder can be quite a handsome tree. The leaves may be 12 × 8 cm and their extreme margins are minutely curved under; some are quite strongly lobed from below the middle.

MERITS: Very rapid early growth and large flowers, fruit and leaves. In its native region the bark becomes silvery and this makes a prominent feature.

LIMITATIONS: This tree needs a damp or retentive soil and then grows very rapidly indeed and may be 12 m tall in 10 years but it is unreliable thereafter and rarely has made a big tree or survived well.

ORIGIN AND OCCURRENCE: This tree ranges from Alaska to California and is very common in valleys at low elevations. Introduced before 1880 it remains rare and apart from a few small experimental plots it is found only occasionally in the larger gardens.

Alnus subcordata
Caucasian alder

FEATURES: A rare tree which ought to have a promising future when it is better known. The bark is smooth, dull-grey and the branches strong, nearly level. In some trees the leaf may by 20 × 10 cm and in others they may be 5 cm long and oval.

MERITS: The most vigorous alder, making a fine tree to 18 m in 30 years with a stout bole. The foliage is a useful variant among alders and is variable among individual specimens, some having lanceolate willow-like leaves. The flowers and fruit are large. As an alder, it is self-sufficient in nitrogen. A seedling planted in a Surrey garden grew a shoot 2 m long in its third and fifth years to reach 6.5 m.

LIMITATIONS: Rapidly becomes a large tree on suitable sites, needing room, light and moisture. Lacks autumn colour. Probably difficult on drying sites.

ORIGIN AND OCCURRENCE: This tree was introduced in 1860 and is native to the Caucasus Mountains. So far it has remained almost unknown and the only specimens are young, even if large, and in a few major collections.

Betula jacquemontii
Jacquemont's birch

FEATURES: There is some confusion in the identity of this tree. The whitest bark is often seen on trees which are botanically *B. utilis* but are known as "B. jacquemontii". The true *jacquemontii* has 7–9 veins each side of the leaf and those with 10–14 veins are *utilis*, which are also pubescent on the veins of the underside. A graceful tree of narrow shape and reasonably rapid growth.

MERITS: The attraction of this tree is the bark which in selected forms is shiny, smooth, pure-white, but the foliage is also of high quality, and the male catkins are long.

LIMITATIONS: A generally tolerant tree, this requires full light and good drainage. It is hardly worth planting unless the bole be made a feature as a single specimen or in a widely spaced group. Care is needed to ensure that stock is of the whitest bark, and even these periodically shed the white and become briefly orange.

ORIGIN AND OCCURRENCE: Native to Kashmir and western Tibet, this tree was introduced in 1880 but was very little planted until recently. Most of the plants now seen in smaller gardens and in parks are grafts and represent but two or three clones, one deriving from a tree of *B. utilis*

in the Royal Botanic Gardens, Edinburgh, with strikingly pure-white bark, but at Wisley, Bodnant and a few other gardens there are trees of independent, seedling origin.

Betula lutea
Yellow birch

FEATURES: The Yellow birch deserves to be known better and planted more. The bark is dark-grey with some smooth and shiny patches of brownish-yellow. The grey areas peel and roll and some are light pinkish-grey. In the open, the crown tends to be globose with level lower branches and ascending upper, but in a group only the ascending branches survive and bear fine, straight shoots. The leaves are ovate-acuminate, irregularly double-toothed and have 12–15 parallel veins each side. The numerous fruit are erect, stout cylinders 3 cm long. Trees of a little over 15 m are found.

MERITS: This is a pretty tree in the summer, with large leaves well spaced and borne well back along the shoots, but it is the autumn colour which gives it greater distinction. In early or mid-October all the leaves turn simultaneously bright gold, usually at its best for three days, but sometimes for a week.

LIMITATIONS: For good growth this requires a reasonably good soil which does not dry out too rapidly. It bears quantities of fruit from an early age and these break up and drop a carpet of bracts and seed which are untidy in a paved area. It is a broad tree for its height unless confined, but will grow well as a group or grove.

ORIGIN AND OCCURRENCE: A common tree in wooded valleys from Newfoundland to Tennessee, this was introduced in 1767 but has been rarely planted except in collections.

Betula maximowicziana
Monarch or
Maximowicz's birch

FEATURES: The Monarch birch is a tree with character. Strong branches ascending at a wide angle bear rich green leaves to 14×11 cm, broadly ovate, resembling those of a lime. The toothing is elegant with fine teeth between each long tooth that is the extension of each of the 10–12 veins each side. Autumn colour is a good yellow.

MERITS: The exceedingly handsome, broad, large leaves are the main attraction, with clean pinkish and white bark on a clear bole. New leaves on young trees emerge orange-coloured and may maintain a tinge of this colour through the summer. It makes a good, single specimen tree. The male flowers and fruit are large and freely borne.

LIMITATIONS: Rather heavily branched for a birch, this needs more room than most and, for proper growth a reasonably good soil, not too acid.

ORIGIN AND OCCURRENCE: This Japanese tree was introduced before 1890. It is found only in a few large gardens and collections.

Betula nigra
Black or River birch

FEATURES: This birch is distinctive in bark, foliage and crown. The crown is rather dense with fine twigs, borne on a few big ascending branches. A few old specimens are known 19 m tall.

MERITS: The bark on young trees is pale orange-brown or pink, with large blackish-brown adhering flakes. With age it becomes deep red-brown or nearly black and strips freely, large rolls hanging from the branches. The foliage of lobulate or very doubly-toothed leaves shiny-green above and somewhat silvered on the underside, is attractive.

LIMITATIONS: This will not flourish on dry sites and seems to be suited only to the south of England.

ORIGIN AND OCCURRENCE: Very common by riversides in eastern America, this birch ranges further south than any other, reaching Florida. It was introduced in 1736 but is still rare and old trees are found only south of the river Thames.

Betula papyrifera
Paper-bark or Canoe birch

FEATURES: This is a warty birch with dark-brown shoots and rather broad, matt leaves, with few veins for their size. The bole, with conspicuous bark grows to an impressive size for a birch.

MERITS: The motive for planting this tree is often the supposedly white bark. In fact this can be a wide variety of blends of white with dark-purple, light-purple, red and orange. The bole can be splendidly smooth-cylindric and the foliage is of substance and quality. Early growth is quite rapid.

LIMITATIONS: This tree prefers good soils, some shelter and sunny summers. There are good trees in north-east Scotland but few in the west. It requires full light and grows a rather broad crown. It is probably short-lived since no old trees are known.

ORIGIN AND OCCURRENCE: The native range is from British Columbia and Alaska across to Labrador and Pennsylvania. Introduction was in 1750, but it has been very little planted.

Betula pendula
Silver birch

FEATURES: The familiar Silver birch is strictly only this species but the name is commonly used to include the Downy birch. From an early age the crown is pendulous and becomes increasingly so. The pale-yellow male catkins, dull-purple and short during winter, open as the leaves unfold. The leaves are broadest below the middle or at the base, and irregularly toothed. The bark of older trees is marked by large black diamond-shaped areas. The tallest tree known here is 30 m tall.

MERITS: A graceful and popular tree, the birch shows within eight or ten years the white bark which is its main feature. The process is accelerated and the bark is whiter if the bole is cleaned of side-branches at an early stage and exposed to sun and wind. Autumn colour is good in most years and the fallen leaves are too small to interfere with drains and gutters. The tree is of great value to wildlife, unless in a paved enclosed area in a city. The aphids on its leaves attract Great, Blue and Coal tits and the ripening seed feeds redpolls, siskins and goldfinches as well as Great and Blue tits. The light shade cast is a good protection for shrubs from late frosts and from sun-scorch, and, on the better soils, suits the growth of herbs and bulbs.

LIMITATIONS: This tree must have full light and good drainage. It is untidy as it drops vast quantities of bud-scales and male flowers in the spring, seeds and bracts in the autumn and barrow-loads of dead shoots all the year. On light, hungry soils its roots travel far to compete strongly with shrubs. Stumps of cut trees sprout strongly. In England it is short-lived and may begin to break up when 60–80-years-old, but it will last twice as long in central and northern Scotland.

ORIGIN AND OCCURRENCE: One of the first natives to recolonise Britain in the wake of the retreating ice, this tree is common on all light soils, especially on sandy heaths. It grows well in suburban areas but less well in centres of cities with polluted air.

CULTIVARS: **'Dalecarlica'** is a highly prized form with smoother bole, whiter bark, more pendulous shoots and deeply cut leaves. It is available only as grafted plants, bottom-worked. It originates from a tree found in 1767 in Sweden which had given rise fifty years later to a local population of similar types.

'DALECARLICA'   'YOUNGII'

'Youngii' arose at Milford, Surrey at the beginning of this century. As usually seen it is grafted on a clean stem at 1.5–1.8 m and forms a dense head of fine shoots with small, dark leaves, the outer shoots becoming long and pendulous. It is rather untidy and not very shapely in this form although popular, and can look well beside a small pool, but occasionally it makes a taller tree with foliage in pendulous layers when it is reasonably attractive.

Betula pubescens
Downy birch

FEATURES: The Downy birch differs from the true Silver birch in having greyish, horizontally banded bark and twisted non-pendulous shoots. It also differs in the shoot and petiole covered in short, silky, white pubescence and the leaf being broadest about the middle and regularly toothed. Some trees are less clear-cut in these features and there are intermediates. Also, sprouts of both species are unreliable in their characteristics.

MERITS: This is the nearest to Silver birch that can be grown on a heavy clay or on sands with impeded drainage. As a native tree it shares the advantages for wildlife listed for *B. pendula* together with fitting into rural landscapes.

LIMITATIONS: This tree has little of the grace associated with 'Silver birches' having a crown of twisting shoots and a greyish bark. It shares the other drawbacks listed for *B. pendula*.

ORIGINS AND OCCURRENCE: Also one of the first natives to return after the Ice Age, this tree is

locally common on heavy soils or where drainage is bad and is more frequent in Scottish glens than is *B. pendula*. It is probably never, deliberately planted in gardens, but has been included in many where housing estates are made in old woodlands.

Betula utilis
Himalayan birch

FEATURES: This splendid birch is closely related to and often confused with Jacquemont's birch. The crown is often rather broad with a few big upswept branches and the leaf is relatively broadly ovate-acuminate 8–10 cm long but may be 14 cm. The flowers and fruit are large.

MERITS: The two best features of this tree are the bark and leaves. The bark can be extraordinarily diverse depending upon origin. In the western parts of its range the tree grades into *B. jacquemontii* and has a beautiful clear-white bark. Origins from further east and into China have rich brown bark, sometimes glossy with large scales, differing shades of red-brown and deep-brown resembling a handsome python-skin. In all forms the leaf is of good size and well-veined, while in some it is a glossy deep green with a red petiole which makes it very attractive.

LIMITATIONS: This tree really needs to be an isolated specimen to show its good foliage and interesting bark to advantage. It prefers reasonable shelter and a soil that is not impoverished. For a birch it casts a heavy shade.

ORIGIN AND OCCURRENCE: This tree was introduced in 1849 and ranges along most of the Himalayan mountains into China and Tibet. It is rare, older specimens being confined to a few specialist gardens but occasional young trees are seen in parks and gardens.

Buxus sempervirens
Box

FEATURES: The box is an evergreen, densely crowned, bushy tree or shrub. In a few natural stands it is a small tree to 8 m with a sinuous, bare bole and often a narrow-spired apex. The bark is pale-brown and grey fissured into square, thick plates. The shoot is square in section. The leaves are in opposite pairs and are glossy dark-green. The flowers open early in spring and are clustered with five or six males around a central female flower and can be a conspicuous yellow.

MERITS: This is one of the very few evergreen native trees and has neat, fairly bright foliage. It is quite pretty in flower and in warm, damp air the foliage exudes a pleasant aroma. It is found naturally on chalk and limestones but will grow on neutral or mildly acid soils. The dense crown gives excellent low shelter or screening and takes clipping very well.

LIMITATIONS: Box will never grow rapidly nor make a big tree even in the south. In the north it will be a shrub.

OCCURRENCE: Box is native but very local on chalk downs and limestone hills from Kent and Surrey to Buckinghamshire and Gloucestershire. It regenerates densely, despite rabbits grazing young plants, at one site in the Chiltern Hills. Abroad it is a tree only of south-west Europe and north Africa.

Carpinus betulus
Hornbeam

FEATURES: One of our neglected natives, the Hornbeam is rarely planted except as a hedge or in the form of a cultivar. The bole is usually short and never straight and the crown is broadly domed. The leaves have prominent parallel veins and sharp, double toothing.

MERITS: One of the best trees for growing on intractable clays, this has good foliage added to all the summer by masses of fruit like Japanese lanterns. The early April male catkins are numerous if not spectacular, preceding the leaves. Autumn colour is very good for a reasonably long period, changing from yellows to warm-brown, occasionally orange. The silvery bark adds interest to the ribbed and pocketed bole with some fine patterns of dark-grey. In winter the crown is distinctive with straight slender twigs in profusion.

LIMITATIONS: A broad-crowned and large tree, to 30 m, this needs space (but see Cultivar) and casts a dense shade.

ORIGIN AND OCCURRENCE: A native tree of late arrival, the natural range extends only from Kent to Somerset and Hereford. Pure hornbeam woods, mostly pollarded, are a feature of Epping and Hainault Forests in Essex and in a few places in Hertfordshire, but elsewhere the trees tend to be more scattered. Although now seldom planted, it is common nearly everywhere, as older trees in parks, around boundaries of larger gardens in suburbs, and in churchyards.

'FASTIGIATA'

CULTIVAR: 'Fastigiata' This is one of the best and most widely useful of all amenity trees. Grown on a clean stem of 1.5 m it makes a dense neatly ovoid-acute crown of radiating straight shoots. It is even more decorative when bare than when in leaf. Autumn colours are good yellow to orange-brown. Cultivated since 1886, some specimens 50-years-old are over 15 m in height. For the first few years it is a narrowly columnar plant.

Carya cordiformis
Bitter-nut

FEATURES: This is a hickory with a shallowly ridged but not shaggy bark. The leaves bear nine leaflets, the terminal one tapering gradually to its sessile base, and the basal pair much the smallest. Male catkins may be profuse but not conspicuous, being green. They divide into three near the base.

MERITS: Hickories are so seldom planted that any species is a welcome variation. The Bitter-nut makes a tall tree (several are 25 m) with slender ascending branches arching out gently at a good height. The foliage is attractive and assumes splendid golds in autumn.

LIMITATIONS: A hardy tree but one which requires hot summers to grow well, this is not advised for planting north or west of the Midlands. It needs space and full light to allow development of the tall crown of gracefully arching branches. The season in leaf is rather short. A sheltered site on good soil is essential. Young plants resent moving but are not hardy enough to plant out when small, so they must be grown in containers.

ORIGIN AND OCCURRENCE: Common but scattered on the middle slopes and sheltered valleys of the Allegheny Mountains, the Bitter-nut extends from Quebec to Louisiana and was introduced in 1689. Although as frequent as any hickory, this is not often seen and is confined to a few of the best gardens.

Carya ovata
Shagbark hickory

FEATURES: Although in cultivation for nearly 350 years, the Shagbark hickory is rather scarce. The very stout shoots, green, then purple-brown, bear leaves to 65 cm long with five leaflets, the terminal three being broad and large, to 35 × 20 cm; the central one with a stout 3–4 cm petiole; of a thick, leathery consistency and usually yellowish green. In mid-June it bears masses of three-parted, green catkins 10–15 cm long and in summer the obovoid green fruit are frequent.

MERITS: In full leaf this is an unusual and quite interesting specimen. The coarsely shaggy bark and the very large leaves are features, but the best one is the brilliant yellow autumn colour.

LIMITATIONS: A broad-crowned tree this needs space and warmth and is suited only to the south and west, although it will survive elsewhere. Out of leaf it is not attractive, being sparsely branched and looking very bare. The big leaves could be a nuisance when they fall.

ORIGIN AND OCCURRENCE: This hickory has a very wide range in eastern America, from Quebec to Texas and was introduced in 1629. It is rarely seen except in the few collections, but there are occasional specimens in western and southern gardens to 20 m × 80 cm.

Carya tomentosa
Mockernut

FEATURES: A hickory with a smooth bark is exceptional but, until quite old, this one is grey and lacks any fissures or ridges. Eventually the bark becomes purple and is divided into smooth ridges. The leaves have seven leaflets and can be over 50 cm long, the terminal leaflet slender, lanceolate and on a slender petiole 2–4 cm long. Crushed foliage yields a paint-like scent. The three-parted male catkins are densely borne and dull-yellow in June. There are specimens over 20 m tall.

MERITS: The Mockernut makes a handsome, tall, fairly narrow crown bearing very large leaves. In autumn it becomes a tower of brilliant-gold for a short period.

LIMITATIONS: This tree needs a relatively sheltered but unshaded position on good soil. It is suitable only for the southern parts of the country.

ORIGIN AND OCCURRENCE: Ranging from Ontario to Texas this tree is nowhere common but occurs in sheltered mountain valleys in small numbers. Introduced in 1766 it is quite rare in collections and major gardens.

Castanea sativa
Sweet chestnut

FEATURES: A very fine parkland tree, the Sweet chestnut has grey and smooth bark on young trees which gradually fissures vertically. After some 100 years the fissures and ridges become more pronounced and begin to twist spirally. When the tree is about 250 years-old and hence about 2.5 m in diameter, the bark is rich dark-brown and the fissures and ridges, now deep, spiral at a low angle. A few trees are 35 m tall and boles of more than 3 m in diameter are known.

MERITS: This handsome tree grows vigorously almost anywhere in these Islands on any light soil. It withstands severe treatment and it coppices readily. Although not native, it fits rural scenery well. Pure woods are not notable for wildlife, but they are frequented by woodpeckers, nuthatches and tree-creepers and chestnut-coppice regularly cut grows an excellent flora, being among the best places for bluebells and nightingales. Towards the end of June, masses of male catkins flower, ivory-white against the dark-green, shiny leaves with an exotic and attractive appearance. In the autumn most trees show good yellows, then russets.

LIMITATIONS: A very large-growing, long-lived tree of vigorous growth, this is entirely unsuited to restricted spaces. It casts a dense shade and sheds large leaves. It will not grow well where drainage is impeded nor on heavy clays.

ORIGIN AND OCCURRENCE: This tree is native to southern Europe, and from north Africa to the Caucasus Mountains. It is thought to have been brought here by the Romans and regenerates itself quite readily on light soils in the south. It is a common parkland tree, and grows well even in the far north-east of Scotland. In fact one near Strathpeffer, Easter Ross, is the oldest known tree of any sort in Britain with a documented planting date, 1550.

Catalpa bignonioides
Indian bean tree

FEATURES: Although it comes from the deep south of the USA this Catalpa will thrive in our much cooler more southerly cities and gardens. The reddish-brown bark is finely scaly. The leaves may be cordate or rounded at the base and are ovate, short-acuminate and up to 25 × 22 cm. The tree is usually short-lived, achieving a bole diameter of 80–90 cm in 100 years but often decaying thereafter.

MERITS: Even before the drastic improvement in London air, Indian bean trees flowered regularly in Piccadilly and Parliament Square. This is thus a tough and tolerant tree. The leaves are noticeable for their size and on young trees are often purple as they unfold. The flowers are the more welcome for being open in late July and August and are rather orchid-like, packed into a large, broad, conic flower-head. They are sweetly scented and appear white from a distance but each frilly-edged trumpet is spotted in pink, yellow and purple. The bean-like fruits may be 40 cm long but only 8 mm across and hang several together through the winter, creating general interest.

LIMITATIONS: Thriving and flowering well only where summers are hot, this is not suited to the cool areas north and west of the Midlands. It has a broad, low crown and the shortest season in leaf of any tree, nor does it show any autumn colour. Highly exotic in every way, this tree is out of place in the rural scene and should be associated with buildings.

ORIGIN AND OCCURRENCE: This native of Florida, Alabama and Louisiana was introduced in 1726. It is frequent in London parks and in southern and East Anglian cities and towns and, in the south is quite common as a garden tree. In

southern Scotland it is a small, largely non-flowering foliage-tree.

CULTIVAR: 'Aurea' has leaves which open bright pale-yellow and, in their short season lose some of this colour, greening appreciably but it is highly effective in June and July. It is less hardy than the green form and is seen only in southern England. Young plants may be scorched by full sun.

Catalpa × erubescens
Hybrid catalpa

FEATURES: The Hybrid catalpa is notable for its very big leaves and late flowering. The crown tends to be narrower than that of C. bignonioides and may be broadly conic, 18–19 m tall. The leaves are thin textured, and bright-green with abruptly tipped lobes. The flowers are no bigger than those of C. bignonioides and, being spread over a taller panicle yet little more numerous, they make less of a splash of colour. The fruit are numerous and may be 40 cm long.

MERITS: Rapid early growth is an advantage for trees suited to courtyards and precincts. This tree has impressive leaves, often more than 30 cm each way, which are deep-purple in the bud. The flower-heads are big, tall and open and the flowers are powerfully scented, opening late – towards the end of August. The onset of flowering occurs within a year or two of planting, since the plants are grafts.

LIMITATIONS: This tree of rapid growth needs shelter from winds and should be considered only for southern areas with hot summers. The crown form is not good for a tree which spends eight months of the year without leaves.

ORIGIN AND OCCURRENCE: An Indiana nurseryman, Mr. C. J. Teas, was growing the Chinese catalpa *C. ovata* together with the native species *C. speciosa* and *C. bignonioides* and fortuitously produced a hybrid in 1874. The alternate parent was first taken to be *C. speciosa* but is now considered to be *C. bignonioides*. Introduced in 1891, this tree has a local distribution here perhaps due to individual nurseries with stock. Big trees are few but three are in gardens near Farnham, Surrey, one near Reading, Berks and one in Sydney Gardens, Bath, Avon. There are also a few in East Anglia.

Cercidiphyllum japonicum
Katsura tree

FEATURES: The Katsura is an elegant and attractive tree notable for its colour in the autumn. The plants are either male of female, the latter bearing innumerable little blue-grey claws of fruit during the summer. The oppositely placed buds are prominently strung along slender shoots and leaf out well back along branches.

MERITS: This is an exceptionally ornamental tree at all times. The better plants make tall, regular and shapely trees with arched branches and straight, slender shoots. When leafing out it is strung with red then pink leaves and bright-red tassels of flower. In summer, the dense foliage of small round leaves is notably elegant, pale grey-green. Autumn colours are variously ruby-red, scarlet, crimson, mauve and yellow.

LIMITATIONS: Frost-pockets should be avoided strictly, for the attractive red and pink unfolding leaves are susceptible to damage by late frosts.

This is a much more vigorous tree than it looks and requires space and light to give its autumn colours. It needs side-shelter and a good, damp soil. It is exceptionally susceptible to drought and is best grown near open water. The eastern coastlines are unsuitable except in sheltered, wet hollows with good air drainage. It casts a dense shade.

ORIGIN AND OCCURRENCE: Although occurring in China as well, it is from Japan that this tree was received in 1865 and the Chinese form was probably unknown here until very recently. The Katsura is frequent in large gardens, especially in the west, and is present at Westonbirt, for example, in a dozen or more groups. It has been much planted more recently. Many trees, even in the east (Sandringham for example) exceed 15 m and some are over 18 m while one crowded in among tall trees in Hampshire is 25 m tall.

M

Cercis siliquastrum
Judas tree

FEATURES: A small tree with spectacular, although irregular, flower display and pleasant foliage. The flowers are typical of the Pea family. The shoots are dark red-brown and bear alternate sub-orbicular leaves 8–10 cm across. Hardy probably everywhere, this is not seen north of the Midlands presumably because growth will be poor and flowering minimal.

MERITS: In good years the display of bright rosy-pink flowers on bare stems, shoots, branches and even boles is spectacular in May. The foliage is light and attractive, small, nearly round leaves. The big, broad pods are deep-purple in summer and the bark has some purple areas.

LIMITATIONS: A climate with hot summers is needed for the display of flowers of this tree and except in East Anglia and the southern counties it needs to be among buildings with south-facing walls to flower well. Only a small tree at best, rarely 9 m tall, it has a tendency to lie down with age and is never shapely as a tree. It may be bushy. The persistent big pods turn dull-brown by winter and are then little ornament.

ORIGIN AND OCCURRENCE: One of the early introductions unrecorded, but around Tudor times, from south-west Asia and south-east Europe, this may have been grown first for use of the flowers as a sweet addition to salads. It is frequent in the south in parks, relatively small gardens and a few churchyards.

Corylus colurna
Turkish hazel

M

FEATURES: A strong-growing tree to over 20 m (65 ft) on a stout bole, this tree maintains a shapely conic crown until mature. It bears large male catkins early in spring and clusters of nuts with involucres bearing rows of short spines and with long, tapered segments. The leaves are large and broad. The bark is rough and flaky, dark brown and is distinctive in winter.

MERITS: This makes a bold, unusual tree with robust early growth. It grows well on alkaline or neutral soils and tolerates very cold winters. The spring displays of catkins is early and good. The crown is well-shaped and it can grow a fine bole. It thrives in warm, dry areas, and in cities.

LIMITATIONS: This is probably not suitable for very acid, peaty soils nor where drainage is poor and rainfall high. With age, the level branching makes a broad crown needing room to develop properly. There is negligible autumn colour.

ORIGIN AND OCCURRENCE: The natural range is from Asia Minor to the Balkan Mountains. The tree was introduced before 1600 but has not until recently been widely planted. Fine specimens exist in the Royal Botanical Garden, Edinburgh and in some collections and large gardens in England.

Crataegus crus-galli
Cockspur thorn

FEATURES: A most distinctive thorn, this tree has pale brown shoots with numerous thorns in rows, 4–8 cm long, slender and curved, of the same colour. The glabrous leaves are obovate, cuneate and rounded at the tip.

MERITS: A low tree that will not grow too big, this is sufficiently robust to grow almost anywhere and is at home on chalk. The flowers are pleasant but unspectacular and the main merits are the autumn colour and persistent fruit. In autumn the foliage is a clear pale-orange, a very unusual colour among trees, and the red fruit remain through the winter.

S

LIMITATIONS: This can never achieve more than about 8 m in height and is often a low bush on a leg. The crown is broader than it is high and is decidedly a tangle of branches. The winter aspect is thus not ornamental. The long, sharp very numerous thorns make this plant unpopular with gardeners and unsuited to planting near paths.

ORIGIN AND OCCURRENCE: A north-eastern American tree ranging from Quebec to Kansas, this was introduced to Fulham Palace in 1691. It is rare, being found sometimes in city parks, and a few gardens. Most, if not all, the trees sold as _C. crus-galli_ are _C. prunifolia_ (see next page).

Crataegus × grignoniensis
Grignon thorn

FEATURES: This is a large-fruited form of *C. lavallei* (see below), with glabrous shoots, and is planted for the display of fruit.

MERITS: The foliage and flowers are reasonably good but the great feature is the fruit. Large bunches of orange-red fruit of good individual size persist until well into the winter.

LIMITATIONS: The coarsely twigged untidy crown render this tree more suitable for planting as one among a varied group than as a single specimen tree.

ORIGIN AND OCCURRENCE: Found in 1873 at Grignon, France, this has recently been planted in a number of decorative schemes and a few gardens.

Crataegus × lavallei
(syn. *C. × carrierei*)
Hybrid cockspur thorn,
Carrière's thorn

FEATURES: Although probably a seedling of the Cockspur thorn, Carrière's thorn differs from it in general aspect. The dark-grey, scaly-barked stem holds a spreading crown of level branches crowded on their upper side with short shoots. The dull green shoots bear few stout 5 cm thorns. The leaves are oblong-obovate, pubescent beneath and dark glossy-green above. The inflorescence has woolly stems with about 20 flowers with a red disc and pink anthers.

MERITS: A tough tree, this has dark glossy leaves and bears dense masses of white flowers which become persistent orange-red fruits. The leaves remain dark-green through the autumn and may turn deep bronzed-red before falling. The dense shoots rising from level branches are a feature in winter.

LIMITATIONS: This tree has no noticeable drawbacks where only a medium-small tree is required.

ORIGIN AND OCCURRENCE: An obscure hybrid known before 1880 and derived from *C. crus-galli* and a related Mexican species, this is frequent by arterial roads and in large gardens.

Crataegus monogyna
Hawthorn

FEATURES: Although familiar chiefly as a hedge plant, the Hawthorn can be a tree 15 m tall and is very long-lived. The bark is dark-brown deeply fissured into rectangular plates.

MERITS: Exceedingly tough and exposure-hardy, this will thrive almost anywhere including in cities. The copious flowering varies but little with the years and in most years the berries, at first orange-red make a good display. They soon become deep-red but are then eaten by birds except in years when they are so prolific (e.g. 1974, 1976) that the inroads of hordes of birds make little impression. The food for birds is but a part of the ecological benefits of hawthorn. A native of long-standing and of varied habitats, it is the host plant of a large variety of insects. Some tree-sized plants may show good, deep-red autumn colours.

LIMITATIONS: Although there are a number of hawthorn trees 12–14 m tall, this cannot be expected to make more than a tall, spreading, far from tidy, bush.

ORIGIN AND OCCURRENCE: Native to woodland edges, scrub, chalk downs, commons and heaths this plant has been the main constituent of farmland hedges since the Enclosures. It is much used in city parks and squares.

Crataegus oxyacantha
Midland thorn

This native tree is grown only as one of the red-flowered forms like **'Paul's Scarlet'**, in which it grows into a 10 m tree with a stout bole, exceptionally useful in city parks.

Crataegus × prunifolia
Broad-leaved cockspur
thorn

FEATURES: This thorn is an adaptable, useful small tree with a low crown. The glossy, purple-brown shoots bear 2 cm thorns of the same colour. The leaf is broad-ovate, glossy dark-green and pubescent on the midrib beneath. The flowers are in small, erect inflorescences and the white buds are tipped scarlet.

MERITS: Colour in the last two weeks in October is outstanding. The leaves turn orange then an added crimson tinge makes a unique colour of polished-copper before the final turn to crimson-purple. The dark-red fruit last only until the winter. A robust plant, this will thrive almost anywhere including on chalky soils.

LIMITATIONS: This is rarely more than a big bush. It needs full light to give its autumn colour. It is shapeless and without merit in winter.

ORIGIN AND OCCURRENCE: A hybrid of obscure European origin, this was known before 1800. It has been planted of late commonly on roadsides, by approaches to garages and in similar places, and older plants, usually bushy, are frequent in large gardens.

Davidia involucrata
Dove-tree

M

FEATURES: The Dove-tree is becoming quite well-known. The usual form is var. _vilmoriniana_ which lacks the white pubescence on the under-side of the leaf and is instead glabrous and shiny. The bark is dark-purple or red-purple flaking finely to pale-brown. The inflorescence itself is a globular head of small yellow flowers, hanging on a stout stalk between the two unequally sized white bracts, which make the conspicuous 'flower'.

MERITS: Chiefly recommended for the unique and striking flower-bracts, creamy-white then pure-white hanging in profuse rows beneath the branches, this tree also has a place as a foliage plant. The leaves are large, jaggedly toothed, deep glossy-green and prominently veined. It is a sturdy tree and grows well on any good loamy soil, even in large towns but doubtfully in polluted air, and not so well in thin hungry soils.

LIMITATIONS: An exposed site is unsuitable for this tree whose floral display is large, hanging bracts. Poor or dry soils also prevent proper development of the tree. There is a marked interval between planting and flowering despite the use of large plants and five or even ten years may have to elapse. Best grown as an isolated specimen, this tree has in early life ascending branches but for profuse flowering it needs to be older, when the branches spread level and quite widely. In winter, the open crown makes a rather gaunt prospect, and there is negligible autumn colour. It is highly susceptible to drought.

ORIGIN AND OCCURRENCE: The var. _vilmoriniana_ was the first form in Europe, sent to Vilmorin's in France in 1897 from central China. The type form was sent to Britain in 1904 by Ernest Wilson also from central China and a few years later the same collector sent large quantities of var. _vilmoriniana_. Trees of these early origins are in many of the major gardens which were collecting at the time. Younger trees are now in many parks and smaller gardens as well. The form var. _vilmoriniana_ usually grows more vigorously than the type.

Eucalyptus gunnii
Cider-gum

L

FEATURES: The Cider-gum is the common hardy eucalypt seen in eastern parts as a big tree. It is distinguished by elliptic leaves on yellow petioles.

MERITS: A tree of exceedingly rapid growth which can grow 2 m in a season, this is a fully hardy eucalypt and is tolerant of very poor soils. When of no great age the tree bears innumerable white flowers like tufts. The stripping bark is unusual as is the blue-grey of the foliage. It grows, but may look thin in cities.

LIMITATIONS: The Cider-gum requires full light and grows very rapidly. In its early years it is liable to be laid over by winds and may have its top blown out, which is however soon replaced. A few trees become thin and leggy. All eucalypts are quite out of place in rural scenery.

ORIGIN AND OCCURRENCE: Native to south Australia and Tasmania the Cider-gum is not there one of the taller eucalypts, tending to be shrubby, but grown here since 1846 it has exceeded 30 m and is often a shapely tree.

Eucalyptus niphophila
Snow gum

M

FEATURES: The Snow gum is one of the few eucalypts to show no juvenile foliage. It has oblong-lanceolate, usually falcate leaves to 14 cm long finely marked red along the margin.

MERITS: Although variable in each respect, the value of this tree lies in its very vigorous growth, in the orange-amber colour of young leaves and in the strikingly bright blue-white bark. So far as is known it is completely hardy. In flower it is spectacular, with very large pure white flowers in bunches.

LIMITATIONS: Like all eucalypts this needs full light and is not concordant with rural scenery.

ORIGIN AND OCCURRENCE: The date of introduction must be recent but is not recorded. The tree ranges up to the tree-line in southern Australia. A few were planted by specialists in about 1950 and since 1965 it has been quite a frequent sight in small gardens.

Eucalyptus nitens
Shining gum

FEATURES: This is the only big-leaved *Eucalyptus* hardy beyond Ireland and Cornwall.

MERITS: The rate of growth has its uses. In Cornwall it has been 12 m in five years and in Argyll, trees in a plot were 20 m in nine years. This proved to be completely hardy until 1979 when many were badly scorched but sprouted again along the bole. Juvenile foliage, retained for some years is blue-grey to green, large, long leaves and quite striking. Adult foliage is still large but less so.

LIMITATIONS: Usually the fastest-growing tree we can grow, this needs space and light.

Euodia hupehensis

M

FEATURES: Euodias have opposite leaves and naked buds. This species has grown over 20 m tall in 50 years in a Perthshire garden. It has a leaf 20–25 cm long with 5–9 leaflets.

MERITS: This splendid tree has a smooth grey bark and a good shape so looks well in winter. The leaves are compound with glossy, cupped leaflets on a deep pink stalk, and very distinguished in summer. The creamy-white broad heads of flowers open usefully late, in August and they are, interestingly, either wholly female or wholly male, more or less at random on the tree. The female flower-heads yield a display of erect berries, red-brown then scarlet in October. With all this, the tree is sufficiently robust to thrive in city parks and is perfectly hardy, and there are specimens in the chalk-garden at Highdown.

LIMITATIONS: None known, beyond rapid growth ruling out small spaces.

ORIGIN AND OCCURRENCE: This tree was found in central China and sent here in 1908. It is fairly

rare but is in some large gardens and in at least two London parks, where the similar *E. velutina* with densely downy shoots and leaves, is also remarkably vigorous and now 19 m tall in St. James's Park.

Fagus sylvatica
Beech

FEATURES: This fine native species is one of the most useful and impressive trees in some difficult situations. Young trees often make shoots of 60–100 cm, usually in two short bursts. The first is in early May when 40–60 cm will expand within two weeks, and the second similar surge of growth is in July. In most areas the mature trees are 25 m tall and in sheltered valleys or in big stands some trees exceed 40 m.

MERITS: An exceedingly handsome tree at all times, it leafs out a bright fresh green, has a long period of rich yellows, russets and browns in the autumn and when bare the silvery-grey bole and branches are much admired. It is a strongly growing tree and withstands quite severe exposure once well established. Far from requiring a chalky soil it thrives equally on gravels, light loams and acid sands. In permeable soil its powerful root-system goes deep so that it can acquire the abundant moisture it needs and makes a fine tree on apparently dry, exposed chalk hill-tops. It is beneficial to a rather restricted range of wildlife but a specialised one and on some sites it can support a bluebell ground flora. The fruit are an important source of food for many mammals, coal-tits, bramblings and chaffinches. It is of inestimable value in general shelter in exposed regions. Almost all the Cornish gardens and many in eastern Scotland rely on extensive shelterwoods of beech.

LIMITATIONS: Potentially a very large tree casting a dense shade over a wide area this is unsuited to close proximity to buildings. Beech is very sensitive to excess moisture and will not grow well on heavy soils nor in damp hollows. Refusing to root into poorly drained horizons, it is, on shallow soils above them, very superficially rooted and becomes unstable. The life of the tree is a little over 200 years and decay and death set in extremely rapidly, due largely to two fungi, *Meripilus giganteus* and *Ganoderma adspersum*. It will collapse very rapidly after death and big branches almost rain down. It is not safe even when still apparently healthy but old, and limbs will easily be torn out by winds and may drop even during calm periods. Leaf-fall is heavy and can cause blockages, and male flowers are shed by the million. For establishment in exposure or on chalky hills a nurse tree, Scots pine, Thuya or Lawson cypress is essential. Grey squirrels may severely damage trees by stripping bark when they are 20–40-years-old.

ORIGIN AND OCCURRENCE: Native to England, the beech was a late arrival after the Ice Ages and did not extend into Wales or Scotland.

L

L

L

Widely planted everyhere now, it is abundant on chalk-lands but also on Exmoor and the southern uplands in shelter-belts, in parks and gardens and there are many thriving even in city parks.

CULTIVARS: **'Asplenifolia'**. Fern-leaf beech. A continental form introduced in 1826 to Knaphill Nursery in Surrey, this has a more dense crown of finer shoots and bears small leaves deeply but variously cut. Where the tree is pruned or damaged, normal and intermediate leaves grow out. It is highly attractive and grows as fast as the type tree but with a broader, more bushy crown.

'Dawyck' is a fastigiate form shaped like a Lombardy poplar but with a few shoots curving out from the crown. Derived from a single tree now 25 m tall at Dawyck garden near Peebles it is an excellent tree where space is restricted or a formal appearance but a countryside foliage is needed.

'Pendula'. A continental form first planted here at Knaphill Nurseries, Surrey in 1826. Four specimens are still there and spread widely. In this form the branches which reach the ground root and send up another vertical stem. Possibly a different clone is slightly less common and may attain 30 m with long hanging branches but without layers. A good isolated specimen where there is plenty of space.

'Purpurea'. An assemblage of copper beeches leafing out pale coppery-pink but dull purple-brown for the rest of the season. These are vastly over-planted and discerning plantsmen agree that they should be given a rest and none planted for a few hundred years.

'Zlatia'. A cultivar from Zagreb in which the new leaves are pale golden colour, soon greenish-gold and then normal dark-green. A splendid variant while the colour lasts and of vigorous growth.

Fraxinus americana
White ash

FEATURES: This is an elegant and fast-growing tree very common throughout the eastern States often as a splendid street tree. The tall, domed crown has stout shoots from a regular rather flat branching system, and pale-brown buds. The leaves are 35 cm long with seven broad, stalked leaflets, the terminal three to 15 × 7 cm. The leaflets are entire in some trees, obscurely toothed or sharply toothed on others.

MERITS. Well-sited, this can grow more rapidly than the Common ash and is a useful variation. The underside of the leaf is white or pale greenish-white, which is an attractive feature. The remarkable bronze-purple autumn colour in America may be shown, if paler, here.

LIMITATIONS: A large, vigorous and spreading tree. Needs room, some shelter and a rich, deep, well-drained soil, to grow properly. In general it has not been the success that was hoped it would be in this country but it has rarely been grown on the deep base-rich soils that suit it best. It grows well in the Royal Parks in London.

ORIGIN AND OCCURRENCE: Common in eastern North America and introduced in 1724, this ash is occasional in parks, a few large gardens and collections but is quite rare.

Fraxinus angustifolia
Narrow leaved ash

FEATURES: This southern tree of very attractive foliage should be planted more in southern England. The dark-grey bark is much ridged and becomes rough and knobbly. The buds are purple-brown and yellow-brown. The foliage is fairly open, the slender, lanceolate leaflets being well-spaced.

MERITS: A good tree in southern city squares and parks with shiny fresh green leaves elegantly strung with slender leaflets. Casts a light, dappled shade.

LIMITATIONS: A large-growing tree requiring room and light, probably unsuited to northern parts with cool summers. The roots will be wide-spreading and invasive. The season in leaf is rather short. Grafted plants must be worked at ground level. Many grafted at 1–2 m have grown exceedingly unsightly boles with a gross change in diameter at the union.

ORIGIN AND OCCURRENCE: Native to the Caucasus and Black Sea region and north Africa this tree has been cultivated here since 1800. It is almost restricted to towns and cities south of the Thames, and is quite rare except in London. At Chiswick House one is 29 m × 97 cm and one in Dorset is 30.5 m tall.

Fraxinus excelsior
Common ash

FEATURES: A native tree coarse and rarely shapely but popular with writers and the public, the ash is in the same family as the lilacs and forsythias but in this species there are no petals on the flowers. The velvety black winter-buds are unique to this ash. The grey-green stout shoots are flattened at the nodes. The flowers expand before the leaves and are at first blackish-purple domes. They then expand to dark-red and the males have masses of tiny, pale-yellow anthers. Supposedly the females are on separate branches or even trees, but frequently the same flowers that bear the stamens expand more fully with much branched green stems extruded 5 cm and the stamens arise each side of ovaries which then open a style and stigma. The tree coppices freely and late shoots and leaves emerge purple. Young trees may grow a metre in a year but old trees increase only in girth and quite rapidly until they die when less than 200-years-old and rarely more than 1.5 m diameter. Many trees achieve 30 m and there have been specimens over 40 m tall.

MERITS: On the best soils a tree of rapid early growth, highly resistant to wind, the ash is capable of some passable growth even in remote areas of the Highlands, near the sea and in cities. In leaf the tree has a bright and rich appearance. There is an associated fauna and the seed are important to bullfinches in the spring.

LIMITATIONS: Not a tree for enclosed spaces or near gardens. It needs to develop to a large size and has a strong and hungry root-system. When not in leaf it has a coarse very bare look and the season in leaf is short, while autumn colour is far more brief. For good growth only the best soils are of use – damp but well-drained, deep and base-rich. Elsewhere cankers can be unsightly, and trees of good shape are rare.

ORIGIN AND OCCURRENCE: A native tree abundant on or near chalk and limestone areas, the ash seeds itself copiously even on poor sandy soils and is common in hedges everywhere, usually as a very poor, cankered, coppiced plant. It is common in town and city parks and in countryside parkland and woods.

CULTIVARS: 'Diversifolia' is an interesting variant, a robust tree with a more open crown of more regular level branches and of quite a poplar-like appearance when in leaf. Each leaf is an oblong-ovate simple leaf on a long 10 cm petiole. It casts a lighter shade than the type tree and can be 27 m tall.

'Jaspidea'. The Golden ash is a tree nearly the size of the type with golden or pinkish-yellow-brown shoots, leafing out yellow and of good golden autumn colour.

Fraxinus ornus
Manna or Flowering ash

M

FEATURES: A species from the small group of ash trees which have flowers with petals and fragrance. The bud is domed, laterally flattened and brown. The leaves are 25–30 cm long and have 5–9 leaflets on 1.5 cm stalks. The fruit are slender, lanceolate, bright-green until autumn and on a wire-thin peduncle. Autumn colour is fleeting pale-yellow and brown.

MERITS: A neat, if broad-crowned, smooth-barked tree covered well in late May with foaming masses of highly fragrant flowers. It thrives by main roads or in towns.

LIMITATIONS: Very few indeed, beyond a preference for good soils and some shelter, and space for a broad crown with a possible eventual height of 20 m.

ORIGIN AND OCCURRENCE: Sent from southern Europe and the Black Sea region before 1700 this is fairly frequent tree in gardens and town parks and by main roads.

Fraxinus oxycarpa
Caucasian ash

M

FEATURES: This species is similar to *F. angustifolia* and often treated as a form of it. It is distinguished by the characteristics given under merits, and, in detail, by the hairs each side of the midrib at the base on the underside of the leaflets.

MERITS: This is a remarkably cheerful, clean bright tree and very shapely. The bark is pale-grey and smooth and the foliage a bright, glossy-green.

LIMITATIONS: This tree should be suitable almost anywhere except on very poor sandy soils and possibly in the coldest areas.

ORIGIN AND OCCURRENCE: The range extends from the Balkans through Asia Minor to Persia. Introduction was in 1815 but old trees are very scarce and younger trees little less so. Currently the planting is largely taken over by the cultivar.

CULTIVAR: '**Raywood**' arose in Australia and has been in commerce since about 1928. Its merits are its very vigorous growth (in Norfolk one was 17 m × 40 cm when 24-years-old); the same features as the type, together with the major reason for planting, the rich display in autumn of purple foliage.

M
'RAYWOOD'

Gleditsia triacanthos
Honey-locust

L

FEATURES: The Honey-locust is a remarkably tough tree tolerant of hot, paved restricted rooting areas. The shoots bear three small spines by each bud, (which is hidden within the petiole until the leaf falls). The leaves are slender and pinnate, often doubly pinnate at the base, 10–20 cm long. The flowers are in male or female inflorescences on the same tree and are unusual amongst the pea family in being regular and campanulate, about 20, yellow-green, on each spike. The pods are very big in hot countries, to

45 cm long, but here are about 25 cm and infrequent, which is an advantage in towns where a heavy crop would be a nuisance.

MERITS: As a tree for hot, rather dry sites this is vigorous and unusual, with elegant foliage of a fresh colour. The branched spines on the bole, with annual additions which are green, are an interesting feature when in a shrubbery or flower-bed out of harms way. This is an exceptionally tolerant tree of extreme city conditions, thriving beneath skyscrapers in New

York, Atlanta and other cities, (in the unspined form 'Inermis').

LIMITATIONS: Worth growing only where summers are hot, in the south-east. The type tree with its ferociously spined bole is not recommended for planting by paths or in open spaces (but see 'Cultivar' below). The tree has a short season in leaf and is somewhat sparse when bare. It grows tall and requires light.

ORIGIN AND OCCURRENCE: Introduced from central USA before 1700 this tree is frequent only in Cambridge and surroundings. It is seen in London parks and in towns to the south. In Cambridgeshire one was 23 m × 48 cm when 44-years-old (Anglesea Abbey) – surprisingly rapid growth.

CULTIVARS: **'Inermis'** grows to the same size as the type and lacks all the spines on the bole,

having instead a more fissured bark with scaly flanged ridges. It is the form usual where the tree is in a street or park.

'SUNBURST'

'Sunburst' is a fairly recent form from the mid-western USA whose potential size cannot be known but would appear to be less than the other forms. In Nebraska, the oldest trees are scarcely 9 m tall but spread widely. Its merit is in leafing out bright-gold then turning a bright yellow-green before becoming more normal-green, with new leaves gold at the tips of shoots.

Griselinia littoralis

FEATURES: As a tree, which in Ireland may be 15 m tall, the *Griselinia* has a stout, curved trunk with a grey scaly bark. The broad, oval leaves vary in size from 3 to 12 cm and are thick, leathery, usually glossy and yellowish-green above, very plain, matt, pale-green beneath. They are oblique at the base. Plants are either male or female but in either case the flowers are inconspicuous and yellowish-green.

MERITS: A bright, cheerful evergreen, this has a distinctive colour and foliage and makes a solid

mound or broad tree very useful for shelter from sea-winds. It will grow on chalk or on acid soils.

LIMITATIONS: Not fully hardy inland in north and east, this is only a shrub except in Ireland and by the west coast.

ORIGIN AND OCCURRENCE: The New Zealand plant has been grown here since about 1850 and is common as a shrub in Ireland and the south-western peninsular and less common in those parts and in North Wales as a tree. Further north and east it remains shrubby and is rare.

Ilex × _altaclarensis_
Highclere hybrid holly

FEATURES: The general features of this group of hybrids are strong purple or green shoots, a solid sturdy crown and bole, and broad, flat leaves to 10×10 cm or more, with few spines or none. The flowers, whether male or female are large for a holly, clustered along the shoots in bunches and pale-purple until they open. Female forms have large berries.

MERITS: As a group these are invaluable as exceedingly tough evergreens, defying sea-winds and town air and tolerant of very poor soils if they are well-drained. The commonest form is 'Hodginsii', a male form with a distinctive grey sheen to the foliage, vigorous and handsome. Most of the green-leafed forms can make sizeable trees to 14–15 m tall. Young plants have a regular whorled crown with a conic spire.

LIMITATIONS: None, beyond that where the surroundings must be kept swept as dead leaves fall during the summer and are unpleasant to handle. Large close plantings of a single form can be dull. Not all the forms bear berries.

ORIGIN AND OCCURRENCE: Hybrids which arose when a tender Mediterranean holly, either _I. perado_ or _I. platyphylla_ was grown in conservatories and, first at Highclere in about 1838 and subsequently elsewhere, moved out of doors in the summer, when they were pollinated by bees from Common holly. The berries were used to raise more plants. The forms mentioned are very common in parks, especially at the seaside and in cities and towns, also in the larger gardens.

CULTIVARS: 'Camellifolia'. Good in a formal planting, this regularly conic tree resembles in outline a bay. The dark, yellowish-green, glossy leaves are mostly entire, and over 12 cm long. They are lanceolate or oblong-ovate. The relatively large flowers are female and give way to large red berries but not in profusion.

'**Golden King**' has spineless or few-spined leaves to 10×5 cm boldly edged rich-yellow and is a female form.

'**Hendersonii**' can be 10 m tall, a rather shapeless high mound of dull yellowish-green leaves, and bears quantities of large bright-red berries.

'**Hodginsii**'. The commonest and probably most robust form, used on the coast and in cities, is a floriferous male with glossy, broad leaves giving it a distinctive sheen from a distance.

Ilex aquifolium
Common holly

FEATURES: This native tree is returning slowly to favour having suffered from over-planting in Victorian days. In shade or with considerable age the crown is broadly domed and somewhat pendulous, but young trees are narrowly conic and may retain a slender spire, when 12–15 m tall. The pale-grey or pinkish, buff-speckled bark often has large blisters or warts. Unlike the Highclere hollies, the spined leaves have strongly buckled edges so that the spines point alternately up and down. Spined leaves are replaced in older trees, above 1–3 m from the ground by plane, unspined leaves but only on strongly-growing trees and seldom in the shade. Occasional trees are 20 m tall.

MERITS: In all forms, a very tolerant, tough plant and with its cultivars, a group with handsome and varied evergreen foliage. Hollies can be useful as a living fence and will grow in moderate shade although they will bear few berries in such a position. The remarkably narrow, slim, spire-like crowns of young trees are very shapely. Hollies bear pruning and mutilation very well, although looking none the better for it.

LIMITATIONS: The type tree can be dull if planted in numbers and single trees may be males and so lacking berries.

ORIGIN AND OCCURRENCE: This holly is native except in the extreme north of Scotland, and is found to 550 m above sea level. It is a common understorey in the better drained oakwoods and in beechwoods probably where these were once of oak. The type and many cultivars are widely planted in town parks and gardens but had been out of fashion during this century until recently.

CULTIVARS: **'Bacciflava'** has pale-yellow berries and nearly black leaves, a splendid tree for an unusual variation.

'Ferox', the Hedgehog holly has small, hooded leaves with several rows of spines on the upper surface. It is fairly frequent, as is the cream-margined form.

'Handsworth New Silver' is a bright, clean plant with broad margins as nearly white as in any holly, on a small leaf with big spines, and on purple shoots.

'Perry's Weeping Holly' makes a long-pendulous mound to 6 or 7 m tall, the small leaves edged nearly white, and can be very attractive.

'PERRY'S WEEPING HOLLY'

Juglans nigra
Black walnut

FEATURES: A fine, handsome tree of considerable vigour and stature in areas with hot summers and on deep rich soils. The buds are pale-brown covered in soft grey pubescence and the shoots brown or orange, densely pubescent. The leaves unfold bright yellow-green and are soon a rich emerald colour. They have 15–23 leaflets well-spaced and may be 45 cm long. The male catkins are thick, long-conic, to 10 cm long. The fruit are large, 5 cm across, globular and green and when bruised or skinned yield a strong, rather sweet scent. They are frequently numerous on the ground beneath the tree in autumn.

MERITS: Many specimens are noble trees, to 30 m tall with long, clear and impressive boles. Although some trees are broader in the crown from short boles, all bear large very handsome leaves showing their numerous, slender leaflets distinctively and a rich bright-green. Fast growing on the right sites, the trees display bright-gold autumn colours and at all times the heavily ridged bark, often black, makes interesting what might otherwise be a somewhat gaunt bare tree.

LIMITATIONS: A tree requiring plenty of space, and deep rich soils for proper development, the Black walnut also needs as much sunshine as possible. It does not thrive in the western half of Britain and except for one in Easter Ross, all the best trees are south and east of a line from York to Exeter. An unsuitable tree for an exposed site on a dry soil.

ORIGIN AND OCCURRENCE: Native to the USA from Massachusetts to Texas, this tree was introduced before 1656 and is infrequent in parks and the larger gardens in the south-east, East Anglia and the Midlands but rare beyond these regions.

Juglans regia
Common walnut

FEATURES: This well-known tree has been intensively sought for its timber so there are few or none seen with good boles. Growth in height soon diminishes as the crown broadens and few attain more than 18 m although one was recently 26 m tall. Growth in diameter is at first rapid and is maintained quite well but senility sets in after about 200 years and perhaps less, and the tree falls to pieces.

MERITS: In early May, the leaves unfold rich deep-red then orange-brown. After some weeks they are bronzed green and eventually a yellow-green. They have the property of repelling flies and although not in the class of the Black walnut for decorative aspect, the foliage is attractive. Another feature is the very pale, grey bark with broad, smooth ridges. The fruit are uncertain in this climate and trees are raided by grey squirrels, but where ripening they are suitable for pickling and in good years for dessert.

LIMITATIONS: A broad tree needing space and light, this also requires base-rich, light, deep soils to grow well, thriving on brick-earths and hop-garden soils below chalk slopes and on the margins of alluvial valleys.

ORIGIN AND OCCURRENCE: Probably native only from the Black Sea region eastwards, to China, this tree may have been brought here by the Romans. Quite common everywhere except in the Highland region it is notably numerous in south Yorkshire, Lincolnshire and Devon, Somerset and Dorset.

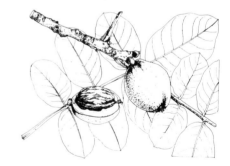

Koelreuteria paniculata
Golden rain tree

FEATURES: An unusual tree with several attractive features, Koelreuteria could well be planted more in the south. The leaves are doubly pinnate and 45 cm long with a red main stalk. The leaflets are highly distinctive in being broad, oblong-ovate and lobed or coarsely toothed. Flowering is late, in August.

MERITS: The singular feature is the large, open panicles of small yellow flowers projecting from the top of the crown. Subsidiary features extending the season are the pink bladder-like fruit and the spring opening of the foliage which is at first deep-red changing to yellow and to nearly white. The ability to grow in paved yards and poor hot sites is useful.

LIMITATIONS: This grows and flowers well only in restricted areas where the summers are hottest. These are East Anglia and around Chichester particularly, and generally in the south-east. It has a short season in leaf and makes but a poorly-shaped tree, unattractive in winter.

ORIGIN AND OCCURRENCE: A tree of China, Korea and Japan, this was introduced from China in 1763. It is grown in the south-east and Midlands of England but is uncommon.

Laurus nobilis
Bay, Poets' laurel

FEATURES: The Bay has a smooth, black bark, wrinkled or cracked, but not fissured until very large. The shoots are dark purple-red and the leaves are lanceolate, hard, dark-green with a crinkled, finely toothed margin. The flowers are in short stalked bunches of 2–6 beneath each leaf, opening in April. In some years, the 8 mm fruit are abundant and turn black when ripe.

MERITS: This splendid evergreen makes a shapely, tapered plant with highly pleasing foliage and bright-yellow flowers clustered on the stems. It is tolerant as to soil but appreciates some side-shelter especially from the north and east. The leaves are used in flavouring some meat dishes.

LIMITATIONS: Fully hardy and capable of becoming a 10 m tree only in the far south and west, this laurel is elsewhere only a tall shrub liable to leaf-scorch in freezing winds.

ORIGIN AND OCCURRENCE: The bay is native to the Mediterranean area and has been cultivated at least since 1562. Whilst trees are frequent only in Ireland, Cornwall, south Devon, south Wales and by the west coast, as a shrub it is relatively frequent everywhere and is commonly used in containers in courtyards and beside doors.

Ligustrum lucidum
Chinese privet

M

FEATURES: This remarkably handsome, tolerant tree is among the most valuable evergreens we have. The bark is smooth, dull-grey, striated with buff. The thick leaf is glossy deep-green, ovate, entire and about 10 × 5 cm. Usually this privet tends to be bushy but there are trees 12 m tall and it has attained 15 m.

MERITS: The attractive, glossy, evergreen foliage is hardy in all southern areas and is for much of the year mixed with panicles of buds or flowers. The flowers open and are intensely fragrant at the useful time of August and continue until January, a remarkable period for

flowering. The crown is a well-marked dome and the tree flourishes on any soil, including chalky ones. It thrives in towns, including London.

LIMITATIONS: It is not reliably hardy everywhere north of the English Midlands, and can be slow in growth. But even when it may grow only into a bush instead of a tree, it is a first class bush.

ORIGIN AND OCCURRENCE: Introduced from China in 1794 this tree occurs also in Korea and Japan. It is infrequent on the outskirts of cities and towns only in the south but it is hardy in Edinburgh.

Liquidambar formosana
var. **monticola**
Chinese sweet-gum

FEATURES: At present only a collector's piece, this fine tree deserves much wider recognition and use. The triangular lobes of the leaf are hard and edged with fine, jagged teeth. The bark is dark-grey and flaky from an early age.

MERITS: A tree of character at any time when in leaf, this is planted usually for its beautiful and unusual autumn colours. The leaves are conspicuously three-lobed and emerge shiny red-brown before turning deep-green, almost black, on dark-red petioles. Autumn colour starts with pale-orange and progresses to scarlet, crimson

and purple, and with its leaves at various stages in this progression, a tree is spectacular. The crown is neat and narrow and growth is reasonably rapid.

LIMITATIONS: Of uncertain hardiness in the north-east this will grow well only on fertile well-drained soils. Under shade it is semi-evergreen.

ORIGIN AND OCCURRENCE: Sent from western China in 1907 this tree is rare and found in collections and some major gardens but in very few smaller ones.

Liquidambar styraciflua
Sweet-gum

M

FEATURES: The Sweet-gum is frequently planted in gardens for autumn colour but it is a fine foliage tree as well. The bark is dark-grey and soon deeply ridged and fissured. The crown is usually well-shaped, conic and tall but some have a low crown of widely spreading branches curving up at their outer ends. The leaves are alternate, five-lobed, 15 × 15 cm with regular small sharp teeth. Growth is only moderate but many trees exceed 20 m in height and a few are 25 m. Some trees grow cork-winged suckers at

the base. These may be used for propagating the tree, but they tend to be very corky and slow growing with small leaves. Seedlings are usually far more vigorous with big three-lobed leaves. For reliable autumn colour, trees should be selected in the beds in autumn and planted where they receive full sun and preferably beside water if possible or somewhere cold autumn air flows down to them but is not a true frost-hollow.

MERITS: The foliage is bold, rich glossy-green and free of disease, but it is the autumn colours which give the tree its popularity. Young trees usually turn scarlet then deep-red but in later life some turn pale-yellow with a few leaves deep-red, others scarlet. Still others remain green until November when some leaves are yellow and others plum-purple or dark-red. When they flower, which is rather seldom here, the globular, spiky fruit hang on long stalks through the winter giving the tree a strange appearance.

LIMITATIONS: The Sweet-gum is unable to grow sufficiently in areas with cool summers to be worth planting in Scotland or the north of England. It also requires a generally deep and fertile soil with adequate moisture. Whilst it grows well in southern cities it rarely shows worthwhile autumn colours there nor where exposed to sea-winds. Without leaves it is spiky and gaunt.

ORIGIN AND OCCURRENCE: A splendid tree throughout the Appalachian Mountains this was introduced in 1681. It is frequent in southern England and the Midlands, in parks and gardens, but scarce further north and hardly makes a tree in Scotland.

Liriodendron chinense
Chinese tulip-tree

A useful slight variation on the common American tulip-tree, where available, the Chinese species differs only in the consistently narrowed base to the main lobe of the leaf, smoother bark and pale-orange flowers without a blue-green zone on the petals. Also the new leaves emerge orange and the petiole is often dark-red. In the south it is equally rapid or slightly more rapid in growth but may be marginally more tender in the north than the American species.

Liriodendron tulipifera
Tulip-tree

FEATURES: This is a handsome foliage tree, rather hiding the flowers from which it gets its name. The bark is grey and well ridged until turning dark-brown when very old by which time the ridges intercross regularly. Young trees are ovoid or conic but with age here, (unlike in America where a conic, open crown is maintained until 40 m tall,) the crown becomes dense and hugely domed with a few heavy, nearly vertical limbs. When about 250-years-old the trees begin to break up although remarkably healthy until then. The leaf-buds are formed by two large and persistent stipules enfolding minute leaves.

MERITS: The Tulip-tree is an exceedingly attractive and, in the south, a vigorous and large tree. In 40 years it can be 23 m tall and 75 cm through the bole and may ultimately attain 35 m × 2 m. The peculiarly-shaped, often large leaves are pale fresh green at first then somewhat darker and held in dense masses. The flowers, pale-orange, banded blue-green are very numerous on old trees in some years. In autumn the leaves turn bright-yellow and unless blown off they turn old-gold and russet before falling. The tree is hardy, once above grass-level, and

popular appeal, the flowers are rather unimportant and will not appear until some 25 years after planting. Thriving most where summers are warm, this tree grows slowly in southern Scotland and attains but moderate size there, seldom flowering much, and is not worth growing north of the Forth-Clyde line. It needs a well-drained, deep fertile soil but can be grown well on a warm sandy soil if helped with some mulching. It grows well in towns, but not industrial cities, and may not give any autumn colour. It casts a deep shade, widely. After flowering the fruit capsules remain during the winter and are not attractive.

ORIGIN AND OCCURRENCE: This tree is common in the Allegheny and Great Smoky Mountains in Virginia and Tennessee and was introduced in about 1650. It is frequent in parks and gardens in the southern half of England; uncommon north of the Midlands as far as Edinburgh and rare further north.

CULTIVARS: 'Aureomarginatum' is a slower growing tree rarely 23 m tall. The margins are broadly marked in pale-yellow making the tree pleasantly but not spectacularly conspicuous.

'Fastigiatum'. Planted first in 1888 at Kew, this tree which is a fairly slender column when young has now, when nearly 90-years-old opened out a little untidily. In a planting which is not too formal it is a valuable plant, giving good, golden, autumn colour.

withstands town air and conditions quite well.

LIMITATIONS: This tree is very vigorous in the south and will make an enormous tree so it is quite unsuited to a restricted space. Despite

---

Magnolia campbellii
Campbell's magnolia

FEATURES: This is a stocky tree with a stout, smooth grey bole bearing many low, wide-spreading branches, sweeping up at their tips. The stout shoots are pale blue-green. The leaves are oblong-ovate, 17–20 cm long, white-pubescent beneath and greyish-green and shiny above.

MERITS: Once it achieves an age to flower fully this is one of the most spectacular flowering trees we can grow. Huge rosy pink tulip-shaped flowers open gradually to the shape of a chalice then the outer petals droop and each flower may be 30 cm across. By this age the tree will be 10–12 m tall and the flowers will be on the outside of a large, domed crown. Trees 18 m tall will bear many hundreds of these flowers, which are over before the leaves unfold. The foliage is bold, if somewhat dull, except when the buds unfold dark purple-red.

LIMITATIONS: A tree for the west and south coast regions and north to the Thames Valley only, although since it does well at Kew it might well be tried a little more widely than it seems to have been hitherto. It needs good side-shelter against winds and a deep, rich soil is preferred, although not essential. Frost-hollows must be

avoided. This tree traditionally needs 20 years from planting to flowering and rarely takes as few as 18. Recent years (1970-76) have been kind to the flowers (in 1975 and 1976 many were fully out by the end of the very mild January) but previously, when the tree flowered only in March, it was quite common for the flowers to be ruined by a sharp frost at that time. Like all magnolias, this resents being pruned or moved and must be planted out early in its life.

ORIGIN AND OCCURRENCE: This magnolia comes from the eastern parts of the Himalayas and was introduced in 1868. It is almost entirely confined to the major gardens of Sussex and along the coast to Cornwall, Gloucestershire, North Wales, Argyll and, particularly, Ireland.

CULTIVAR: 'Charles Raffill' is the most frequent (to date) of a number of crosses between M. campbellii and its pale-flowered variety mollycomata. This hybrid was raised in 1946 and is much planted, the early plants now being quite big trees (15 m and over) since they grow rapidly. This hybrid flowers at an earlier age than M. campbellii, the flowers a little smaller and bright purplish-pink. The leaves are to 20 cm long and oblique at base.

Magnolia denudata
(syn. *M. conspicua*)
Yulan lily

FEATURES: A splendid large-flowered white Magnolia, this was formerly much more planted than it is now. The crown is broad and twiggy, sometimes over 10 m tall. The grey-haired flower-buds are prominent in the winter. The flowers have thick petals and open to 20 cm across.

MERITS: In the south, a welcome change from *Magnolia × soulangiana* and a true tree, it is magnificent when covered in its large, pure-white flowers. It is good in towns and can be grown against a wall.

LIMITATIONS: This magnolia is suitable only for the south of England. It needs shelter from the wind and may suffer damage to its flowers if frosts come in the period between the opening of the bud scales and the end of flowering, in March. It shares the cultural disabilities of other magnolias.

ORIGIN AND OCCURRENCE: This Chinese species was introduced in 1789. It has not been widely planted recently and large trees are seen only in old-established gardens in southern England.

Magnolia grandiflora
Southern magnolia,
Bull bay

FEATURES: This evergreen makes a magnificent tree to 30 m tall in Alabama and grows well in southern cities here. The bark is nearly black and is smooth. The leaf is thick, hard, leathery and obovate-oblong with a waved margin, bright, glossy-green above, thickly pubescent, rich rusty-red beneath (but differs from this in the various cultivars and is highly variable in that respect in the wild).

MERITS: A luxuriant-looking evergreen of distinction, this makes a neat small tree, with glossy foliage. The flowers are sparse but open over a long season from July to November (some were out in March in 1975). They are very big, to 30 cm across, well-formed and highly fragrant.

LIMITATIONS: Really only a plant for a wall except in the south-west of England and probably East Anglia and the Home Counties, where it has too rarely been tried. In Devon and Cornwall, a free-standing tree of slow growth. The large, hard leaves are shed during the summer and can be a nuisance. Flowering is sporadic, never copious and, in seedlings needs 20 year's growth.

ORIGIN AND OCCURRENCE: This tree makes a very tall, imposing specimen within its natural range. It was introduced in 1734 and is found against walls quite commonly all over England except in the north-east, in Wales and Ireland. As a free-standing tree it is confined to the south-west and near the south coast.

CULTIVARS: **'Goliath'** is the most popular form for its larger flowers borne earlier in life but probably only because these plants are not seedlings. It also differs from the type in its much broader leaf, green beneath.

'Exmouth' is similar, with a narrower leaf.

Magnolia salicifolia
Willow-leaved magnolia

FEATURES: There are several forms of this tree, some with much broader leaves than others. The fruit are curved, lumpy cylindric, 8 cm long and bright yellow-green.

MERITS: Extremely effective when the delicate, tall crown is a cloud of pure-white flowers, this tree can have a broad crown 14 m tall. The flowers open in late April when there is much less chance of their being damaged by frost than is the case with most other tree-magnolias. The foliage is not only rather elegant, narrow leaves but these have distinctive grey-brown tints and red petioles and when crushed they exude a strong, sweet, heliotrope or aniseed scent.

LIMITATION: This tree needs a warm and sheltered site, preferably on good soil and is unsuitable for the north.

ORIGIN AND OCCURRENCE: This tree was introduced from its native Japan in 1892 and is found almost entirely in the major gardens of southern England.

Magnolia sprengleri 'Diva'

In some respects a superior tree to *M. campbellii* this will flower within 15 years of planting by which time it is a shapely tree 15 m tall bearing 500 superb bright rosy-pink flowers. It was sent from China in 1907.

Malus × atrosanguinea

A useful variation on *M. floribunda* and equally floriferous, this hybrid, (probably *M. halli-nana × M. sieboldii*) differs from that tree in the brighter red buds and richer pink flowers.

Malus floribunda
Japanese crab

FEATURES: Always grown as a standard, this tree has a dark-brown, scaly bark. The shoot is green and densely pubescent. The lanceolate leaf, on a pinkish petiole, crimson at base, is sharply toothed on the outer third, shallowly on the remainder.

MERITS: In flower, unfailingly spectacular, the densely held red buds and pink flowers fading to white, foam all over the crown. In some years there are numerous, small, yellow fruit. This tree gives an early and welcome sign of spring in unfolding its small, bright-green leaves very early, usually in March but in 1975 in January. Like other apples, this thrives on chalky soils and is tolerant of towns and streets.

LIMITATIONS: A low tree, never making a tall crown, but rounded and broader than it is tall. This crown is rather an untidy, confused mass when not hidden by leaves. Fitting only an urban landscape, this tree must have full light and adequate space to make a worthwhile plant.

ORIGIN AND OCCURRENCE: Introduced from Japan in 1862 this tree is very common in streets, front gardens in towns, in parks and larger gardens, throughout England but rather less so in Scotland.

S

Malus × purpurea
Purple crab hybrids

FEATURES AND CULTIVARS: The common cultivars are seemingly distinguishable in books by their time of flowering, red-ness and double-ness, but in the field it is usually difficult to say which is which. 'Aldenhamensis' should be late in flower, deep-red and semi-double. 'Lemoinei' should be stronger growing, more purple and larger in the single flower and 'Eleyi' should be the reddest in flower. 'Profusion' is a rather deeper red with flowers in long sprays and is to be preferred also for much superior foliage, but there is little to choose among the others.

MERITS: Briefly in April the leaves emerge a respectable deep-red and the flowers in dense clusters open from red buds to dark purple-reds in great profusion. The trees are very hardy and tolerant of almost any soils.

LIMITATIONS: Few trees can have such badly shaped, sprawling, formless and tangled crowns as this group of very similar trees. In leaf, after flowering except 'Profusion', they are dowdy, dark-green, badly tinged purple, and have no change to autumn colours. Near red brick even the flowers are a disaster.

ORIGIN AND OCCURRENCE: These all owe their colouring to the Siberian *Malus niedwetzkyana* and are selections from various hybrids with this species. The named forms have arisen since 1912. So far as can be told, all are frequent or common in streets, front gardens and parks in and near towns.

S

Malus hupehensis
Hupeh crab

FEATURES: The Hupeh crab is a sturdy broad tree of great worth. The stout bole is orange-brown fissured into coarse plates. The crown is both tall and spreading.

MERITS: Coming into flower this is entrancingly beautiful. Among good green leaves, numerous, large, pale-pink buds open to inverted cups of large, white, golden-bossed flowers, later opening widely. Small trees have branches wreathed in the long-stalked flowers and large trees make white clouds against the sky. The fruit are numerous, small, globular and bright, shining, deep-red. It grows well in chalky soils. It is a triploid and will not cross with other apples so it comes true from the seed, and grows strongly.

LIMITATIONS: This is a broad, fairly tall tree of rapid growth (for an apple) and needs plenty of room. Not noticed in towns, it may need rather better conditions than some other apples.

ORIGIN AND OCCURRENCE: Sent from Hupeh, central China in 1900 this lovely tree has not yet been widely planted but is in the better gardens and parks. The form grown always has pubescent flower-stalks so is not the true *M. hupehensis*. It has not yet been named.

S

Malus tschonowskii
Pillar apple

FEATURES: This is one of the exceedingly few trees to be fastigiate in wild populations. The small number of trees of appreciable age are 14–16 m tall and have variably narrow, erect crowns. The leaves are 10–12 cm long, ovate-oblong, thick and leathery, glossy deep-green above and felted with white pubescence beneath.

MERITS: The slender, upright crown makes this tree singularly fitted to planting in streets, courtyards and where space is confined. The foliage is large for an apple; the flowers and fruit are pleasant if unspectacular, but the glory of the tree is its brilliant autumn scarlet and gold. It is sufficiently robust and unfussy about soils to flourish in the difficult sites to which it is so well suited. It withstands well, being planted when big enough for the lowest branches to be out of normal reach except at their very tough bases, and is therefore little damaged by the usual forms of vandalism. It has few fruit and small, unlikely to be a nuisance on pavements. It comes into leaf silvered by dense hairs.

LIMITATIONS: Not particularly inspiring in winter.

ORIGIN AND OCCURRENCE: This Japanese tree was introduced in 1897 but was little planted until adopted by road authorities in the last ten years. Bigger trees are in only a few nurseries and major gardens, therefore, but young trees may now be seen in town streets, by arterial roads and feeder roads to motorways, and in precincts, parks and car-parks.

M

Malus
'John Downie'

FEATURES: A neat tree, spectacular in spring and autumn, 'John Downie' is an adaptable tree of great value. The leaf is glossy rich-green and lanceolate or ovate. The top height seems to be about 8 m.

MERITS: Young trees are upright, narrow at first and highly attractive when covered in pale-pink buds and clear white flowers in profusion. Older trees are more spreading, bearing arched branches, also splendid in flower. An even greater merit, is the fruit which are prolific, conic-ovoid and brilliant-yellow and scarlet in long-stalked bunches making a unique display. Like other apples this is tolerant of any well-drained soil, especially chalk. The fruit will make a first class jam for flavour, clarity and colour.

LIMITATIONS: None, but this will never be a big tree.

ORIGIN AND OCCURRENCE: Raised at a nursery near Lichfield in 1875, 'John Downie' is being planted in small gardens in large numbers. Bigger trees are less frequent.

Malus 'Golden Hornet'

FEATURES: 'Golden Hornet' is the only weeping apple normally grown but is otherwise undistinguished until in fruit. The flowers are white, in quite good number.

MERITS: The reason for growing this rather than another apple with more or better flowers is the fruit. These are strung down the weeping branches in bunches of six or more and are a good bright pale-yellow.

LIMITATIONS: Room is required beneath this tree for the pendulous branches.

ORIGIN AND OCCURRENCE: This seedling was selected in a Surrey nursery before 1949 from a variety of a rare Japanese species. It is now popular for planting in small gardens, in parks, around trading estates and in similar urban situations.

Nothofagus dombeyi Dombey's Southern beech

FEATURES: Apparently the finest tree in Chile, Dombey's Southern beech is a promising tree here. The bark is dark-grey or black and smooth, striated grey until the tree is large when it breaks into dark-brown, thick, square flakes which are shed leaving red patches. The crown is a fairly dense ovoid with upper branches swept up almost to vertical. The leaves are variable in shape, diamond-shaped, oval or lanceolate, always doubly and jaggedly toothed, hard, shiny and 2.5–4 cm long. The underside is matt, smooth, pale-green with only the midrib showing. Flowers are borne by trees when about 10 m tall, the male flowers being like small Fuchsia flowers, cream or pink-tinged tubes 6 mm long with protruding stamens.

MERITS: One of very few broadleaved evergreens with tiny leaves, this makes a highly decorative plant. Where thriving it grows with great vigour – in Co. Wicklow two trees 36-years-

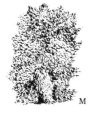
M

old are 27 × 1 m diameter. Even at Kew in sheltered shrubberies it has grown reasonably fast and has not been damaged during cold winters. As a dark background for early cherries it is excellent, the mature foliage being nearly black.

LIMITATIONS: Not a tree for eastern areas or exposures, this evergreen can be scorched by cold winds. Except in the west or in sheltered or warmer parts of the east, the growth can be cut back considerably by real winters. Probably not a success on chalky soils.

ORIGIN AND OCCURRENCE: Introduced from Chile, where it ranges south to Tierra del Fuego, in 1916, Dombey's Southern beech is found as a big tree frequently in large Irish gardens and in some in Cornwall, Devon, Wales, Cumbria and Argyll. It is uncommon or rare further east except in Sussex.

Nothofagus obliqua Roble beech

FEATURES: The Roble beech is the only broad-leaved tree able to grow as fast as the best conifers on very acid, poor soils at Bedgebury in Kent. The bark is smooth and pale-grey at first, gradually ageing to dark-brown square, curling plates. The leaves are ovate-oblong varying much in size and in depth of lobules but with 7–11 pairs of veins even on the biggest leaf, which distinguish it from a small leaf of *N. procera* of the same size, (see p. 63). The slender shoot is dark-red above and slightly hairy.

MERITS: The Roble beech is of great value as a broadleaved tree conformable with the native woods yet of exceedingly great vigour and highly attractive. It has arched sprays of alternate, slender shoots in herring-bone patterns high

L

against the winter sky; pretty leaves and good yellow and crimsons in autumn. It is fairly tolerant with regard to soil if well-drained.

LIMITATIONS: This tree should grow with great rapidity and requires much room to develop. It has long ascending and arching branches which may be damaged in exposed places. It needs reasonably good soils either acid or somewhat alkaline, on a sheltered site. Young trees may be cut to the ground by the hardest winters. A few trees together will often seed themselves prolifically and the young plants can be a nuisance in a garden.

ORIGIN AND OCCURRENCE: This Chilean tree was introduced in 1902 and although nowhere common as yet, it is seen as large trees in many

Irish, western and southern gardens and occasionally in small forest plots. Several trees are more than 25 m tall and one is over 1 m in diameter, while at Windsor one has attained 26 m in 22 years.

Nothofagus procera
Rauli

FEATURES: The Rauli is in many areas the fastest-growing of all trees and makes a splendid specimen. The bark is silvery-grey and remains this colour on the oldest trees, becoming marked by deep, narrow, dark, long fissures. The crown is at first somewhat upswept to an ovoid with an acute tip where the leading shoot dominates, but with age becomes a regular, hemispheric dome

when given the room. The shoots are stout, for a *Nothofagus*, green and much roughened. The leaves are various sizes with the larger ones 8 or occasionally 12 cm long, oblong-ovate, finely toothed, lobulate on small leaves, and prominently marked by 15–18 pairs of veins. Flowers are profuse from about the 20th year, the males yellow and greenish-brown globules hanging on short stems in mid-May.

MERITS: A remarkably handsome tree with a sturdy bole and strong branches, this also bears big leaves beautifully veined, an attractive orange colour when freshly unfolded and giving good yellows, oranges and some red in autumn. Conformable with native countryside trees, this is of great value for its exceedingly rapid growth. In Devon, trees have been 14 m in 9 years from seed. Although generally best in western gardens, one of the oldest and best is near the Suffolk coast and is 28 m × 86 cm when 60-years-old and a monumental tree. In Here-fordshire, shoots of 2 m have been grown and in Surrey a bole is 73 cm in diameter when 39-years-old. Although the big trees are all on slightly acid soils or neutral, young stands have grown very strongly on thin soils over chalk.

LIMITATIONS: This Chilean beech needs plenty of room to make a hugely domed crown in a relatively short time. It does not grow well on poor, acid soils and is slightly less able to withstand hard winters than is *N. obliqua*. It is not suitable for exposed places.

ORIGIN AND OCCURRENCE: Introduced from Chile, where it spreads through the Andes into Argentina, in 1913, the Rauli is confined as a big tree to Irish, western and Sussex gardens (and East Bergholt Place, Suffolk, see above). Since 1950 and increasingly recently it has been planted, when available, in forest-plots and in gardens more generally, but it remains quite scarce.

Nyssa sylvatica
Tupelo

FEATURES: This is a tree of moderate growth and size which develops in early years a dull-grey, deeply ridged bark. The leaves are entire at the margins, obovate or elliptic and of a glossy yellowish-green at first then darker. The flowers are inconspicuous greenish-yellow, the males and females separate on the same tree.

MERITS: The Tupelo is attractive in its summer foliage but it is of greatest ornamental value in the autumn. The foliage becomes glossy yellow and scarlet then uniformly deep ruby-red. In the early phase it is one of the best and brightest of all the trees colouring in autumn.

LIMITATIONS: The Tupelo needs a hot summer and a rich, deep and moist soil to be worthwhile as a specimen. This limits its range as an effective plant to the south-east of England and the Midlands on sheltered, fertile sites. The winter aspect of the tree is of little attraction being rather gaunt.

ORIGIN AND OCCURRENCE: Native to the Allegheny Mountains of North Carolina and Virginia, the Tupelo was in cultivation before 1750 but had not been planted in any but small numbers until in 1907 about 150 trees were placed around the lakes at Sheffield Park, Sussex. There are two trees around 18 m tall at Chatsworth, Derbyshire but it is very rare so far to the north. Old trees are highly exceptional,

one in Hampshire dating from 1810 and 25 m tall had no close rivals, but blew down recently.

Paulownia tomentosa
(syn. *P. imperialis*)
Foxglove-tree

FEATURES: This tree is of unusual aspect, foliage and flowers. The smooth, grey-barked bole is soon very stout and the crown broad, irregularly domed. All the late summer and winter the flower-buds covered in golden-brown hairs stand on protruding panicles. Adult leaves are long-acuminate triangular to 35 × 25 cm, opposite and densely hairy beneath, on a pink densely

where one is not wanted, the shoot can be cut to the ground annually and the plant will throw up another each year with outsize leaves. Although needing some space and full sunshine, this is an excellent tree for southern towns and around buildings.

LIMITATIONS: This tree grows stout shoots 2 to 2.5 m long in its first few years and these are invariably nipped at the tip by frost. Next year there will be two or three shoots and these need to be reduced to one strong one. It is quite unsuited to exposed places both because of its large leaves and its brittle branches. For good growth and even more for reliable flowering it requires hot summers so is best planted only in East Anglia, the southern Midlands, south coast, London area and parts of the south-west. The flowers being at the tips of the shoots are seen well only when looking down on the tree and so it is sometimes planted beneath ramparts, castle-walls or bridge-approaches. The roots are largely confined in the first few years to large turnip-like tap-roots with very few subsidiary feeding-roots, so moving the tree is difficult. Later rooting is strong and superficial. The tree prefers a hot, dry soil to a damp, cold one but is otherwise fairly tolerant. In a long season out of leaf this is a gaunt tree. It is short-lived and its branches become riddled with woodpecker holes.

ORIGIN AND OCCURRENCE: Native to China, the Foxglove-tree has long been grown in Japan from which it was introduced to Europe in 1838. In 1907, Wilson sent seed from central China and the Westonbirt tree together with the other big specimens are of that origin. Large trees are relatively frequent only in Cambridge, London, Bath and a few other southern cities.

M

pubescent petiole 10–15 cm long. One tree, in a very sheltered avenue at Westonbirt, Glos. is 28 m tall but very few elsewhere exceed 12 m.

MERITS: From the first year this is a striking plant with leaves up to 45 × 45 cm hanging from the unbranched stem. After a few years it flowers and the pale-mauve or purplish-blue trumpets, maybe ten to a panicle, each 6 cm long, are spectacular in late May just before the leaves unfold. Where there is no space for a tree or

---

Platanus × acerifolia
(syn. *P. × hispanica*)
London plane

L

FEATURES: This tree is probably the first inter-continental hybrid tree to arise and it exhibits good hybrid vigour. The checkered, pale-yellow and brown bark is not long retained on the bole (except in one rare clone) and big-boles are dull orange-brown rather finely ridged. Leaves vary with the clones, the earliest (perhaps original trees in Britain) bearing large, broad leaves about 20 × 20 cm with a long, straight base briefly cuneate to the petiole and big lobes cut more than half way, with a few big teeth on each side. 'Pyramidalis', commonly used in cities and streets has a small leaf, about 15 × 15 cm, with a very cuneate base and shallower lobes. This form also bears only 2–3 fruit per stalk whereas most others bear mainly 4–6. The male catkins bear yellowish, small flowers, whilst the females bear crimson heads in mid-May. The copious seed is highly fertile and gives rise to a range of leaf-variants.

MERITS: The London plane is extraordinarily tough and robust and can grow rapidly in conditions of smoky air and root-runs under impermeable surfacing where most trees could scarcely even survive. It is so wind-firm that few have ever been known to blow down and it is very rarely if ever guilty of dropping a branch from a live tree. Many trees are at least 200-years-old and in full health and vigour while two may be nearly 300-years-old and are equally thriving. This tree withstands almost any mutilation inflicted upon it by a wide variety of authorities with problems arising from street plantings. It is free of disease except for sporadic outbreaks of "anthracnose" when new shoots and flowers wilt as if frosted, but this disease (*Gnomonia veneta*) has little if any lasting effect. The new leaves are covered in pale orange-grey hairs but are soon a clear, bright-green and the shiny, darker green of summer is a splendid foil

to the greys of Portland stone so frequent in cities. As a tree to make the largest possible specimen in a city park, the London plane has no rivals. Open-grown, single specimens in southern England make the most enormous, tall, broad domes, often reaching down to the ground.

LIMITATIONS: Rapid growth continued without perceptible decrease for at least 200 years makes this potentially one of the biggest of all trees. With an enormous crown of densely held big leaves it casts a vast shadow and can only be tolerated in confined spaces by continuous pruning which becomes expensive and frequently visually outrageous. The leaves are tough and make roads slippery and block gutters and drains. The fruit break up in May and release the seed which have a ring of hairs at one end. These hairs, or fragments of them, are carried by the wind, and can cause irritation to the eyes of people who are sensitive to them. The roots are powerful and far-reaching and can damage underground services and structures. Although wonderfully adapted to growing there and decorative among buildings, the London plane is on many counts the least suitable of all species for growing in streets and small city squares. In open countryside the tree is somehow incongruent, with harsh greens, and a crown alien among other trees. In cities, this tree can suffer much damage with a south-facing aspect where early growth is encouraged by sunny weather and then long periods of cold winds follow. North of the Midlands, except in south-east Scotland, cool summers decrease growth to the point where it is not worth planting. There is negligible autumn colour.

ORIGIN AND OCCURRENCE: The origin of this tree is still uncertain. In the literature, until 1919 when Henry and Flood made good distinctions, there is complete confusion among Oriental, London and American planes. It is impossible to tell unless the tree is still known, exactly to what earlier writers are referring. For long the London plane, where separated at all, was regarded as a variant of the Oriental plane – var. *acerifolia*. This view is now held again by some botanists. In 1919 the idea was promoted that it was a hybrid between the American and the Oriental planes, and this seemed highly satisfactory in explaining the leaf-shape and number of fruits per stem as intermediate between these two species. The hybrid was stated to have arisen at Oxford Botanic Gardens in 1670, based on a paper by the Director, Bobart. Later there was concern that the American species is hopelessly unthrifty in Britain, could not be established at Kew with decades of attempts, and so could not have flowered here. The result was the acceptance of the first cross having occurred [in about 1650] in Spain or southern France where the American species will grow well. In America, plants acceptable as London plane have recently been raised by hybridising Oriental and American planes, so the hybrid origin probably is the correct one.

The biggest London planes are in gardens and rectories south of the Thames, as at Witley Rectory, Surrey (35 × 2 m) Mottisfont Abbey (35 × 4 m but a double stem) and Bryanston School (50 × 1.7 m). Few in London are of this size but a tree possibly dating from 1680 at Ranelagh, Barnes is 34 × 2.4 m and one at Carshalton is 39 m × 2.5 m. The tree at the Bishops Palace, Ely, also reputed to date from 1680 is 35 × 2.7 m. This vast tree has continued to grow so fast in girth that the reputed date is almost certainly untenable. Further north, the species lacks the warm summer needed for full growth and few exceed 25 × 1.3 m but it is not uncommonly used as a street tree in Edinburgh.

CULTIVAR: **'Suttneri'** is an exceedingly rare form (three trees of some maturity known in Britain, one in Ireland) in which the leaves are boldly variegated cream and white whilst leaves inside the crown are often all white. With so much leaf-surface contributing nothing to the photosynthesis this is understandably slow-growing and has reached no great size, but one at Puttenham, Surrey is 22 m × 75 cm. Probably hard to obtain, this is a valuable, attractive tree.

Platanus orientalis
Oriental plane

FEATURES: The Oriental plane differs from the London plane in having deeply and acutely lobed leaves, usually more fruit on each stalk and a lower, broader crown. Many old trees have recumbent or layered branches and form wide mounds. Others have stout, short boles with pale red-brown bark.

MERITS: This tree is ultimately a large feature which can occupy as much as a tenth of a hectare as a mound of recumbent or layered branches. The foliage, boldly divided into long acute lobes is excellent and in autumn turns to unusual bronzed brownish-purple. The growth is vigorous and disease-free.

LIMITATIONS: A very large, widely spreading tree quite unsuited to enclosed space, the Oriental plane also casts heavy shade and sheds big leaves. Like the London plane, but probably even more, it requires hot summers for good growth and does not thrive away from the south and Midlands.

ORIGIN AND OCCURRENCE: This tree ranges from the Eastern Mediterranean, Cyprus and Crete through Asia Minor. Its date of introduction was probably around 1550. It is fairly frequent in parks and gardens from East Anglia southwestwards but uncommon, becoming rare to the north. A few specimens are more than 30 m tall and one is 2.5 m in diameter.

Populus alba
White poplar

FEATURES: This tree is often confused with the much sturdier, bigger-growing Grey poplar and has almost the same foliage. The bole is rarely straight, usually leaning and sinuous. The bark is white and cream over large areas, marked by rows of diamond-shaped black pits. The leaves on strong shoots and young trees are divided into acute lobes; those on mature branches nearly round, with incurved teeth. Male trees have short catkins, dark purple until they pollinate when they are dull-yellow. Female trees bear catkins of green fruit which become woolly before they are shed in June.

MERITS: This is a valuable tree in exposed coastal areas which are low-lying, of blown sand or restricted drainage. In the sand the suckering habit allows the plant to keep pace with the deposition of blown sand, although it will be more a series of large bushes than a tree. Alone or amongst other trees the new growth in spring makes a bright silvery feature and to a lesser extent is maintained in summer by the pure-white undersides of the leaves. In autumn the foliage turns bright-yellow, if usually only briefly.

LIMITATIONS: This should not be planted where a large specimen is required or where numerous and persistent root suckers are inconvenient. It is not a tree for restricted spaces, nor does it thrive in cities, and is short-lived.

ORIGIN AND OCCURRENCE: A tree widespread in Europe, this has been grown here so long that there is no record of its coming, which may have been in Roman times. Locally common in some coastal areas it is relatively infrequent but usually seen around the edges of fields and margins of copses, rarely more than 20 m tall.

CULTIVAR: **'Richardii'** is an almost rare form in which most of the crown is of bright-yellow leaves. It is extremely attractive.

Populus candicans 'Aurora'

FEATURES: This is the only poplar grown outside one of two specialist collections which has variegated foliage. The variegation is not on all the leaves, some of which are uniformly dark-green but is mainly concentrated on the mid or late season growths. The variegated leaves may be largely white or cream or white tinged pink, and in midsummer some trees have all the fully developed leaves green and the newly emerging ones white, like a water-lily flower at the tip of each branch. The colour thus increases as the season advances. The leaves are triangular and have dark-red petioles.

MERITS: 'Aurora' has great value as a well-marked variant of rapid growth for a patch of damp soil.

LIMITATIONS: As with other poplars, care must be taken to see that none is planted on a heavy, clay soil within about 30 m of a building. This tree may lose much of its attraction when it attains large size, due to poplar canker; it is fairly short-lived.

ORIGIN AND OCCURRENCE: The parent species, *P. candicans* is a balsam of unknown origin cultivated since 1755. It is probably of north-eastern American origin. 'Aurora' was raised in Europe and has been marketed in Britain since about 1950 so no large trees are known. It is occasionally planted in small roadside gardens and more frequently in large gardens and in parks, whilst in Devon it has been used as a roadside tree in a few places.

Populus canescens
Grey poplar

L

FEATURES: The Grey poplar is a much stronger-growing, bigger version of the White poplar and often mistaken for it. The stout bole is nearly straight: it can be long but usually bears big upcurving branches within 6 m of the ground.

The bark is silvery-grey and white or cream, prominently pitted black in horizontal rows. In old trees the lower parts become dark-grey with prominent knobs and deep fissures. Leaves on young trees or sprouts are shallowly lobed and on old trees they are orbicular-ovate, indistinguishable in shape from those of *P. alba* but the undersides are greyish-white and not bright pure-white. The crown is a high multiple dome, somewhat pendulous on the periphery. The tree can attain 38 m in height and 1.6 m in diameter and is frequently over 30 m tall.

MERITS: For rapid growth into a noble specimen of fine proportions and distinctive aspect few trees are better than the Grey poplar. The male tree, which is almost universally the one seen is dark-purple all the winter with abundant catkins. When coming into leaf the whole crown is a sparkling silvery-grey. In autumn it is bright golden colour. It grows well in the far north of Scotland, even by the seashore.

LIMITATIONS: This should never be planted in a restricted space as it needs much room to develop rapidly its tall, broadly-domed crown and also it suckers widely. For full growth it needs damp but well drained soils, nearly neutral or somewhat alkaline, and grows poorly on dry sands or acid soils.

ORIGIN AND OCCURRENCE: This tree is a hybrid between *P. alba* and *P. tremula*. Since only the latter is native it is probable, although not a necessity, that the tree was introduced rather than is native. If so its introduction was long before such records were kept. It is frequent in broad valleys in and near chalk lands and in the limestone regions of Ireland as well as on alluvial soils generally, in parks and a few gardens. There are big trees as far north and east as Sutherland but few in the north-west.

Populus × euramericana 'Eugenei'

FEATURES: This poplar is one of the most easily distinguished in this large group of hybrid black poplars. The narrowest in the crown, and lightest in branching, this is a male clone. Old trees develop somewhat pendulous outer shoots.

MERITS: A singularly shapely specimen, neat and conic with light branching and of great vigour until it exceeds 35 m in height. After that the crown becomes more broad and loses its regularity. It casts less shade than other poplars of its size owing to the rather open crown and small leaves.

LIMITATIONS: On clay soils this should never be planted within at least 30 m of a building. It requires a good, neutral or alkaline soil, preferably deep and moist, and warm summers. Autumn colouring is negligible or fleeting.

ORIGIN AND OCCURRENCE: A hybrid between P. 'Regenerata' and the Lombardy poplar, this arose in the Metz nurseries of Simon Louis in 1832. The oldest in the British Isles are the 1888 plantings at Kew, Edinburgh and Glasnevin (Dublin) where they are 35 × 1 m. At one time infrequent on rich, moist valley land, this tree is now rarely seen except in collections, but could well be used for variation amongst other poplars in amenity plantings.

Populus × euramericana 'Robusta'

FEATURES: The 'Robusta' poplar is in several ways the best of the hybrid black poplars for general plantings. The crown until 25–30 m tall is a regular, rather broad, ovoid-conic with upcurving lower branches. The catkins (male) are prolific, large and deep-red, often identifying the tree at a distance by their profusion in early April.

MERITS: The growth is very rapid indeed in height and diameter (to 31 m × 46 cm in 22 years for example, in Herefordshire) and the crown is fairly regular and pointed. In May the new leaves emerge bright red-brown and become spectacularly orange-brown for a week. The crown is more dense, with heavier foliage than in others of this group, which gives better screening, sound or dust-filtering qualities. In this it most resembles its American parent, Populus deltoides. The prolific male flowering is an attractive feature.

LIMITATIONS: As for 'Eugenei'.

ORIGIN AND OCCURRENCE: This hybrid between P. deltoides and a P. nigra 'Plantierensis' arose in France in 1895. It is frequently seen in south-east England in small plantations, screens and some roadside plantings, and has attained a height of 40 m.

Populus × euramericana 'Serotina'

FEATURES: The first of the intercontinental poplar hybrids to arise, P. 'Serotina' was once widely planted but now newer hybrids are replacing it. The bole is clean and may be 10 m long. It has a pale-grey bark with deep parallel ridges and fissures which remain continuous for 10 m or more. The crown tends to become cup-shaped with a few large branches curving upwards and inwards particularly on the weather side. The last poplar and the last countryside tree in leaf, it shows up dull orange-brown for some weeks as the leaves emerge. Catkins (male) are late, bright-red and soon shed.

MERITS: A very vigorous tree of some character with light grey-green foliage which flutters in light winds. As a male clone it causes no troubles with woolly seeds. The broad crown makes it effective as a screen on the largest scale.

LIMITATIONS: As in the preceding two, with the additional one that it is not suitable for places much resorted to for picnics or games by the public. This is because it rapidly achieves a great size (to 40 × 2 m) with very big branches and then starts dropping the branches and generally collapsing, within a hundred years of planting.

ORIGIN AND OCCURRENCE: This hybrid between *P. nigra* and *P. deltoides* arose first in France in about 1750. It is much used in city parks and is commonly used as a large screen. Big individuals stand out in some broad, south-eastern valleys. Often seen much pollarded in parks.

CULTIVAR: **'Serotina Aurea'**. Golden poplar is a much slower-growing form, rarely attaining 25 m. It is infrequent but occurs in parks and gardens locally. All summer it remains a good golden yellow and is a very effective tree for providing this variation among large trees. The largest trees are over 30 m tall. This tree thrives in towns and is the largest tree available with golden foliage.

Populus nigra
var. *betulifolia*
Black poplar

FEATURES: The native Black poplar is generally overlooked as a Black Italian poplar but differs in important ways. Old trees bear heavy arching branches sweeping down with dense masses of rather upswept shoots. The bark is brown and has short, big ridges and the bole usually has sprouty burrs on it. The leaves emerge pale, brownish-green then become bright, shiny-green.

MERITS: A native becoming rare in the wild and so of great interest to botanists, but common as a city and industrial area plant in north-west England as a male clone, the 'Manchester poplar'. It is tough and healthy and of but moderate vigour, after a very rapid start for 20 years or so, and is easily kept in check by regular pruning. Autumn colour is a pleasing yellow.

LIMITATIONS: A broad, and not very tidy, tree from the early years, this requires room and needs to be an isolated specimen to show its features well. The other constraints for poplars apply (see *P.* 'Eugenei' above). Also, female trees will distribute woolly seeds in June.

ORIGIN AND OCCURRENCE: Native, large, old trees now very rare, are in a few south-eastern valleys and, evidently planted, a few in the west and in Wales. As a small, usually pruned tree, it is common in the industrial north-west.

L

Populus nigra
'Italica'
Lombardy poplar

FEATURES: The public concept of a poplar is centred on this tree, but it is a striking departure from the normal form. Moderately fast-growing, although slow for a poplar, these trees are seldom as tall as they look. Few trees exceed 35 m and none exceeds 37 m. The columnar crown is pointed until height growth ceases and then may consist of several parallel shoots, usually dead. Some trees are more ovoid than truly columnar and there is considerable variation in shape (but see 'Gigantea' below). A male clone that bears numerous, small, deep-red catkins in late March.

MERITS: The Lombardy poplar is useful as an occasional spot plant in a sheltered hollow, or, on a large scale, as a group, particularly in a city park. It sheds neither woolly fruit nor dangerous branches, and is remarkably wind-firm.

LIMITATIONS: See *P.* 'Eugenei'. A singularly poor choice for lines or avenues as very liable to breakage, disease, and lightning damage.

ORIGIN AND OCCURRENCE: A fastigiate form of Black poplar apparently arising in northern Italy, this was first brought to Britain from Turin in 1758 and planted at St. Osyth Priory, Essex. Common everywhere except in mountainous regions, this seems to thrive best in the London and middle Thames area and in East Anglia.

OTHER CULTIVARS: **'Plantierensis'**. This arose in the Simon Louis Nurseries at Metz in 1855. It differs little but is identifiable by shoots which are first pubescent. It also seems to be more robust and healthy and have a more strictly columnar crown. Some of the big trees in the Severn Valley and Herefordshire are of this form.

'ITALICA'

'GIGANTEA'

'Gigantea' or **'Italica Foemina'**. This female form has a bushy crown narrow at base broadening towards the top and bears large curved catkins in late April. A more effective screen although less shapely than 'Italica'.

'Vereecken' is a particularly well-shaped vigorous clone forming a regular, broad, columnar crown, conic towards the apex.

Populus trichocarpa
Black cottonwood
Western balsam poplar

FEATURES: The Western balsam poplar can rapidly make a large but not particularly shapely specimen. The bark is dull grey and finely ridged and the bole soon bears sprouts. The leathery leaves vary in size and shape with vigour of the growth which bears them but are usually ovate-lanceolate and may be 20 cm long. The underside has a thick, paint-like cover of greenish-white. Male catkins are stout green and red and are shed early. Female trees bear green long catkins which bear fruit with woolly tufts, shed in mid-summer. The tree is known to reach 37 m and can be 30 m in 15 years.

MERITS: Exceedingly rapid growth on almost any damp soil. As a young tree the crown is narrow and the bold leaves whitish on the undersides are a feature. Growth is vigorous even on acid soils and where summers are cool. Autumn colours may be brief but of good yellows. The balsam scent is popular and is most evident on warm days when growth starts in April but may be perceived on any hot day in summer.

LIMITATIONS: Those given under *P.* 'Eugenei' apply even more strongly here. This tree is even more vigorous and has more powerful roots. It is also liable to produce root-suckers over a considerable area. The bole is normally untidy with sprouts and snags, and branches break. The usual forms are susceptible to bacterial canker.

ORIGIN AND OCCURRENCE: Native of western North America, where it is the biggest broad-leaved species from Alaska to Oregon, this tree was not introduced until 1890. It is common in most lowland areas, in gardens as single trees and along roadsides in lines, as far north as Dingwall.

CULTIVARS: **'Fritzi Pauley'** and **'Scott Pauley'** are shapely, very vigorous, and free of disease.

Populus 'Balsam Spire'
(syn. *P. trichocarpa* × *balsamifera* '32')
Hybrid balsam poplar
(TT32)

This cross between Western and Eastern balsam poplars received in 1948 from Ontario was selected for its extreme vigour and narrow crown. It frequently makes a shoot 2.5 m long each year for some years and usually at least 2 m. The branches are at nodes only so are widely spaced and are light and ascending. Growing to 20 m in 10 years or so, this is useful as a variant wherever Balsam poplars are planted or can be used where space (above ground) will not allow a broad-crowned tree.

Prunus avium
Gean, Wild cherry, Mazzard

FEATURES: The Gean is a tree of great merit in flower and autumn colour as well as a source of food for birds. The crown of a young tree is made up of annual whorls of branches, level at origin then somewhat upcurved. The leaves are oblong-elliptic, abruptly acuminate and sharply toothed. The white flowers are in bunches of 5–6 on stalks 4 cm long. A few old specimens exceed 25 m in height and one is 1.4 m in diameter of bole, but it is not a long-lived tree and the majority never attain such dimensions.

MERITS: This is a tree of vigorous and shapely growth on suitable sites when young; specta-cular flowering in mid-season for cherries and excellent colour in the autumn. It has the advantage of being a native species with its associated fauna and provides quantities of small fruits for blackbirds and thrushes in July or August. The timber is also excellent in appearance and qualities.

LIMITATIONS: A tree of considerable vigour when young, this has a powerful but superficial root-system which lifts pavings and throws up suckers. It thrives best on a soil with some lime or a good loam and is short-lived on shallow or dry, sandy soils. It is prone to a fungus causing a witch's broom which bends down branches with dense, precocious-leafing, non-flowering shoots which are unsightly. It needs considerable space to develop its full crown.

ORIGIN AND OCCURRENCE: This tree is a native found at its best on the margins of southern chalk and limestone areas. It is widely planted in streets, parks and gardens.

CULTIVAR: '**Plena**'. Double white cherry. This form makes a slightly smaller tree of less open growth. The flowers open two weeks later than in the wild form and are fully double, hanging as globes of white. They last longer and are among the finest cherry flowers.

Prunus dulcis
(syn. *P. amygdaloides*, *P. communis*)
Almond

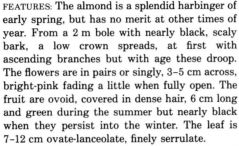

FEATURES: The almond is a splendid harbinger of early spring, but has no merit at other times of year. From a 2 m bole with nearly black, scaly bark, a low crown spreads, at first with ascending branches but with age these droop. The flowers are in pairs or singly, 3–5 cm across, bright-pink fading a little when fully open. The fruit are ovoid, covered in dense hair, 6 cm long and green during the summer but nearly black when they persist into the winter. The leaf is 7–12 cm ovate-lanceolate, finely serrulate.

MERITS: When in flower this tree is of great beauty and is the first spectacular flowering tree of the season, being in full flower (in London, which is very early) in February or in some years, in January. It appreciates a soil with some lime.

LIMITATIONS: The almond is very dull when out of flower and of poor shape. In early summer it is likely to suffer from Peach leaf curl, a fungal disease in which every leaf buckles and becomes in part red then the centres wither. It is also liable to the diseases which cause flows of gummy resin, and is short-lived on the whole.

ORIGIN AND OCCURRENCE: The original range is not fully known as the tree has been cultivated for a long time, but it is thought to have ranged from the Black Sea region to North Africa. Less planted now than formerly, the almond is still common in parks and gardens but, being short-lived, is less seen in old gardens than in the newer ones.

Prunus maackii
Manchurian cherry

FEATURES: The Manchurian cherry can grow to 19 m tall in woodland but in the open it makes a low, broad crown. The leaf is small, about 8 × 5 cm almost entire with widely separated minute peg-like teeth, and dark-green above. The flowers are on nearly erect 4 cm globose spikes, opening towards the beginning of May, are fragrant and 1 cm across.

MERITS: The bark is the attractive feature. In young trees it is smooth and has a soft gloss which shows up the honey colour or pale-orange well. The vigour of growth has its advantages and the flowers are pleasant when observed.

LIMITATIONS: This is a remarkably vigorous

tree with spreading crown and roots so it requires plenty of room. Grown only for its unusual and attractive bark, it loses its *raison d'etre* rather quickly since in 40 years the bole can be expected to be 75 cm in diameter and wide grey fissures open in the bark which remove most of the attractive smooth area. The flowers are white, small and not spectacular.

ORIGIN AND OCCURRENCE: Found in Manchuria and Korea, this tree was introduced in 1910. It is occasional in old large gardens as a fairly big tree (to 15 m × 80 cm) and has been more widely planted recently.

Prunus padus
Bird cherry

FEATURES: This is a small tree, often having many stems from low on the bole, with light branching. It comes into leaf a fresh green quite early but is among the last cherries to flower. The flowers are white and scented, densely packed on axillary spikes and ripen to small black berries.

MERITS: A native tree and bearing fruit relished by birds, this cherry is of value in rural plantings to encourage wildlife. It is also an attractive tree with clean, smooth shoots, and shapely leaves which colour pale-yellow, some tinged crimson or turning red early in the autumn. In late spring it is highly ornamental in flower. It grows wild on limestones so it can be planted on alkaline soils but also tolerates more acid, sandy soils.

LIMITATIONS: The Bird cherry is one of the possible winter hosts of the aphid *Rhopalosiphum padi*, which is a vector of the Barley yellow dwarf virus. Hence in those rural areas of central and central southern England in which cereals are an important crop, and Bird cherry is not a native tree, the growing of this tree is not recommended.

ORIGIN AND OCCURRENCE: The Bird Cherry is considered to be native in Britain north and west of a line roughly from the mouth of the Humber to the Severn, and in the northern half of East Anglia. It is locally abundant in the Craven and Pennine limestone districts.

CULTIVARS: '**Colorata**' has dark-purple leaves

opening around spikes of rich pink flower buds which open to pale-pink, when it is exceptionally attractive. It is a small tree, so far, of recent origin. The form 'Watereri' is a much stronger growing form making a sturdy bole and widely sweeping branches. It has bigger, darker leaves but the chief feature is the much longer flower-spikes which curve out all round the shoots. In flower it is very ornamental but at other times it is rather a coarse tree.

Prunus sargentii
Sargent cherry

FEATURES: Sargent cherry is a splendid all-purpose tree for towns. In winter the bark is distinctive, purplish-brown and smooth with horizontal rows of prominent lenticels. The leaves unfold reddish-purple during flowering and become yellowish before maturing dark green. They are ob-elliptic with an abrupt, acuminate tip and hang somewhat. Autumn colour starts in early September and many are brilliant, dark-red or scarlet, all over by the middle of the month. A few colour later and are dark-red in early October.

MERITS: A strong growing tree unusual in being of the first class both in early spring flowering and in autumn colour. In flower the tree becomes a light cloud of good pale-pink. It is rarely attacked by bullfinches and the autumn colour is reliable and in most trees very early, although a minority colour at the normal time. It is a tough tree, able to grow in any normal soil and in towns and streets.

LIMITATIONS: Although upright at first, for a full crown in later years this tree needs plenty of space. It will spread widely if of seedling origin or if grafted low down. A vigorous grower, it can become a reasonably large tree to 13 m × 80 cm but is not very long-lived. The union of stock and graft can be unsightly, and with the rootstock always P. avium there may be strong sucker-shoots around the bole and further afield.

ORIGIN AND OCCURRENCE: Wild in the hills of Japan and Sakhalin, this cherry was introduced in 1890 and is very common around towns in private and public plantings.

HYBRIDS: The most frequently used hybrid is 'Accolade', a cross with P. subhirtella raised in 1927 in Surrey. This has a low crown of widely spreading, arched branches profusely hung with semi-double bell-shaped soft-pink flowers early in the season, two weeks before P. sargentii is in flower. It has a glossy bright-green leaf which gives yellow, orange and red colours in the autumn, but it is thinly foliaged in summer with a poor crown.

'Shosar' is a more upright growing tree with a dense array of deep-pink flowers with a purple calyx and smoky purple in bud, a very desirable tree.

'Kursar' is similar with bright pale-pink flowers in profusion from deep carmine buds and an upright growth. It was named as a hybrid of P. sargentii and P. kurilensis but the raiser, Capt Collingwood Ingram asserts that it is P. campanulata × P. kurilensis.

Prunus serrula
Tibetan cherry

FEATURES: This tree with the unique bark is becoming well-known. It has a low crown and rarely attains 10 m. The long-pointed leaves are mixed in size but small and finely toothed. The flowers are prolific, two or three together, small (2 cm across) and white but open only when the tree is in full leaf.

MERITS: A tree growing well and placed well, so that the bark is frequently rubbed and kept smooth, has a rapidly expanding bole with beautiful bark. This is usually rich-mahogany and glossy between bands of lenticels but in some of the later Chinese collections it is orange-brown or red. In all cases it is prominent and attracts much admiration.

LIMITATIONS: This tree needs to be well grown to make its one effect, and this means a good medium or alkaline loam. Specimens on dry, or acid soils tend to be thin and poorly shaped. The crown, even when the plant is well suited, is untidy and spreading, rather dull in leaf, the flowers partially hidden by foliage and there is little, if any good colour in the autumn. Graft-

S

union must be made at ground-level but some plants are worked at anything up to a metre above ground. Where *P. avium* is the rootstock, which is usual, the root-system becomes strong and superficial, and suckers may need removing.

ORIGINS AND OCCURRENCE: This tree ranges from western China into Tibet and was introduced in 1908. It is seen increasingly in gardens and a few parks but older trees are confined to specialist collections.

Prunus serrulata
Japanese cherries

A large group of highly selected cultivars originating in Japanese gardens, is of unknown and mixed parentage. Most of them, however, apparently have *P. serrulata* among their ancestors and they have, until recently, been listed under *P. serrulata* or *P. longipes* or *P. lannesiana*.

They are referred to collectively as 'Sato sakura' and their cultural requirements, and demerits are the same, so they will be treated as a whole and the particular merits and features of a selection of them will be given separately.

MERITS: The forms selected are extravagantly beautiful in their various ways when in flower. Every year they are densely laden from an early age and in some years they are even more floriferous than in normal years. They all show considerable autumn colour and some are spectacular. They grow well on limestones or on soils thinly covering chalk and tolerate a wide range of soil conditions except poor drainage and dry or acid sands.

LIMITATIONS: The Sato cherries are, with the exception of 'Amanogawa', trees which soon have wide-spreading, rather low and poorly shaped crowns. They are all grafted plants, usually on *P. avium* stock at 1.5 or 2 m and some tend to show the union, and sprouts from the stock may join the crown of the selected form unless a watch is kept and they are removed. After flowering they are all exceedingly dull, shapeless trees, difficult to screen partially without obscuring their display of flowers. They are all totally alien to the countryside and should be associated with buildings and the highly ornamental plantings which are not part of the countryside. They are all relatively short-lived and apt to lose the ability to flower in profusion when about 50 years old. They do not grow adequately on dry or acid sandy soils and are not suitable in exposed positions.

ORIGIN AND OCCURRENCE: Almost all the Sato cherries originated in Japan (some probably via China a long time ago) and they have been introduced over a long period. One, 'Pink Perfection' is a hybrid which arose in Surrey. The first to be sent here, 'Hokusai', came in 1866. Many others came between 1890 and 1905; the ubiquitous 'Kanzan' in about 1913 and several still rare were brought after 1930. All but one or two given below are very common in and around towns, parks and gardens.

A SELECTION OF SATO SAKURA
'Amanogawa'. Strictly fastigiate, opening out from the top when some 20 years old. Mid-late season; semi-double, large, fragrant, pale-pink flowers among leaves opening pale bronzed-green. Summer foliage pale-green; autumn pale-yellow and pink, turning orange mottled red. Valuable in confined space; avenues, etc.

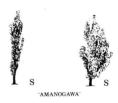

'AMANOGAWA'

'Fugenzo'. Low, spreading, drooping crown with deep-red buds and leaves, then double, deep-pink flowers in short-stalked trusses at the end of the season, Resembles 'Kanzan' but is lower, redder and in full flower as 'Kanzan' fades.

'Hokusai'. Broad low crown. Mid-early season, densely bunched large semi-double pale-pink flowers among pale red-brown leaves. Autumn colours orange and scarlet. A useful extension of the season of 'Kanzan' which opens about two weeks later.

'Horinji'. Upright then spreading crown of long branches. Late season; big pale-pink flowers from dull pink buds and calyces, fading white very attractively. Resembles 'Hokusai' but more open, upright crown, later flowering, brighter buds and paler flowers. Very attractive but little known.

'Kanzan'. Ascending branches when young; curved and broad, arching widely when older. Flowers mid-late season, dull pink buds among deep-red leaves, always in immense quantities, semi-double bright-pink. Autumn colours pale-yellow, amber, pink, sometimes red. Reliable and spectacular but not very original.

'Kiku-shidare'. Also known as 'Cheal's weeping cherry'. Low rather gaunt plant with sparse branches arching down to the ground. Flowers early, very large, double, bright pink, in clusters among leaves at first slightly bronzed then pale-green.

'Okiku'. Spreading globular crown bearing large clusters of frilled, double, large, pale-pink flowers green-eyed in mid-season. A beautiful and spectacular plant, almost unknown and very rare.

'Pink Perfection'. Hybrid 'Kanzan × 'Shimidsu' 1935. Crown globular, flowers late, red buds, long-stalked bunches of large double flowers deep-pink fading to pale-pink below, leaves at first slightly bronzed. Exceedingly pretty and prolific with a long late season, but has off-years.

'Shimidsu'. ('Longipes'). Crown low, spreading, mainly level and slightly drooped; buds pink in long-stalked bunches opening pure white, large and double beneath bright green leaves very late in season. Supremely beautiful in flower.

'Shirofugen'. Similar to 'Shimidsu' except for having a more pendulous crown, red-purple unfolding leaves and flowers at first pale-pink, then pure white then pink when fading. Equally beautiful, but different.

'Shirotae'. The first Sato cherry of the season; crown low, spreading, eventually arched; flowers early mid-season (for Prunus in general) large, pure white with red centre, mixed semi-double and almost or quite single, with the bright-green leaves. In summer the foliage is distinctively large and bright, glossy green.

'TAI-HAKU'

filamented teeth than the others in this group. In autumn many trees turn bright scarlet and gold.

'Ukon'. Similar in growth to 'Tai-haku' but quite distinct, early in flowering as the flowers open pale-yellow among pale-brown foliage in mid-season about a week later than 'Tai-haku'. Later they are white with a red eye very like 'Tai-haku' but markedly smaller and semi-double.

'Tai-haku'. This superb tree was known only from a Japanese embroidery of 1750 until discovered in a Sussex garden, acquired among a job-lot of Japanese plants in 1900. Crown upright then long branches spreading widely, wreathed in the largest cherry flowers of all, early mid-season 6–8 cm, single, pure white from a pink bud among unfolding deep-red leaves. The leaves become 20 × 8 cm with even more

'UKON'

Prunus subhirtella
'Autumnalis'
Winter-flowering cherry

FEATURES: A well-known and much planted tree valued for its show of flowers right through the winter. The spreading crown of slender shoots bears small sharply-toothed leaves. The flowers are in bunches of two to five and the earlier ones are rather tight against the shoot but later in the season they are on short stalks, whilst the last flush of flower comes from tighter bunches at the tips of the shoots. The flowers are very pale-pink (deeper in 'Rosea') and have fringed petals.

MERITS: The flowering season is extraordinarily extended, starting before the leaves turn yellow in October and ending as the new leaves expand in April. Flowering mainly

therefore on leafless shoots and often in fair profusion much of the winter, this tree is invaluable, if spectacular only in a few extra good seasons (as in 1974–75). Amenable to planting in streets, it is also best in a busy area (no bullfinches) but may then incur damage from picking by the public.

LIMITATIONS: A very untidy, twiggy tree all summer unrelieved by flowers, this is also liable to extensive damage by bullfinches in sheltered places.

ORIGIN AND OCCURRENCE: Introduced from Japan before 1909 this tree is common in streets, parks and gardens everywhere.

Prunus subhirtella
'Pendula'
Weeping rosebud cherry

FEATURES: This form is usually grafted at 2 m height on a bole of *Prunus avium* and shows a marked unconformity between the stout straight bole and the smaller bunch of sinuous spreading branches arising at the point of grafting. It can be a 9 m tree from such a graft but it is also seen as a low mound worked on a rootstock not far from the ground. The crown is internally rather a confused mass of shoots but the exterior is of long pendulous shoots. The foliage is small and can be sparse.

MERITS: When in flower, this tree is a highly ornamental, often spectacular plant crowded densely with small, single white flowers. It will grow well in alkaline soils.

LIMITATIONS: Like most cherries, this one is not a success on very acid or very light sandy soils but needs a good medium loam to thrive. When not in flower some of the taller plants are scarcely attractive. It is slow in growth and remains small.

ORIGIN AND OCCURRENCE: The Weeping rosebud

cherry was raised long ago in Japan and was brought to Europe and America in 1862. In the north-eastern States it is common as quite a tall plant. In Great Britain it is infrequent and mostly seen as a more shrubby plant.

Prunus × yedoensis
Yoshino cherry

FEATURES: The Yoshino is a spectacular tree when in full flower, but is a poor plant for the rest of the year. The crown is made up of stout branches curving low. The flower buds are pink and sometimes (probably in warm seasons) the flowers are pink for some days.

MERITS: The one great merit of this tree when untroubled by bullfinches is the great display of fragrant single white flowers early in the season, in March in early years. The flowers wreathe every shoot and are in short-stalked bunches of five or six. They are 3–3.5 cm across and mature into small obovoid glossy scarlet and yellow fruit.

LIMITATIONS: There is no point in planting this tree where bullfinches are active, but it will flower well in busy streets, precincts and estates. Out of flower this is an exceptionally poorly shaped tree. It is unable to thrive adequately on dry sandy sites.

ORIGIN AND OCCURRENCE: The origin is Japanese but somewhat obscure as it is not old at Yoshino, and is little known in Japan, but is believed to be a hybrid with *P. subhirtella* as one parent. It was introduced here in 1902 and is quite frequent in gardens and by roads in towns.

HYBRIDS: 'Pandora' (*P. × yedoensis × P. subhirtella*) is a vigorous tree with erect ovoid crown densely covered in February or March with pink buds opening to clear white single flowers. Flowers and crown-shape are altogether superior to the common Pissard's plum (*P. cerasifera* 'Atropurpurea') which flowers a little before it. A first class tree.

Pterocarya fraxinifolia
Caucasian wing-nut

FEATURES: The Caucasian wing-nut is a splendid vigorous tree but is suitable for only a limited range of sites. The buds of wing-nuts are peculiar in being small naked leaves, densely red-brown pubescent. Axillary buds are borne on long stalks or minor shoots. The expanded leaf has usually 15–21 leaflets, smallest towards the tip and the base, stalkless and finely toothed. Old trees to 35 m tall occur in southern England and the bole may be 1.8 m in diameter.

MERITS: This tree has exceptionally handsome foliage, the bright-green pinnate leaves can be 60 cm long and they turn bright-gold in autumn. The female catkin is decorative, to 15 cm long decked with pink stigmas and lengthening to 30–60 cm so that throughout the summer the tree is hung with bright yellow-green strings of circular winged fruit. The very vigorous growth in the right places is also a considerable merit.

LIMITATIONS: It is essential that this tree be given a wide area free of obstruction above and below ground. It has a broad crown of level branches and may, unless singled, grow a dozen boles. It can also be an intolerable nuisance near flower-beds or lawns for the extensive root system sends up innumerable suckers over a wide area. Cattle are the best means of keeping these down. For the full vigorous growth a good moist soil is needed and a position near open water gives good results. In winter this is a rather gaunt tree.

ORIGIN AND OCCURRENCE: This tree grows wild in the southern Caucasus Mountains extending along the Elburz range in north Persia. It was introduced to France in 1782 and to Britain probably by 1800. It is infrequent but may be seen in some London parks, a few other city parks and in many large gardens in England.

Pterocarya × rehderana
Hybrid wing-nut

FEATURES: The Hybrid wing-nut is a tree of remarkable vigour which limits its use rather severely. It is a tree on a single bole, although rarely more than 3 m long before bearing wide spreading level branches. The rachis of the leaf is deeply grooved, usually throughout the leafy part but sometimes only by each pair of leaflets, and often slightly flanged.

MERITS: The extraordinary vigour of this tree is valuable in itself and this is shown on a somewhat wider range of soils than suits *P. fraxinifolia*. At Kew Royal Botanic Gardens one planted in 1953 in poor gravelly soil near the Main Gate, was within fourteen years of planting, 13 m × 48 cm and after 28 years it was 22 m × 77 cm. One on a rich, damp site in Ireland is 26 m × 90 cm when planted 42 years. The handsome foliage is enhanced all the summer by innumerable long strings of fruit with elliptic membranous wings.

LIMITATIONS: As with *P. fraxinifolia* (above) but emphasised more strongly as it is an even more vigorous tree. It is, however, rather less given to root-suckers, and does keep to a single bole.

ORIGIN AND OCCURRENCE: This hybrid arose from a cross between *P. fraxinifolia* and the Chinese *P. stenoptera* growing near together in a French nursery, the seed being sent to the Arnold Arboretum, Massachusetts in 1879. It has arisen in the same way many times at Borde Hill, Sussex. The Chinese species has broad, toothed flanges on the rachis and this is inherited by the hybrid in varying amounts, and distinguishes it from the Caucasian species (and from the Chinese by its much reduced appearance). Introduced in 1908, this tree was until recently seen only in botanic gardens and major collections but it is now being planted more widely.

Pyrus calleryana
'Bradford'
Bradford pear

FEATURES: This and 'Chanticleer' (below) are selections made in the USA of a Chinese species which is seen only in a few collections. 'Bradford' is distinguished by its neat ovoid crown and smallish ovate leaves.

MERITS: This is a most shapely, attractive tree with pale greyish-green leaves following early flowers. It should give good autumn colouring. A most valuable point is the extreme adaptability to soil and site. It is used quite frequently in very hot cities like Memphis and Atlanta, but also flourishes in Montreal where winters are long and very cold. It should thus be adapted to any urban area in Britain.

LIMITATIONS: This will probably not grow to a large size, or it may lose its shape if it does, but beyond this there seem to be no limitations.

OTHER CULTIVARS: **'Chanticleer'** is another selection, with a narrower, taller and more open, conic crown and longer leaf. This is now planted occasionally in Britain. In a mild winter it may have some leaves orange and scarlet and others still green and remain like this until spring, and a number of flowers may open in October among the leaves. Normally it colours well and sheds leaves by November and the flowers open in April, just ahead of the silver-haired emerging leaves. It is one of the most adaptable, tolerant, shapely and decorative of all trees.

Pyrus salicifolia
Willow-leafed pear

FEATURES: A small tree useful in planting schemes for its silvery foliage, this pear is now well-known. The slender, mostly pendent branches bear narrow, entire leaves 3–9 cm long covered at first in silvery hairs but dark, grey-green above later in the season. The flower-buds are tipped scarlet and the fruit are 2–3 cm long.

MERITS: A tough, hardy tree which thrives on almost any soil, this is planted for its silvery foliage shown to advantage on the pendulous exterior shoots. It has good flowers but being white they have little effect amongst silvery foliage.

LIMITATIONS: Known only rarely to 12 m, this needs full room to develop its pendulous crown without which it is of much reduced value. Out of leaf it is not attractive.

ORIGIN AND OCCURRENCE: Grown as *P. salicifolia* 'Pendula' this seems to be the type tree as all are pendulous. It is native to the Black Sea region and was introduced in 1780. It is fairly common in parks in town and city and in gardens.

Quercus acutissima
Sawtooth oak,
Japanese chestnut oak

FEATURES: This is one of the best oaks for foliage and is a very unusual, attractive tree, planted much in America. The pale-green shoot bears lanceolate leaves 20 cm long with some 15 well-marked pairs of parallel veins each ending in a long-spined tooth. The bark is dark-grey and rough with ridges and scales early in life. The acorns are almost hidden in deep cups surrounded by long, curved, hard projections.

MERITS: A cheerful bright-green, glossy and strikingly bristle-toothed leaf gives the foliage distinction. Unusual oaks are among the most interesting and attractive additions to the range of ornamental trees and this one, of moderate size and growth should be grown more.

LIMITATIONS: Without foliage this is a gaunt dark-grey tree and for the effective display of foliage it must be growing strongly and healthily. For this a good medium loam is required and a position of moderate shelter and good air drainage. In northern regions with cool summers this will not be expected to be a success.

ORIGIN AND OCCURRENCE: This tree is found from the Himalayas to Korea and Japan and was first sent in 1862. It is rare but there are a few good trees in botanic gardens. It is a tree which has done well in trials in the eastern USA and is now planted in many car-parks and streets. The rapid growth there, however, may relate to the regular and continual summer temperatures of 90°F and above.

Quercus canariensis
(syn. *Q. mirbeckii*)
Mirbeck's oak

FEATURES: Mirbeck's oak is a vigorous, shapely and handsome tree, to 30 m tall. The bark is grey, pale on scales and dark in fissures which are numerous and well developed. The leaves may be hooded on some trees, quite flat on others and have regularly toothed acute tips.

MERITS: Most young trees and some much older have regular, ovoid, acute crowns which are peculiarly neat and shapely for an oak. A very sturdy plant with stout shoots bearing substantial, healthy and shapely leaves, about half of which remain evergreen, enough for good shelter or screening in winter, it grows rapidly on any normal soil and it fits the rural scene well.

LIMITATIONS: Not suitable for high altitude nor for poor sandy soils.

ORIGIN AND OCCURRENCE: Native to North Africa and Spain, this tree was introduced in 1844. It is rare, being found only in some large gardens and parks in the south of England and in a few collections elsewhere.

Quercus castaneifolia
Chestnut-leaved oak

L

FEATURES: The original specimen at Kew shows this to be one of the finest trees in form, foliage and vigour of growth. The bark of young trees is black and shiny, and with age fissuring appears and ridges divide into short blocks. The lateral buds as well as the terminals bear short whiskers.

MERITS: A tree of remarkable growth and handsome foliage, this is an outstanding addition to amenity trees that fit into our countryside. The original tree, growing on poor gravelly soil at Kew is 31 m tall and 2 m in diameter when 135 years old, while another not far away was 18 m × 68 cm when 28 years planted. The leaves are up to 20 cm long, oblong-lanceolate with ten or more pairs of parallel veins each vein ending in a triangular tooth. They thus have some resemblance to those of the sweet chestnut.

LIMITATIONS: Suitable only where a tree of the largest dimensions is required and growing best where summers are fairly warm, this tree seems able to grow fast on a fair range of soils but not dry sands. It casts a heavy shade.

ORIGIN AND OCCURRENCE: The main population is in the Caucasus and Elburz Mountains around the south of the Caspian Sea but there is a variety found in Algeria. The tree was introduced in 1846 and the original tree is still growing rapidly. Some collections and a few gardens have specimens (mostly derived from that at Kew) but it is a rare tree.

Quercus cerris
Turkey oak

FEATURES: The Turkey oak is a familiar countryside tree although it has been growing here only 240 years. The crowns of young trees are narrow and tall and in old trees they are broadly domed with branches moderately straight but swollen at their origin on the bole. The buds, both terminal and lateral are conspicuously whiskered and the shoot is densely pubescent. The leaves are irregularly lobed and very variable in depth of lobing and size. The acorn is slender in a cup with scales drawn out into long-pointed curved tips. Male flowers hang in dense bunches, crimson before they open.

MERITS: The very vigorous growth of this tree is attained in any lowland area in Britain and on light soils as well as reasonably heavy clays. It fits into the rural scene, seeds itself like a native and thrives in city parks.

LIMITATIONS: The Turkey oak grows rapidly into a very large tree and needs the room to do so.

ORIGIN AND OCCURRENCE: Native to southern Europe, this tree was introduced in 1735 and the first trees were planted in the Exeter area. Now common everywhere in the lowlands and seeding itself widely it is much seen in large gardens and parks as well as in hedgerows.

Quercus coccinea
Scarlet oak

FEATURES: The crown of Scarlet oak is more open than that of the Red oak, with a few branches spreading widely from a sinuous bole. No bole is likely to exceed 1 m in diameter and few trees 30 m in height. The leaf, glossy on both surfaces, lacks prominent tufts in the angles of the veins beneath, differing in this from *Q. palustris*. After leaf-fall a few of the lower branches retain their dead leaves until the New Year.

MERITS: The popularity of this tree and the selection grown as 'Splendens' is due to the bright-scarlet then deep-red assumed by the foliage in autumn. This sets in on a branch or two before the rest of the crown turns colour. The foliage in summer is pretty, being deeply lobed and bright, shiny green.

LIMITATIONS: Unless growing well this tree is of poor form and is no ornament. It succeeds in reasonably good soils, preferably in areas with warm summers. It will not make a tree of the largest size and is relatively short-lived. For autumn colour a sunny position is best.

ORIGIN AND OCCURRENCE: Widely spread in the eastern USA, the Scarlet oak is not common in this country although first grown here in 1691. It is mainly seen in large gardens and parks in southern England.

CULTIVAR: **'Splendens'** was selected in a Surrey nursery and grafts of this tree are quite commonly planted. It was selected for superior autumn colour and is distinguishable from the type in leaf by much larger leaves with small but distinct tufts of hair in the vein axils beneath. It is usually more vigorous than the type.

Quercus frainetto
(syn. *Q. conferta*)
Hungarian oak

FEATURES: The Hungarian oak is a most distinctive tree in its foliage and makes a majestic specimen. The bark is pale-grey, finely divided into blocks on a smooth straight bole. Leaves may be 25 cm long with 7–10 lobes each side, each being somewhat lobulate itself. Original, very early trees and many recently planted are grafted at base on to *Q. robur* which

usually grows sucker shoots. A tree planted 44 years ago near Cambridge was 19 m × 80 cm and the largest are now 35 m tall and 1.3 m in diameter.

MERITS: There is no finer tree than a well-grown Hungarian oak. Showing great and sustained vigour on reasonably sheltered, damp sites anywhere in the lowlands they have shapely crowns on radiating straight branches and large, deeply and much lobed leaves. The prominently cut leaf-margins give the crown, even at some distance, a distinctive and highly decorative appearance.

LIMITATIONS: This tree is suitable only where there is about 30 × 30 m space and where large leaves are no problem.

ORIGIN AND OCCURRENCE: This tree is native to south-east Europe from southern Italy to Hungary and was introduced in 1838. Fine specimens are in some large gardens and estates mainly in the east of England and Scotland with fewer in the west and in Ireland.

Quercus × *hispanica* 'Lucombeana'
Lucombe oak,
Exeter oak

FEATURES: The Lucombe oak is by far the most frequent tree whose foliage is sent to be identified, so it is yet to be generally known. There are six or so forms in cultivation divisible into two groups of differing general aspect. The original form is not unlike *Q. cerris* but the bark may be quite corky, the large leaves have a deep-green, glossy, upper surface and those on the periphery of the crown remain green through the winter. The other group resemble *Q. ilex* in their lower, more dense, fully evergreen crown and small leaves. Some of these have pale, thickly corky bark, others have dark-grey, non-corky bark. The leaves 4–6 cm long are about half the size of those in the first group.

MERITS: One of the very few evergreen (or largely evergreen) trees reliably hardy anywhere and attaining a large size. The bark may be an interesting feature if the tree is one of the forms with pale, thick corky bark. It is an excellent tree for high shelter against wind, even near the coast. The more evergreen forms show a pleasant silvery shade in June when the new leaves unfold, and then dense sprays of purplish-grey male catkins.

LIMITATIONS: This should not be planted where a large evergreen tree will obstruct the light unacceptably. In numbers or groups it can be too sombre.

ORIGIN AND OCCURRENCE: A hybrid between *Q. cerris* and *Q. suber* raised at Exeter in 1762, propagated by grafts at first, then seedlings. These are very variable and three were selected in 1792 at Lucombe and Pince's Exeter nursery

for general use. Common in south and east Devon and Cornwall on estates and in parks and gardens; frequent in East Anglia and the Midlands but scarce further north and in Ireland.

Quercus ilex
Holm oak

FEATURES: The Holm oak has an almost black bark with thin scales and the crown is dense with slender, straight, ascending branches. Leaves on young trees and on some sprouts have spined lobes resembling those of holly but on adult trees they are quite entire. The shoot and the 2 cm stalk bearing acorns are covered in dense white hairs like the underside of the leaf while the upper surface sheds white hairs within a month or so to become shiny, deep-green. The normal leaf is narrowly elliptic but there are less frequent cultivars with broader leaves and others with narrower, lanceolate leaves often curled down at the margins. In the south-west of England specimens are 25–27 m tall but elsewhere 20 m is a good height.

MERITS: The foremost value of this tree is for tall permanent shelter against sea-winds. In this respect only the Lucombe oak is a serious rival amongst broad-leaved trees. The Holm oak tolerates a wide variety of soils and pH values provided drainage is good.

LIMITATIONS: Although sufficiently robust to be grown in almost any difficult situation, the constant deep shade cast and the dark crown make it unwise to use these qualities except with circumspection. It is rarely advisable near buildings while group plantings need careful spacing and avenues should be avoided. The rate of growth is slow. Hard dead leaves fall in quantity during the summer. It has little appeal to wildlife except, to some extent, goldcrests.

ORIGIN AND OCCURRENCE: A western Mediterranean tree, the Holm oak has been grown here since the sixteenth century. Particularly common in coastal areas, and in the south-western peninsular, it is frequent everywhere in parks and gardens.

Quercus macranthera
Caucasian oak

M

FEATURES: This fine oak is almost a Mirbeck's oak with persistent hairs. The shoots are stout and covered in orange-brown pubescence. The leaf is similar to that of the Sessile oak but larger (15-23 cm) and like Mirbeck's also sometimes hooded, pubescent beneath, and of hard consistency. The bark is pale-grey with a tinge of purple; it flakes coarsely.

MERITS: A tree of good, sturdy growth and handsome foliage, which blends well with native trees in rural areas, and has foliage much superior to that of Common oak.

LIMITATIONS: A reasonably good soil and plenty of space are requisites for this tree.

ORIGIN AND OCCURRENCE: This tree ranges from the Caucasus Mountains to north Iran and was introduced in 1873. It is found only in collections and some large gardens and parks north at least to Edinburgh

---

Quercus palustris
Pin oak

FEATURES: The Pin oak is a red oak with typical, deeply lobed leaf with large, whisker-pointed teeth. It is distinguished from others in this group grown here by conspicuous tufts of hairs in the axils of veins on the under surface of the leaf. As a young tree it has a straight bole with a silvery smooth bark and a lower crown of drooping and splayed out shoots making a distinctive crown.

MERITS: The Pin oak has an unusual and shapely crown with fairly densely held, very attractively deeply cut foliage. In the autumn the leaves near the tips of the branches turn scarlet whilst the remainder are a fresh green then the entire crown becomes scarlet, crimson and then dark red. It is a useful tree for ill-drained soils and will grow quite rapidly on ordinary soils. It will ultimately make a fine tree over 35 m tall, with a good bole.

LIMITATIONS: This tree comes from regions with very hot, long summers and thrives only in the south and east of England. In Scotland it makes insufficient growth to be a shapely tree.

ORIGIN AND OCCURRENCE: The Pin oak is found from around Missouri and Illinois to New York and is widely planted as a street tree in southern States. It was introduced before 1770 and is not common anywhere here but is in some of the larger gardens and a few parks. It could be planted much more in urban areas and in streets generally, in the south.

Quercus petraea
Sessile oak,
Durmast oak

FEATURES: The Sessile oak is, at its best, easily distinguished from the Common oak. One feature is the crown of straight branches radiating to form a big dome. The leaves are flat, not crinkled; lanceolate not obelliptic; have a 2 cm yellow petiole, a cuneate base, regular lobing and are thick and leathery, rarely encumbered by galls. The acorns are usually borne directly on the tip of the shoot but may be on a short peduncle. Big trees are 40 m tall and some boles are 2.9 m diameter.

MERITS: Early growth is generally markedly more rapid than that of the Common oak and the crown is more shapely on a better bole. The foliage is much more healthy and handsome. In

general a splendid tree, a native, easy to grow, healthy and long-lived, highly beneficial to wildlife. Sessile oak woodlands in western hill regions have a specialised fauna - pied fly catcher, redstart and wood warbler.

LIMITATIONS: Unsuited to the heavy clays which grow Common oak, and needing good drainage, this tree also needs plenty of moisture and usually grows best in the higher rainfall areas of the west. It needs plenty of space in which to develop its full crown.

ORIGIN AND OCCURRENCE: A native species and early colonist, the Sessile oak is predominant over the northern and western hills. It has been replaced on the southern clays by the later immigrant, Common oak, but survives mixed with that species on lighter soils. In some parts of the north and west a range of hybrids between the two species occurs. Most of the venerable old oaks in Powys and a few of those in Herefordshire are Sessile oaks. Sessile oak has a large outlier from its main range in the area of the old Enfield Chase, predominating in woods and parks on the west side of the River Lee.

Quercus phellos
Willow oak

FEATURES: The distinctive Willow oak is more robust and vigorous than its appearance suggests. The crown of slender shoots bears strap-shaped leaves 7–8 cm long which unfold pale-yellow in June. The female flowers are in axils on the middle sector of the new shoot and, during the first summer, the acorns remain 2 mm long to ripen the following year and grow up to 1 cm long.

MERITS: This makes an unusual and interesting tree. Although in America the foliage is deep-green, it is in this country a pale- often yellowish-green and is delicate and attractive. The bark is smooth and growth is quite rapid.

LIMITATIONS: Coming from a region with long hot summers, the Willow oak is unlikely to grow well where summers are cool and it thrives best in the east and south. Unless thriving, it looks thin and makes a poor specimen.

ORIGIN AND OCCURRENCE: Ranging widely in the eastern USA this tree was introduced in 1723. It is found only in some of the larger gardens where the biggest are 25 m tall and 1.2 m diameter. In Georgia trees are 50 cm diameter in 20 years. It has been tried on a large scale as a tree for city streets and is a success in Atlanta, Georgia and in New York where summers are long and hot, also in cooler areas of New England.

Quercus robur
(syn. *Q. pedunculata*)
Common English oak

FEATURES: The Common oak is the dominant countryside tree of most of lowland Britain. The crown is composed of heavy, twisting branches making an irregular shape or a number of domes. The leaves are irregularly lobed and have an auricle each side of the very short petiole. By autumn the undersides are often completely covered with the little green discs of Spangle-gall which are shed before the leaves. The acorns are in twos and threes on slender 5 cm peduncles. There are few specimens much taller than 30 m but one of 41 m is known. Unpollarded boles may be 3 m in diameter in a few of the well-known veterans but most of the old trees are pollards and range to 3.7 m in diameter, all very hollow.

MERITS: The Common oak is the best tree for wildlife as a whole, supporting a wider range of fungi and insects and hence birds than any other, although relatively few birds actually nest in oaks. A sturdy, tolerant tree, this oak although supporting such a range of fauna and flora, remains generally healthy to a great age. This is the main tree of the heavy clay lowlands and is never out of place in the rural scene. It is, despite lore to the contrary, of quite rapid growth and in 50 years it should be about 20 m × 0.5 m diameter. Autumn colours are varied, usually good russets, and very late, the majority rarely colouring before November.

LIMITATIONS: Unless grown as a group, this oak requires some 30 m space to ensure an unconstricted crown. The roots can be invasive

and may unsettle buildings in thick clays.

ORIGIN AND OCCURRENCE: A native tree of relatively late arrival, this is abundant wherever there are trees on the heavier soils in the south and east. It was favoured against the Sessile oak in planting for the Navy so was spread into other areas. It is also abundant on higher ground in some places, Dartmoor and Exmoor for example, and in valleys in the Scottish Highlands.

CULTIVARS: '**Concordia**' The Golden oak is very rare and difficult to propagate. Were it available it would be a splendid tree for decorative planting as it leafs out bright golden-yellow, greening only a little by August.

'**Fastigiata**'. The Cypress oak is an exceptionally good tree for occasional formal use,

L

'FASTIGIATA'

blending in foliage so completely as it does with the surrounding countryside trees. The usual form is shaped like a Lombardy poplar and is a graft of the original German tree but much broader trees and some only upswept, not fastigiate, arise when acorns of the true Cypress oak are sown.

Quercus rubra
(syn. *Q. borealis*)
Red oak

L

FEATURES: The common Red oak is sometimes known here as the 'Spanish oak', a name applied in America to the closely related *Q. falcata*. Male flowers, slender yellowish catkins, can be dense in some years. The female flowers are on short stalks in the axils of the new leaves in the middle sector of the new shoot. The acorns remain very small, pale-brown during the first summer and winter and expand and ripen in their second year.

MERITS: Rapid early growth on a variety of soils and in moderate exposure enables this oak to attain good proportions within a relatively short period. The usually short bole is soon stout and has slightly silvery-grey bark until it is of good age. It bears a hemispheric crown of large, handsomely lobed and toothed leaves which unfold pale to bright-yellow for two weeks in May. The autumn colours are always good even if not always red (see below). Rapid growth is attained on soils more open and sandy or acid than suit most oaks and remarkably good growth has been made on a peaty mountain-side.

LIMITATIONS: This tree is exceedingly vigorous when well-grown and cannot be used in confined spaces. It needs good drainage. Autumn colour is variable, the desired reds being frequent on young trees but rare on old trees. Many, however, show highly attractive bright-orange and gold but many turn yellow and brown. This oak is not known to be of any particular attraction to wildlife. It casts a dense shade over a wide area and sheds large leaves.

ORIGIN AND OCCURRENCE: Native to the eastern half of North America from Nova Scotia to Texas, this oak must have been introduced many times from different regions and is very variable in cultivation, as it is in the wild. The first introduction was in 1724. Locally abundant where it seeds itself on sandy soils in southern England, this oak is common in parks and gardens everywhere. Several of the largest exceed 30 m in height and a few are 35 m while boles are frequently 1.3 m in diameter and known to 2.0 m

Robinia pseudoacacia
Locust-tree, Robinia,
False acacia

L

FEATURES: The Locust-tree is all too often called the 'acacia', but has two good correct names to choose from. The bark is smooth, dark red-brown on young trees and shoots, and soon becomes grey with deep, rough-sided fissures among intertwined ridges. There is a pair of short, spiny stipules at the origin of each leaf and the swollen

base of the petiole encloses the bud. The leaves are 15–20 cm long, composed of 13–15 oval, entire, minutely spine-tipped leaflets. The flowers are of the sweet-pea form, white in hanging clusters which largely obscure the foliage. The seed-pods 5–10 cm long, persist dark-brown into the winter. The roots bear nodules wherein are nitrogen-fixing bacteria; hence the ability to thrive where nitrogen is lacking. An occasional tree in shelter is 28 m tall but few exceed 25 m and clear boles, which are infrequent, are seldom more than 1 m diameter.

MERITS: A tree which can survive and thrive in city streets, on industrial waste tips and on soils devoid of nitrogen must have its value. The pale fresh green of new foliage looks well against the greys of Portland stone and the fine pattern of small leaflets is a foil to the massive blocks of city buildings. In a good year for flower, the tree is a fine sight and emits a powerful fragrance. In some surroundings the rough, gnarled misshapen aspect of old Robinias is acceptable and adds interest. It has a useful ability to grow strongly in hot dry sands.

LIMITATIONS: This is another of the trees which grow and flower well only where our summers are hottest, unable to receive here the high and continuous temperatures to which they are accustomed. Southern England, the Midlands and East Anglia have the hottest summers and as a flowering tree this Robinia is not worth planting anywhere else. The season in leaf is short, autumn colour is almost nil and the winter aspect is gaunt. Vigorous small-spined sucker-shoots will often arise at considerable distances

'FRISIA'

M

from the bole. Even in the regions best for flowering, a cold spell from mid-May can disrupt flowering and a cool season yields few flowers.

ORIGIN AND OCCURRENCE: The Locust-tree grows wild in the Allegheny Mountains of eastern America but is rarely much better than scrub except in damp sheltered hollows with deep soil. It was brought to France in 1616 and to Britain about 20 years later. It is common in town parks and gardens in the south-east, less so in the south-west and north of the Midlands.

CULTIVARS: Of many cultivars at Kew, few are seen elsewhere, or deserve to be, but one **'Frisia'** is now very commonly planted. This has golden foliage retaining a good colour until leaf-fall and is an excellent feature in a strictly ornamental planting, although it goes green in the hottest summers.

Salix alba
White willow

FEATURES: The White willow is an imposing, billowing mass of dark grey-blue leaves in summer by many a riverside. In young trees, the crown is ovoid with an acute apex and with age the pointed apex tends to be retained when the crown is a number of tall domes. The leaves are lanceolate 8×1 cm, silky, white pubescent beneath and are borne on slender pubescent, light pink-brown shoots. Big trees are 27 m $\times 1.4$ m diameter.

MERITS: On the right sites early growth is extremely rapid (especially in the cultivar 'Coerulea', see below). The crown of small, markedly grey-blue foliage is attractive. This tree withstands severe and frequent pollarding and pruning.

LIMITATIONS: The White willow needs free access to abundant moisture and can find this really only by watersides, deep ditches or in very damp receiving areas. In places where there is no surface water, the roots travel far and are invasive and can damage buildings on clay sites. White willows need full light and space and grow very fast indeed. Female trees shed quantities of woolly fruit in midsummer.

ORIGIN AND OCCURRENCE: Native to all of Britain except north-west Scotland, the White willow is common along some lowland rivers and by open water in parks and gardens but is rarely planted elsewhere.

CULTIVARS: **'Chermesina'** The Coral-bark willow is an exceptionally useful plant for striking winter colour. Less vigorous and invasive than other forms it can be used with fewer constraints and thrives adequately on any normal soil. The bright coral-red of the shoots from the turn of the year until April is shown best on one-year wood so the brightest colours are obtained by cutting back annually. This leads to a club-headed pollard or a stool, but young trees make enough annual growth to show good colour for many years when left to themselves.

'Coerulea' the Cricket-bat willow has purple shoots and a narrower, more open ascending crown and is even more vigorous. In 15 years trees may be 19 m tall and 0.5 m in diameter.

'Tristis' (*S. × chrysocoma*) the Weeping Willow grown in Britain is not the Chinese

species *S. babylonica* which is widely grown in the eastern USA, but is either a hybrid between that and *S. alba* or is a form of *S. alba*. This grows vigorously on almost any soil, even relatively dry sands, but has invasive and extensive roots and may damage any underground pipes in its quest for water. It also rapidly grows too large for confined sites, but is a good tree where there is room, coming into leaf very early.

L

'TRISTIS'

M

Salix caprea
Sallow, Pussy willow

FEATURES: Often only a shrub, the Sallows can achieve 15 m on a single, if slightly sinuous bole in shelter on a rich damp soil. Male plants are prominent by late March with upswept shoots densely bearing golden flowers, ovoid and about 3 cm long. There is a wide range in time of flowering of individuals, a few sometimes starting in January and many still in flower well into April. The flowers of the female are silvery-green and lengthen as they ripen until in June they show white wool which may turn brown before the fruit are shed.

MERITS: The sallow is tolerant of almost any soil and grows very rapidly for a few years. It is a natural pioneer but can persist in the shade of moderately open woodland. It starts to flower within a few years from seed. For all these reasons, sallow is of great value as a first planting on an open site with rubbly or rough soil, to give early shelter for other more permanent and later planting. It is also a good plant where tall shrubs or low trees are required for merging high forest to grassland or water.

LIMITATIONS: In the summer sallow is of no particular attraction and the female with brown wool in untidy tufts is unsightly for a short while. It is usually a short-lived tree, bushy and with stout shoots.

OCCURRENCE: The sallow is a common native throughout Britain, at its best on damp soils in oakwoods but readily invades any disturbed soil.

Salix daphnoides
Violet willow

FEATURES: The Violet willow could be a useful tree on many sites. The new shoots are dark, glossy purple soon bloomed blue-white and bear lanceolate leaves 8 cm long, finely toothed and glaucous grey beneath. The leaves remain green into November.

MERITS: Within one year of planting this makes the long shoots which give a winter display of blue-white bark. The same colour is present during the summer where, seen amongst the dark-green, shiny, white-veined foliage, it makes an attractive picture. This tree does not get very big as the early rapid growth is not sustained. The foliage has a very long season.

LIMITATIONS: To be attractive this must be growing rapidly and it will do this only on rich damp soils. It then makes long shoots for a few years but soon becomes slow and is often very short-lived. It is therefore a plant which is best cut back or replaced every five or ten years.

ORIGINS AND OCCURRENCE: The Violet willow has a wide range across southern Europe and mid-southern Asia to the Himalaya. Introduced in 1829 it is not at all common and is found in a few gardens and parks usually beside water.

Salix fragilis
Crack willow

FEATURES: This willow is frequently seen on river-banks where it was formerly pollarded regularly, but has now grown a large crown. A short rugged bole, usually leaning, has dark-grey, prominently ridged bark. The somewhat stout, yellowish shoots bear glossy, bright-green leaves as much as 19 cm long tapering to a twisted point and grey-green beneath. The shoots snap cleanly and suddenly when bent a little further away from the main shoot. The crown is a low dome, often about 15 m tall but rarely more and usually has heavy contorted low branches, or numerous erect branches from 2 m up the bole where it had in the past been pollarded.

MERITS: The early rapid growth and the large bright, shiny, green leaves are the main attractions. This is also a good species from the aspect of encouraging wildlife for, a native of long standing, it has a large associated flora and fauna.

M

LIMITATIONS: The Crack willow is a tree for waterside or very damp sites well away from buildings. Early growth is very rapid and plenty of room is required. Female trees shed great quantities of woolly seeds in June. The winter aspect is not attractive except in the particular case of pollards along a stream.

ORIGIN AND OCCURRENCE: This tree is native and widespread. It is the commonest riverside willow in most lowland valleys.

Salix matsundana
'Tortuosa'
Corkscrew willow

FEATURES: The Corkscrew willow is now quite popular and usually causes comment. The branches are sinuous; large shoots more so and minor shoots curled. The crown is upright but outer shoots are pendulous in older trees. The leaves are 8 cm long lanceolate and twisted.

MERITS: A tree of unusual and always interesting aspect, this willow grows rapidly and comes early into leaf a good fresh green and stays in leaf often until December.

LIMITATIONS: This tree makes very rapid early growth and has somewhat invasive roots. On dry sandy soils it will make difficulties for other plants in a shrubbery. It is not a tree for rural positions. It is susceptible to anthracnose of willows (*Marssonina*) and may lose its first crop of leaves during May.

ORIGIN AND OCCURRENCE: A cultivar of Japanese origin of the Pekin willow of northern China. This was introduced in 1925. Propagated very easily as cuttings, it is now frequent especially in new gardens.

Salix pentandra
Bay willow

FEATURES: This splendid tree is the only native willow to flower when in full leaf. There are some young trees already 18 m tall in Copley Square, downtown Boston, so it must be much more adaptable than has been thought. The leaves of the Bay-willow are up to 10 cm long, oblong-lanceolate, finely toothed and deep glossy green; beneath they are glaucous. The bark is brownish-grey finely fissured.

MERITS: This tree has highly attractive, glossy dark foliage with yellow veins on olive-green glossy shoots, to recommend it. It makes a clean little dome of dense foliage and male trees have short bright-yellow catkins. As a native tree it is acceptable anywhere.

LIMITATIONS: In warm southern areas this may perhaps thrive only in damp hollows or by water preferably sheltered from drying winds. It is usually slow growing and rarely exceeds 12 m in height. In winter the crown shows little shape.

ORIGIN AND OCCURRENCE: Native to the northern half of these islands, this tree is infrequent anywhere but may be found by stream sides. It is very rarely planted.

Sorbus aria
Whitebeam

FEATURES: The native Whitebeam has long been planted in streets, more recently mainly in the form of cultivars. The leaves emerge densely covered in silvery hairs showing the undersides on which this is most developed. The upper surfaces lose their hairs and become deep yellowish-green. The leaves are elliptic and about 8 cm long. The flowers are white in heads 8 cm across and the fruit are globose 1 cm and scarlet. Autumn colours on chalk hills are orange-brown and gold, with the silvery undersides still present.

MERITS: A fairly neat tree, tolerant of acid sands or thin soil over chalk as well as paving over its roots, this is decorative when coming into leaf, flowers well, bears scarlet fruit and, on chalk hills especially makes a good but brief display in autumn. Unusually decorative for a native tree.

LIMITATIONS: There may be places where a tree like this, susceptible to fire-blight disease, is not recommended or where the streets have been planted with it in such numbers that more would be monotonous. Birds usually eat the fruit early and autumn colours are fleeting.

S

ORIGIN AND OCCURRENCE: The Whitebeam is native to southern England and part of western Ireland, growing on chalk, limestone and some sandy beds nearby. It is widely planted in town streets but is less common in large gardens.

CULTIVARS: 'Chrysophylla' has large, long leaves grey and pale-golden above and has been planted by some roads. It is not a bright nor a uniform gold but makes a pleasant and unusual tree.

'Decaisneana' ('Majestica') has large elliptic leaves 15 × 9 cm, thicker and tapering to a cuneate base, and larger fruit. It grows fast and can attain 20 m × 70 cm diameter.

'Lutescens' has a neater, more dense ovoid crown, dark-purple shoots and more silvery leaves. It is common in streets and small gardens.

Sorbus aucuparia
Rowan

FEATURES: The buds of the Rowan are large with a curved tip, purple, covered in long grey hairs. The leaves are over 20 cm long and bear about 15 leaflets. The flowerheads are 10–15 cm across bearing creamy white, fragrant flowers 1 cm across in May. A few trees exceed 20 m and old boles may be 80 cm diameter.

MERITS: The rowan grows well on chalky soils or on acid, peaty soils and is exceedingly hardy and resistant to exposure. Young trees have neat erect crowns. The foliage is attractively pinnate and from an early age the tree flowers freely. The fruit are copious in most years and turn orange-scarlet early in August so are visible for a short while before being attacked by birds. In the far northwest the rowan is magnificent in October as the leaves turn scarlet and crimson.

LIMITATIONS: On dry acid sands this tree is short-lived and may look thin for years. On banks which dry out it may lose its leaves in a long drought and may die. It is susceptible to fire-blight disease and birds make a mess beneath the tree from eating the fruit. Good autumn colour is uncommon except in the mountainous northwestern regions.

ORIGIN AND OCCURRENCE: This native tree

grows higher up the mountains of Scotland and Ireland than any other, reaching 1000 m. It is abundant lower on the hills in the north-west and is planted very commonly in streets, small gardens and town parks.

S
BEISSNERI

CULTIVARS: 'Beissneri' is a highly attractive form in great demand. It has an upright crown with copper-pink bark overlain by grey wax which when wet allows the bark to shine bright-orange. The leaflets are deeply toothed and colour clear yellows in autumn.

'Xanthocarpa' has abundant flowerheads more domed than in the type and opening a little later. The fruit ripen yellow-orange and may be less attractive to birds. This form is now being planted in car-parks and similar places.

Sorbus cashmiriana
Cashmere rowan

FEATURES: The Cashmere rowan has upright main branches and slender minor ones arching

down from them. The leaves are 15–20 cm long with 17–19 leaflets deeply serrated.

MERITS: The foliage is good and the flowers are unusual in being pale-pink but it is the fruit which gain this tree a place in the list of ornamentals. About 30 large fruit 13 mm long hang in a bunch, white with a protruded apex, soon made prominent by the leaves falling.

LIMITATIONS: The Cashmere rowan depends for its effects on bearing good heads of fruit so it must have a sunny position for it to flower well. It is not good on dry sandy soils, and is rather lacking in vigour. The leaves fall early and it is not long-lived.

ORIGIN AND OCCURRENCE: This tree from the western Himalayas was probably introduced around 1900 but there seems to be no exact record. It is infrequent, perhaps rare.

Sorbus cuspidata
(syn. *S. vestita*)
Himalayan whitebeam

FEATURES: The Himalayan whitebeam has an upright crown bearing very substantial leaves bright silver-white with hairs beneath, thick, shallowly toothed, often somewhat lobulate and to 22 × 14 cm. The crown is acute and shapely in the biggest tree known so far which is 18 m × 76 cm diameter. The white flowers are strongly scented of hawthorn.

MERITS: A splendid foliage tree of vigorous growth, tolerant of a wide range of conditions.

LIMITATIONS: There are few places where this tree will not grow well but probably a dry sandy area in an exposed place would be an unwise choice. In winter the branching and shoots are a little stout and gaunt.

ORIGIN AND OCCURRENCE: Found in the Himalayas, this tree was introduced in 1820 but no tree nearly so old is known. Until recently it was very rare but there has been some planting in large gardens and parks.

RELATED FORM: *Sorbus thibetica* '**John Mitchell**'. The tree known for 40 years as *Sorbus* 'Mitchellii' was thought at that time to be a hybrid raised at Westonbirt by W. J. Mitchell. It is now found to be a distinct form of *Sorbus thibetica*, a species ranging from Bhutan through Burma to Yunnan Province, China. A very sturdy tree, it has massive orbicular leaves to 20 × 18 cm and has been planted recently in large gardens for its handsome foliage.

Sorbus domestica
True service tree

FEATURES: The True service tree is a tree of character, very distinct from other rowans. The bark is dark red-brown deeply fissured into narrow ridges, which with age grow broader and break into grey, orange and brown, rectangular plates. The leaves are large and hanging, 15–22 cm long with 13–21 leaflets of a distinctive dark yellowish-green colour. The buds are glossy with resin, ovoid and bright-green. The dull cream flowers in large flower-heads yield globose or pyriform fruit 3 cm long, green, ripening tinged brownish-red.

MERITS: A reasonably fast growing tree with attractive bark and bold foliage, this also bears exceptionally large fruit.

LIMITATIONS: This tree seems to need a good damp loamy soil and fairly sheltered position to thrive and becomes thin on poor soils.

ORIGIN AND OCCURRENCE: Native to southern Europe and south-west Asia this tree has long been cultivated and is sometimes held to be native here. It remains rare but a few fine specimens grow in large parks, gardens and collections.

Sorbus commixta
'**Embley**'
Chinese scarlet rowan

FEATURES: 'Embley' is the most frequent and probably the best of a number of Asiatic rowans notable for brilliant autumn colours. The bud is long-conic and deep ruby-red. The leaf is 17 cm long with 11–15 narrow, oblong-lanceolate, long acuminate leaflets. In autumn the outer parts turn rich deep-purple then the whole leaf turns scarlet, gradually changing to deep ruby-red. The fruit are bright orange-red. In summer 'Embley' is distinct from other rowans in its fine, lace-like foliage on branches arching from erect to horizontal.

MERITS: A pleasing tree with good foliage, flowers and fruit but also spectacular and reliable scarlet, crimson and purple autumn colours. This tree tolerates most kinds of soils, town air and pavings over its roots and is a healthy plant.

LIMITATIONS: No real constraints are evident but it may be fairly short-lived.

ORIGIN AND OCCURRENCE: A Chinese tree whose origin is not fully known, named from a tree which once grew at Embley Park, Romsey, Hants. It is now widely planted by roads, buildings and in parks while a few large gardens have older big specimens. The best are 17 m tall and nearly 0.5 m in diameter.

Sorbus hupehensis
Hupeh rowan

M

FEATURES: The Hupeh rowan is a tolerant tree with handsome foliage and strikingly unusual fruit. The leaves are large, to 25 cm, the pink rachis deep-red at base, bearing 11–13 oblong leaflets deeply toothed on their outer halves; pale, glaucous beneath. The flower-heads are hemispheric, rather open, about 15 cm across, and the flowers have pale-purple anthers. The berries borne in large numbers are white, variably flushed pink.

MERITS: A strong growing and tolerant tree with large foliage of an unusual tint of grey, good flowers and strikingly effective and unusual berries. It seems to thrive and be in good health on a wide variety of sites, and moves well when semi-mature.

LIMITATIONS: This is a reasonably vigorous tree of which many of the older specimens are about 15 m in height. It is therefore suitable only where there is room for a moderately large tree.

ORIGIN AND OCCURRENCE: First sent from Hupeh Province in western China in 1908 this tree has recently become popular with public authorities. Older trees are in a few large gardens as far north as Aberdeenshire.

Sorbus intermedia
Swedish whitebeam

FEATURES: A sturdy tree making a dense, broad dome, occasionally to 15 m, the Swedish whitebeam has leaves with small triangular, toothed lobes regularly decreasing in size from base to apex. The flowerheads are 10 cm across; each flower 1.5 cm with dull, white, circular petals and pale, pink anthers.

MERITS: A very accommodating tree of only moderate size this is a fine sight when covered in white flowers in May. The fruits become scarlet and contrast with the deep-green of the upper surface of the leaf and the silvery-white of the lower, but may be taken by birds very soon after changing colour.

LIMITATIONS: In some urban outskirts this tree has been planted sufficiently numerously already. In numbers the summer aspect is a little dark.

ORIGIN AND OCCURRENCE: Native to a wide area across the north of Europe this tree was introduced at an early unknown date. It is common in some urban areas, by arterial roads in town parks and streets but is uncommon in gardens generally.

Sorbus
'Joseph Rock'

FEATURES: 'Joseph Rock' is as yet an unusual, small, very narrow tree. The leaves are narrow, 15 × 6 cm with about 17 small, oblong leaflets, dark yellowish-green in summer on a dark-red rachis crimson at the base. They are borne rather densely and the flowerheads are small but numerous.

MERITS: The great point about this tree is its display in autumn. The small fruits become a clear yellow and the foliage turns scarlet, deep-red and purple. It is a neat tree tolerant of any normal soil.

LIMITATIONS: This is of rather slow growth and will probably never make a big tree, but has no other known defects.

ORIGIN AND OCCURRENCE: The origin is rather a mystery and no attempt is made to assign this tree a specific epithet. It arose as a single tree planted at Wisley Gardens, Surrey (11 m × 33 cm in 1981) derived from a batch of seeds of another Sorbus species sent by Joseph Rock from China to Edinburgh in about 1930. All true 'Joseph Rock' plants are grafts from this tree, but a number of seedlings are also grown.

Sorbus sargentiana
Sargent rowan

FEATURES: Sargent rowan is another Asiatic rowan notable for autumn colour, in this case with very large leaves. These may be 35 cm long with 9–11 leaflets to 13 cm long. The shoots are stout with big, deep-red, terminal buds glossy with exuding resin.

MERITS: The very large leaves make this a handsome foliage plant and in autumn they turn reliably scarlet then ruby-red which is spectacular. The flowerheads are big, to 20 cm across and later bear more than 200 small, bright, red berries.

LIMITATIONS: A broad, low-crowned tree with

stout branches; this is not attractive in the winter especially if grafted high on *Sorbus aucuparia* when the union becomes swollen.

ORIGIN AND OCCURRENCE: This tree was sent from western China in 1908 and is found in many of the larger gardens and a few parks.

Sorbus torminalis
Wild service tree

FEATURES: This hitherto much-overlooked native tree is now the subject of a national survey and of some popular interest. The leaves resemble those of a maple in a general way, having a large pair of lateral lobes spreading then small forward lobes to the tip. They are hard and deep, shiny-green both sides with a slender, yellow petiole 2–5 cm long. The white flowers have yellow anthers and yield obovoid fruit ripening brown.

MERITS: A native tree of considerable interest, this is unusual and attractive in foliage and autumn colour when it becomes deep-red and purple. It grows well in chalky soils as well as sandy loams.

LIMITATIONS: A reasonably good soil, deep and moist, preferably not too acid is needed for good growth. Can become a large tree, to 26 m tall.

ORIGIN AND OCCURRENCE: This tree is a rather rare native to chalk and limestone areas from Kent to southern Yorkshire and northern Lancashire. It had not been much planted until very recently.

Sorbus 'Wilfrid Fox'
(Hybrid *S. cuspidata* × *S. aria*)

FEATURES: 'Wilfrid Fox' is a handsome useful tree but has to compete with the similar *S. thibetica* 'John Mitchell'. The leaves are variable but mainly elliptic about 15 cm long. The fruit are large, globose 2 × 2 cm, ripening pale-orange or brown.

MERITS: This tree is grown for its strikingly large leaves, silvery at first then deep, glossy green above and white beneath. It will grow on alkaline soils and is very robust.

LIMITATIONS: A sturdy tree rather gaunt when young with few stout shoots; this is probably not suited to dry, sandy soils in exposed positions.

ORIGIN AND OCCURRENCE: This hybrid was raised in about 1920 at Winkworth Arboretum, Surrey. It is uncommon but young trees are being planted in many gardens.

Tilia cordata
Small-leaved lime

FEATURES: The Small-leaved lime is one of the few native trees of great stature, with much to recommend it. The dark red-brown shoots with red buds bear small leaves about 6 cm across, usually nearly circular, deeply cordate with an abrupt, acuminate point but sometimes long-triangular. The underside is pale grey-green with orange tufts of hairs in the main vein-axils. The flowers are about eight together at various angles on a short pedicel, erect in some trees, from a small pale-green bract.

MERITS: A native tree of vigorous early growth; this bears elegant foliage and a mass of fragrant flowers much visited by bees. It grows in any well-drained soil and thrives in the hottest cities, being the standard street tree of such places as St. Louis, Indianapolis and Columbus. It is a particularly excellent tree for genuine rural landscapes.

LIMITATIONS: This becomes a very large spreading tree with a dense crown casting much shade. It is rarely tidy or shapely as a mature tree, the bole tending to have burrs and suckers and heavy branches arch far out. There is little autumn colour.

ORIGIN AND OCCURRENCE: The Small-leaved lime is native to England and Wales but is frequent only in the few undisturbed woodlands on limestone cliffs and on lowland clays, and is rare elsewhere unless planted. It has been planted only occasionally as a street tree in Britain but is found in some parks and large gardens. The largest trees are 37 m tall and 1.5 m diameter.

Tilia euchlora
Caucasian lime

FEATURES: The Caucasian lime has a silvery-grey bole which tends to be clear and smooth for 2 m then bears many branches. The leaves are rounded-ovate, abruptly acuminate, prettily toothed and rich, glossy green. The underside is pale-green with conspicuous tufts of buff or orange hairs in the main vein-axils. Increase in height is very slow above 16 m and few have attained 19 m. The flowers are yellow, 3–7 from a large greenish-white bract, opening in July.

MERITS: The foliage of this lime is glossy and handsome and is free of the swarms of aphids which make the Common lime such a liability. Young trees are vigorous and shapely and the winter-shoots, bright olive-green are distinctive. Like other limes, this tree is tolerant of poor root-runs in city streets and any reasonable soil. Some branches give bright-yellow autumn colouring.

LIMITATIONS: Beekeepers claim that the flowers of this (and of *T. petiolaris* and *T. tomentosa*) are toxic to bees. Bees are much attracted to the flowers of all limes and it may be that these encourage excess more than do the commoner species but it has been observed that hive-bees are not usually the victims. With age the crown of *T. euchlora* becomes domed with outer branches pendulous and stout, and so unattractive. There is also a severe die-back from a canker occurring on some trees.

ORIGIN AND OCCURRENCE: Probably a hybrid between another Caucasian lime and the Small-leaved lime, this tree was introduced in about 1860. Old trees are rare but there has been much planting in streets and parks in the last 40 years or so, particularly since about 1960.

Tilia mongolica
Mongolian lime

FEATURES: The Mongolian lime is a highly desirable addition to the limes and only the difficulty of acquiring it could retard its widespread use. The leaves are small and cut into deep triangular teeth, some of them distinctly lobed, and very deep-green. The flowers are abundant but small, 30 or more on each bract. The shoot and petiole are dark-red.

MERITS: The coarsely toothed or angularly lobed leaves are highly unusual and attractive. Little is known of the cultural requirements of this species but it seems to be tolerant in general.

LIMITATIONS: This tree is fairly vigorous and needs space.

ORIGIN AND OCCURRENCE: Northern China and Mongolia is the range but British trees were brought from France in 1904. Until very recently only three original trees at Kew and very few in other big collections were known, but the attractions of the tree have become known and it is now in demand. Grown among other trees, two specimens have been found over 18 m tall in Sussex.

Tilia petiolaris
Silver pendent lime

FEATURES: The Silver pendent lime is always grafted, usually at 2 m from which point two or three rather sinuous limbs grow erect. The shoot, petiole and under-surface of the leaf are covered in dense, fine, white hairs. The leaf is flat and rather thin in texture, deeply and unevenly cordate on a slender petiole of about the same length as the blade, varying from 6 to 12 cm (see *T. tomentosa*). A few trees are 32 m tall.

MERITS: A majestic tree of excellent foliage where well grown, the Silver pendent lime leaves are rarely infested with aphids, grow large and some hang displaying the silver, pubescent underside. The crown is narrow but tall, broadly columnar with pendulous outer shoots. The flowers are late for a lime, in late July, very

fragrant, large and yellow. Some branches may show good autumn golds.

LIMITATIONS: This can be grown only where a very tall tree with a heavy crown of foliage can be accepted. It makes poor growth on dry, shallow or poor sandy soils. The flowers are considered toxic to bees (see *T. euchlora*).

ORIGIN AND OCCURRENCE: The origin of this tree is uncertain. Grown here since before 1840 it may be a rare native of the Caucasus region or it is, more probably a garden selection of a form of *T. tomentosa*. This tree is frequent in town parks and in big gardens in southern and central England but infrequent further north and west.

Tilia platyphyllos
Broadleaf lime

FEATURES: The Broadleaf lime is a common tree but is not often distinguished from the Common lime. New shoots and leaves are covered in pubescence although by the end of the summer only the shoot-tip, petiole and veins of the leaf still carry a cover of firm hairs. The leaves may be no larger, or can even be smaller than those of Common lime, distinctively matt, dark-green and often curved down towards the margins. The flowers are in bunches of only 3–5 and the fruit are large, 8–10 mm and densely pubescent. The tallest specimens are only 33 m tall, and the biggest boles 1.8 m in diameter.

MERITS: A very tolerant tree, this scores heavily over the Common lime in very rarely sporting a mass of sprouts at the base or higher on the bole. It has a clean bole without burrs and is very shapely as a young tree and fairly so with age. It is the first lime to flower and the flowers are large and fragrant while there are forms which bear exceedingly abundantly. It grows well in cities and streets. As a native tree, this lime suits rural areas.

LIMITATIONS: This tree requires plenty of room. It lacks autumn colours and is somewhat dull in numbers when out of flower. In streets its roots may lift pavings. Its foliage carries aphids in great numbers.

ORIGIN AND OCCURRENCE: The natural range includes Britain to the Welsh borders and Yorkshire but it is rare in woodlands. It is common in towns, streets, parks and gardens but less so than is the Common lime.

CULTIVARS: 'Rubra' the Red-twigged lime has dark-red shoots in winter and paler leaves in summer. It is common and can be a big tree.

Tilia tomentosa
Silver lime

FEATURES: The Silver lime has a short bole and, when mature, heavy limbs. The shoot, petiole and underside of leaf are felted in white down. The leaf is thick, very oblique at base, rather crinkled above and often turned down towards the edges, about 12 × 10 cm with a petiole of 5 cm. Many specimens are over 20 m tall and one is 30 m and 1.4 m in diameter.

MERITS: A very sturdy tree, the Silver lime rapidly makes a good bole and regular hemispheric crown. The foliage is attractive, showing here and there the silver underside of the leaf amongst the deep-green upper sides. It is capable of good growth in city parks and thrives in central London and in cities in the north-eastern United States. The bole and base remain free of suckers unless it is grafted on other limes but this is rarely seen and is unnecessary. Young boles grow with remarkable vigour sustained until maturity.

LIMITATIONS: This tree grows rapidly and has a broad crown, casting a dark shade. The foliage is not entirely free of aphids and the flowers may be toxic to bees.

ORIGIN AND OCCURRENCE: From a wide range over south-eastern Europe to the Caucasus region, the Silver lime was introduced in 1767. It is reasonably frequent in southern and midland England but becomes rare much further north.

M

Ulmus carpinifolia
Smooth-leaved elm

FEATURES: The Smooth-leaved elm occurs in a number of distinct forms of local distribution brought here in pre-Roman times. In most forms, the bark is distinctively deeply fissured and ridged vertically, grey or pale grey-brown. The shoots are slender, shining brown with chestnut-brown ovoid buds and the leaves are typically ovate-lanceolate, small, neatly toothed, leathery

L

smooth above and with white tufts in the main vein-axils beneath. Specimens are up to 40 m × 1.8 m.

MERITS: This tree makes a fine specimen tree with a fairly light crown of small, neat glossy green leaves.

LIMITATIONS: At the present time, no elm can be recommended for planting owing to the continuing and rapid spread of Dutch elm disease. As the English elms succumbed and became more scarce, the increasing population of Elm bark beetle ranged more widely in its choice of elm for feeding. Other elms which, until 1976, had hardly been affected, later suffered severely. With the loss of nearly all elms in some areas, the beetle population must fall sharply but planting cannot yet be recommended. The Smooth leaved elm is a large and vigorous tree needing room and a good depth of neutral or slightly alkaline loam.

ORIGIN AND OCCURRENCE: Native to most of Europe, this tree was probably brought by Iron Age tribes and its distribution reflects this. It replaces English elm in east Kent and East Anglia but has been planted here and there through the Midlands and, uncommonly, in the south.

VARIETIES: Var. *cornubiensis*. The Cornish elm, probably derived from Brittany, replaces the English elm west of a line from Barnstaple over

CORNUBIENSIS

Dartmoor to Plymouth and is abundant in east and south Cornwall. It is mixed with English elm from Plymouth to near Kingsbridge and is rarely seen north or east of Exeter although a few farms and estates in the Midlands and one in East Anglia were planted with it in numbers, and it was used commonly in the Regents Park area of London. It is the dominant elm over a large area of counties Cork and Waterford in southern Ireland. It has a highly distinctive crown with few ascending large low branches and arching upper branches splaying out, with foliage close along the branches. The bark is dark-grey, deeply fissured into vertical ridges and the leaves are narrow, small and bright-green. It is the last elm into leaf and is known to 36 m × 1.4 m

Var. *sarniensis*. The Wheatley or Jersey elm was introduced from Jersey in 1816 and has been extensively planted in avenues and along roads and drives, also in parks all over Britain north to

Edinburgh but with few further north. It is particularly frequent in the Midlands of England. The bark is darker, browner and more broken into plates than others of this species. The crown is very distinctive, densely conic with upswept branches and a persistent central stem. The leaves are darker than those of the Cornish elm and more ovate. The largest trees are 37 m tall and 1.8 m in diameter. This tree resisted elm disease while English elms were dying all round it in southeastern England, but most succumbed in 1980. It remains frequent in the Midlands in 1981, and in Glasgow and Edinburgh in 1983.

SARNIENSIS

Ulmus glabra
Wych elm, Mountain elm

FEATURES: The Wych elm is the only elm truly native to these islands where it is common in the hilly regions of the north and west, especially beside streams. It is uncommon in the south east. It has harshly pubescent green shoots and a nearly sessile leaf very rough on the upper surface. The shoots are distinctively short-jointed and perpendicular. The red flowers in February are replaced in March by the bright, pale-green fruits which are prominent until the leaves unfold. They turn brown and in June they fall. The crown is broadly domed supported by heavy low branches up-swept and by arching high branches.

MERITS: In the absence of disease, a tree of imposing stature and big leaves suitable in the wildest landscapes. Any rather damp but not ill-drained soil, alkaline or neutral, is suitable and the tree stands a moderate degree of exposure and urban air. It is the dominant tree in parks and squares in Edinburgh.

LIMITATIONS: The Wych elm is only suitable where space is plentiful.

ORIGIN AND OCCURRENCE: Widespread in Europe and north and west Asia. Native to Britain; often as a component of woodland. Most common in Scotland, Wales, North-east England and Devon.

Ulmus glabra
'Camperdown'
Camperdown elm

FEATURES: This is a tortuous-branched, creeping form of Wych elm that when grafted on a 2 m stem of normal Wych elm makes a hanging bower to ground level from a low crown of much-contorted branches. The leaves are very harsh to touch, bigger than in the normal tree and may be 20 cm long.

MERITS: The Camperdown elm has a place in semi-formal and formal plantings, at the edges of lawns. It is also an interesting single tree for the centre of a small quadrangle where it will not block the light to upper storey windows, or at a crossways among shrubs where a small tree is suitable. The flowers open in February and, in April, before the leaves emerge, the fruit are fully developed as large bunches of bright yellowish-green discs and are attractive. Any normal soil from moderately acid to considerably alkaline suits this tree and it is remarkably resistant to town and city airs. It resisted Elm disease in affected areas for many years but has usually been attacked in the end and few survive in the southeast.

LIMITATIONS: Dutch elm disease has taken its toll of these trees here and there. Although in some districts none is affected it must be assumed to be at risk until the disease abates. As a tree of peculiar form this has to be used with moderation and placed with care.

ORIGIN AND OCCURRENCE: This oddly shaped tree arose at Camperdown Castle in Angus in 1850. As a seedling it crept over the ground and it makes the typical mound-shaped tree only when grafted on a straight stem of ordinary Wych elm. It is quite common and is mostly seen in urban and suburban parks and church-yards.

CULTIVARS: 'Lutescens' (Golden Wych elm). A broad crowned, usually low tree with good bright-golden foliage. This has been much planted along streets in Devonshire and less so elsewhere. A few survive.

Ulmus × hollandica
'Vegeta'
Huntingdon elm

FEATURES: This distinctive hybrid has a pale-grey bark occasionally dark-brown, with broad, prominent flat ridges interweaving, separated by deep fissures. The leaves are up to 15 cm or more long with 2 cm yellow and pink petiole and a very oblique base. They are firm, leathery and smooth above. The shapely bole bears remarkably straight ascending lower branches which identify the tree at a distance.

ORIGIN AND OCCURRENCE: This hybrid was raised in 1765, a cross between *U. carpinifolia* and *U. glabra*, in Huntingdonshire. It was common in the Midlands and Cotswolds as an avenue, park and roadside tree, and in some London parks but elsewhere it is infrequent. The Cotswold trees were killed by 1980, having withstood the disease well until then, like the fine trees in Oxford. In Cambridge many survive but those along The Backs had to be removed late in 1981.

L

Ulmus parvifolia
Chinese elm

FEATURES: This elm flowers in autumn before shedding its leaves. The crown is domed and dense; the leaves only 3–4 cm long, somewhat oblique at base, narrow elliptic with neat toothing. It is known to 16 m × 45 cm.

MERITS: A highly attractive tree of moderately small size. The leaves are nearly evergreen but fall in December and are small and dainty. The bark seems to be of two forms – in one it is pale-orange and brownish-pink and exceedingly scaly, in the other it is dull grey-brown and heavily

ridged. In warm climates it becomes blue-white with orange scales.

LIMITATIONS: Although resistant to Dutch elm disease, trees have died of honey-fungus recently at Bath and Kew. It probably is not long-lived.

ORIGIN AND OCCURRENCE: The Chinese elm ranges through to Korea and Japan. It was introduced in 1794 but is not seen in this country except in collections. It has been planted in some cities in the eastern United States and in California.

Ulmus pumila
Siberian elm

FEATURES: The Siberian elm is rarely seen in Britain but is a vigorous tree with good foliage. The elliptic, acuminate leaves are scarcely oblique at base, 5–8 cm long and up to 5 cm across. They are irregularly toothed. The biggest trees are 20 m tall, 65 cm in diameter.

MERITS: Similarly neat in foliage, this resembles the Chinese elm but never has the colourful form of bark. The crown is more open and slightly pendulous. It flowers in spring before the leaves unfold. A very tough tree of

vigorous growth, this is suited to street and squares in hot cities, and is resistant to Elm disease, as well as drought and great heat.

LIMITATIONS: The crown is of a poor shape, not attractive when bare of leaves.

ORIGIN AND OCCURRENCE: Ranging widely from Turkmen to Siberia and Korea, this elm was introduced in 1860. It is confined to collections in southern England and Ireland, often in the var. *arborea* which has more slender leaves and makes a better tree.

Zelkova carpinifolia
Caucasian elm

FEATURES: The Caucasian elm is better named the Caucasian Zelkova because in China and Japan there are both elms and Zelkovas. The bole of this *Zelkova* is deeply fluted, or at best far from circular in cross-section and in the open rarely more than 2 m long, but in woodlands it may be over 10 m. The leaves have very short, pubescent petioles and are harsh above, elliptic, acute but not acuminate, regularly and coarsely crenate-toothed and dark-green. The fruit are sometimes numerous, four-ridged, globose, 5 mm long. The biggest trees are over 30 m tall and nearly 2 m in diameter.

MERITS: A tree of character, this *Zelkova* may grow a unique crown, a huge, upright ovoid shape composed of scores of vertical limbs, but it can be less remarkable. It is well able to grow in cities, good trees being in Hyde Park and Regent's Park, London. In autumn the foliage turns a good russet colour. Once established, this is a tree of vigorous growth.

LIMITATIONS: This tree suckers widely, very

L

like the English elm but less consistently, and needs a great deal of space to develop its typical crown. It needs a deep soil, not too dry or sandy. Old trees often carry much dead wood. Saplings are very slender and slow to establish. The apparent resistance so far to Dutch elm disease is due to its beetle vector preferring to feed on elms but when the elms become very rare this may not hold.

ORIGIN AND OCCURRENCE: This *Zelkova* is found in the Caucasus Mountains and was introduced in 1760. It is seen in only a few parks and large gardens, north to Edinburgh. The unique crown form usual in Britain is apparently unknown in the wild. Trees of a form like other trees, with a single bole, are scarce here but grow in London (Hyde Park), and Slough (Langley Park).

Zelkova serrata
Keaki

M

FEATURES: Unlike *Z. carpinifolia*, this *Zelkova* has a normal, domed crown on spreading branches. The shoot is soon smooth and red-brown, and bears rows of alternate leaves 5–12 cm long with a slender point and about ten curved, whisker-tipped teeth on each side. The petiole is glabrous, pale-yellow and 1.5 cm long. The fruit is a 3 mm capsule.

MERITS: The Keaki is an attractive tree able to thrive in cities as polluted as London was 30 years ago. It has a smooth, colourful bark after some years and until maturing, and has elegantly toothed and long-pointed leaves held in a distinctive manner. It colours very well in the autumn; yellow, pink, orange and red. A highly adaptable, tough and attractive tree.

LIMITATIONS: Very few, but probably severe exposure and acid peats will prevent good growth.

ORIGIN AND OCCURRENCE: This is a Japanese species which was introduced in 1862. It is planted in a few towns and city parks and squares and is otherwise confined to the larger gardens. The biggest trees are 20 m tall and nearly 1 m in diameter.

Zelkova sinica
Chinese zelkova

FEATURES: Known only as a small tree so far to 10 m × 35 cm this is distinctive in the entire, cuneate base to the leaf and small, sharp, distant teeth.

MERITS: The orange-pink bark of young trees is a feature in winter. The small, attractive leaves may have crimson petioles and veins and colour yellow and pink in the autumn.

LIMITATIONS: This probably thrives only in southern and eastern regions where summers are warm, and needs a reasonably good soil.

ORIGIN AND OCCURRENCE: Sent from China in 1908, this attractive tree is very rare and can be found only in collections and an occasional garden once owned by a plantsman with access to the Chinese imports.

CONIFERS

Abies alba
Silver fir

FEATURES: For nearly 100 years the Silver fir was the tallest tree in Britain but it has yielded this position to north-western American species since 1965. The bole is long except where neglected trees in the open have been allowed to develop enormous branches low on the bole or have suffered damage. The crown is columnar, conic at the apex until it flattens or splays with age. The shoot is dull-grey and has sparse, dark pubescence, and bears the leaves in several layers widely parted to each side; each leaf 0.5–2 cm, deep-green above with two narrow white bands of stomata beneath.

MERITS: Where well grown this can be among the tallest and biggest trees in the country and of imposing appearance. It tolerates much shade when very young, at the expense of growth, and it withstands very considerable exposure, especially to sea winds, when established.

LIMITATIONS: It is not worth planting this tree for amenity away from the particular regions in which it thrives. These are North Wales, the Lake District, Ayrshire, Argyll north to Wester Ross, and on the east, from the Perth area northwards. In Ireland it grows well in the east and the south-west. Elsewhere it makes poor growth and is liable to disease and premature death. It needs a deep soil with plenty of moisture, and allowance must be made for its rapidly developing growth in height. Early growth is slow and needs high shade, as it is very susceptible to damage from spring frosts.

ORIGIN AND OCCURRENCE: The Silver fir is probably native in Normandy and ranges from the Pyrenees through the Alps to the Balkans and the Tatra Mountains. It was introduced in 1603 but was not planted widely until about 1770. It is rare in south-east England; reasonably common, usually dead at the top, in Devon and Cornwall and very common only in Perthshire, Argyll and Inverness-shire, also quite frequent in south-west Ireland.

Abies bracteata
Santa Lucia fir

FEATURES: This fine, rare tree has a nearly black bark which is smooth except for the branch-scars which are prominently ringed by several circular cracks. The bud is unique among Silver firs in its length and long acute point. The leaves are hard, spine-tipped and deep-green with two bright white bands beneath; 5 cm long, parted each side of the shoot. A few of the oldest trees have borne cones. These are small, 10 cm ovoids surrounded by twisted filaments of protruding bracts 5 cm long. There are several young trees in south England over 20 m tall and one a 100 years old at Bodnant, North Wales, 39 m tall when it was blown down.

MERITS: This fir bears handsome, large foliage in elegantly drooping, fanned sprays and has a tall, slender crown. It grows with great vigour where it thrives at all and is a conspicuous tree.

LIMITATIONS: Although coming from an area with hot, rainless summers, the Santa Lucia fir likes a good damp loamy soil, and can be very slow to establish. It is not a tree for high altitudes, exposure, or a frost hollow.

ORIGIN AND OCCURRENCE: Found native only in a few valleys in the dry Santa Lucia part of the Coast Range of California, south of Monterey, this tree was introduced in 1854. Nowhere at all frequent it is found in large gardens, collections and occasionally smaller gardens north to Aberdeen.

Abies cephalonica
Grecian fir

FEATURES: The Grecian fir has a bark with an orange tinge until maturity when it is grey with squarish plates. The leaves are stiff and stand out all round the orange-brown shoot. They have spined tips and bright but narrow white bands beneath. In old trees the branches spread widely and droop, when they are liable to break off, bearing a load of brown, cylindric, domed cones 15 cm tall. The tallest tree is 41 m and there are boles 1.6 m in diameter.

MERITS: Given good establishment, this tree rapidly builds a good ovoid crown and a sturdy bole. It is tolerant of most soils except drying sands. The foliage is quite bold and young shoots are bright, fresh green. It is among the best Silver firs in warmer drier areas, notably, in East Anglia, and near towns. In woodlands or flanked by similar sized trees it can grow a very fine clean long bole.

LIMITATIONS: As the Grecian fir is among the first firs to flush, it is highly susceptible to damage from spring frosts and needs good air drainage, preferably with temporary high cover, to become established. Unless in woodlands, this tree becomes hugely spreading with age and too heavy in the branches. It may begin to break up when about 120 years old and is by then a coarse tree, liable to be blown down.

ORIGIN AND OCCURRENCE: This tree is found in Greece and to the north intergrades with *Abies alba* through an intermediate species (*A. borisii-regis*). It was introduced in 1824 and is found in many large gardens and collections everywhere.

L

Abies concolor
White fir

FEATURES: The White fir is much less successful or frequently seen than its geographical form, Low's fir. The bark is grey, smooth except for blisters, and only lightly ridged and shallowly fissured with age. In early years the crown is conic, regularly whorled with nearly level layers of branches. The leaves are 5 cm long, blue-grey on both sides, arising from a stout yellow shoot. The cones are big, smooth, domed, to 15 cm tall.

MERITS: A thriving, small tree is decorative, its long blue-grey leaves held erect from the shoots making a distinctive plant. A healthy big tree is a fine specimen with a straight, cylindric bole and regular, columnar crown. One in Northumberland is 48 m tall and several in Argyll have exceeded 40 m.

LIMITATIONS: Unexpectedly, in view of its origin in a region of hot, dry summers, this tree is only worth planting where the summers are damp and cool. On damp sheltered sites good early growth is achieved everywhere but vigour and health decline by the time the tree is 15 m tall and thereafter survival is a gamble except in the favourable areas. In general, large specimens are found only in Northumberland and Argyll but there seems no reason why Perthshire and Inverness-shire should not grow this tree equally well.

ORIGIN AND OCCURRENCE: The typical White fir ranges from Mexico to Utah and, probably South California, although these last may be nearer the variety *lowiana* (see below). It was introduced in 1873 and is scarce, big trees occurring only as stated above.

CULTIVAR: '**Violacea**' is more decorative than the type, its foliage being a brighter blue-grey. It is also more at home in the warmer and drier southern and eastern areas. It is moderately slow growing and has attained only 18 m so far, and is proving to be somewhat short-lived.

Abies concolor
var. *lowiana*
Low's fir

L

FEATURES: The most impressive bole in many a pinetum is that of the Low's fir. In one form the bark is nearly black and is deeply ridged whilst the crown of green leaves is columnar. In the other form the bark is corky, usually brown with deep, wide fissures, sometimes pale and little fissured, and the crown is markedly conic and somewhat blue-grey. Many trees now exceed 40 m and a few are 50 m tall. The largest diameter of bole is currently 1.9 m.

MERITS: Low's fir shows remarkable tolerance of soils and exposure. Young trees may make shoots of 1 m even on poor acid sands and older trees tower out of plantings near cities. Young trees are handsome with their long, green leaves to 6 cm held flat on the shoots or grey-green with a blue-white band, in rows parted by a 'vee' of varying angles. (There are two main forms of this tree in cultivation.) Mature trees can have imposing, long cylindrical boles, and regularly conic, spired crowns.

LIMITATIONS: This fir should be planted only where a very tall tree can be accommodated. In exposure and near big towns it will reach considerable heights but looks thin and becomes somewhat ragged.

ORIGIN AND OCCURRENCE: Low's fir was discovered and described in 1851. It is an intergrade between *A. grandis* in the north and *A. concolor* in the south and is common in central Oregon, the Siskiyou Mountains and down the length of the Sierra Nevada, California. It is grown in many collections and big gardens and some smaller, in all parts, but rarely from East Anglia to Yorkshire.

Abies grandis
Grand fir

L

FEATURES: The Grand fir is now one of the two tallest trees growing in the British Isles. The bark is smooth and blistered for many years. In old trees it is either dull-grey broken into small, shallow squarish plates or dark purple-grey, fissured vertically. The leaves are rich green above and from 2–5 cm long, the shorter ones in inner rows, all lying flat each side of the olive-green shoot. Annual shoots are seen exceeding 1.3 m; 40 m can be reached in 50 years; numerous specimens in Scotland exceed 50 m in height and several exceed 55 m. The biggest boles are over 2 m in diameter.

MERITS: Few trees can in so short a space of time contribute so much to a landscape or attain such height and bulk. Very rapid growth can be

achieved on sands if they are deep, and on thin loams over limestone, but is maintained longer in deep, moist, mineral soils. Young trees are decorative with luxuriant rich green foliage and narrowly conic regular crowns. Growth is generally extremely healthy.

LIMITATIONS: In moderate to severe exposure and on thin soils, the Grand fir does not make a good tree. It is not suitable on chalk or in the long term on superficial limestone. It should be planted only where a very large tall tree can grow rapidly without hindrance. The tops of tall trees are brittle and may blow out, which does not stop the tree from resuming rapid increase in height, but may be inconvenient. It is no use at all near cities or industrial areas. It is rarely long-lived, and when 100 years old and 45 m tall, may in England die or be struck by lightning. In Scotland, particularly in the north, the oldest trees are still shapely, healthy and vigorous.

ORIGIN AND OCCURRENCE: The natural range of the Grand fir has been much fragmented by clearance. West of the Cascades it is a tree of lowlands from Vancouver Island to Mendocino County, North California and ranges eastwards at higher altitudes only in southern British Columbia, in Washington, Montana and Idaho, but seldom as pure stands. It was introduced by David Douglas in 1831 and is common in large gardens, collections and Scottish estates. Stands of Grand fir of more than 20 years in age are infrequent but younger stands, often underplanting a crop of another species, are now commonly seen in commercial forestry.

Abies homolepis
Nikko fir

FEATURES: A sturdy tree, when young, the Nikko fir has stout ascending branches and when old it has a broadly columnar crown. It has a bark with fine papery scales and a pink tinge to the grey. The leaves are broad and lie in many ranks usually parted centrally by a narrow 'vee'. The best growth is made on deep, damp soils in some shelter and here the best trees are, at 80 years, some 25 m tall and 80 cm in diameter while the biggest, in central Perthshire is 39 × 1.2 m.

MERITS: The Nikko fir is the most resistant of all the *Abies* to industrial and city conditions. It will not grow where these are severe but can make a reasonable tree where other silver firs fail. It is a sturdy tree, growing rapidly and, so far, continuously in good conditions, and has attractive foliage with pinkish-white, stout shoots and the leaves have undersides brilliantly banded silvery-white. Cones of Silver firs are usually confined to shoots 30 m above ground but some of the Asiatic species bear fine violet-purple cones at or near eye-level. The Nikko fir does this only when it is fairly mature, when the lower crown may bear a scatter of blue-purple, resinous cones, 8 cm tall.

LIMITATIONS: This fir is only moderately resistant to exposure. It needs to be thriving to be ornamental. As a young tree the outline is a little stark, the whorls of branches rising at 45°.

ORIGIN AND OCCURRENCE: This tree was introduced from Honshu, Japan in 1861 although the oldest trees now date only from an import in 1880. It is a frequent tree in Scottish estates and in collections and large gardens everywhere.

Abies nordmanniana
Caucasian fir

FEATURES: The Caucasian fir can be a good specimen tree with luxuriant foliage. Establishment is best where there is temporary, high, light shade. The shoots are grey-green to olive-brown variably pubescent bearing yellowish-green to rich, deep-green leaves, 2–4 cm long, rising and lying forwards along the shoot and covering it (not parted as in *A. alba*). Cones are frequent but only around the tips of trees over 25 m tall. They are slender, 15 cm tall, cylindric and pale-green ripening brown. The oldest trees are tending to die back at the tips except in central and northern Scotland, and these tips remain acute unlike those of senile *A. alba* or *A. grandis* which splay out or develop twisting, spreading branches. The best trees are 40–44 m tall and the biggest boles are 1.4 m in diameter.

MERITS: In the better forms, the foliage is handsome with large, leathery-textured, rich green leaves, well banded with silver beneath. Young trees are shapely and of good colour. In suitable sites good trees will grow rapidly, with shoots up to 1 m long, and attain 30 m or more with a conic, fairly regular, acute-topped crown. It is a healthy tree until mature, usually avoiding the *Adelges* infestations which can plague European species, but grown in plots it will occasionally suffer attacks.

LIMITATIONS: This tree is very variable in the luxuriance of its foliage and some specimens have little amenity value as the sprays of foliage are as thin as those of *A. alba* and growth is not good. Exposed positions, thin soils, industrial or urban surroundings or concentrations many miles upwind, chalk or lime-stone near the surface all preclude good growth. After a few

L

years' growth, full light and space for a tall tree are requisites and in low rainfall areas growth will be good only in damp hollows.

ORIGIN AND OCCURRENCE: This fir was introduced from the Caucasus Mountains in 1848 and in large quantities just after 1850. It is in some areas the commonest Silver fir in large gardens and is present in most Scottish castle surrounds and gardens.

Abies numidica
Algerian fir

FEATURES: The most notable feature of the Algerian fir is the dense rows of short, stubby leaves, deep blue-green, banded with white above or white-tipped. Second year shoots are orange-brown. Cones are often numerous around the apex and are slightly ovoid cylinders narrowing to an abrupt conic tip, smooth, very pale-green tinged lilac.

MERITS: A sturdy and reasonably attractive tree remarkably tolerant, for a Silver fir, of hot summers and dry air, and of urban surroundings. The biggest specimens are in East Anglia and are over 30 m tall.

LIMITATIONS: A tree which at a short distance has very dark foliage. Algerian fir can be expected to grow well almost anywhere but should be planted in only small numbers.

ORIGIN AND OCCURRENCE: This fir occurs in a very limited area of the Atlas Mountains in Algeria and was introduced in 1862. It is found only in collections and a few large gardens.

Abies procera
Noble fir

L

FEATURES: The Noble fir is a distinctive tree with blue-grey foliage. The stout bole is silvery-grey with few fissures and small areas shallowly cracked into small plates, but in exposure it may be deep-purple. The stout shoots are densely covered in fine orange-brown hairs and are hidden from above as the leaves are swept upwards above and partly spread forwards over them. The leaves have two grey-white stomatal bands on each surface, those beneath more clearly marked. The cones are very big, to 25 × 8 cm, ovoid-cylindrical, purple but largely hidden by the downward bent long bracts which are pale-green tipped gold. They are borne around the apex, often in such numbers that their weight bends or breaks the branches, and sometimes may be found on trees only 5-6 m tall.

MERITS: A well-grown Noble fir is well named. A clear blue-grey at all times, and often (var. *glauca*) strikingly so, young trees growing rapidly have regularly whorled branches and neat, narrowly conic crowns. Older trees soon achieve big, imposing boles with silvery-grey bark and, in the cool north and west, continue, to become majestic trees of great size. The colour of the foliage is a change from the greens which predominate among conifers. The tree succeeds at a higher altitude than other potentially very large conifers. The male flowers, often abundant on low shoots are a rich crimson colour and large.

LIMITATIONS: A good, deep, damp soil is necessary except in cool areas of high rainfall for the Noble fir to grow well, and it is quite unsuited to hot, dry sites. Shapely specimens over 25 m tall are rarely seen except in west Wales and in Scotland. Elsewhere on good sites the trees look well for many years but lose their tops and may have thin crowns and become gaunt. Noble firs require plenty of space, unless grown in a group to make long, clean boles, as they become broad in the crown with age. In some apparently suitable gardens growth is so slow, scarcely 15 cm a year, that they fail to make a tree worth its place. Old trees are liable to be blown down or to become ragged at the top. In towns or near industrial areas the tree is spindly and poor.

ORIGIN AND OCCURRENCE: The Noble fir is confined to two small areas of the Coast Range in Washington and Oregon and to the Cascade Mountains from Washington to the northern border of California. It was introduced by David Douglas in 1830 and is in almost every estate and large garden in Scotland, where it often seeds itself freely, and in Wales, and is common but less frequent in Ireland and England except near the east coast. Several are now 50 m tall.

Abies veitchii
Veitch's silver fir

FEATURES: A deeply fluted bole is characteristic of Veitch's silver fir. The crown is narrow and, unless the top breaks out it remains a narrow spire even in the older trees. The leaves are 2.5 cm long and broaden gradually to an abrupt and notched tip. They are bright, shiny-green above and brilliantly white-banded beneath. When only three years old, the plants may grow slender shoots of 30 cm or more and for some years they may add 70–80 cm annually. After reaching 20 m, growth in height becomes slow and few reach 23 m before death or damage intervene. Due also to the short life, boles more than 80 cm in diameter are rare.

MERITS: As the last Silver fir into leaf, Veitch's silver fir is very rarely damaged by frost and can establish in the open. It is also usually the fastest Silver fir in height-growth in its first few years. A well-grown tree has an elegant, conic crown with downswept branches sweeping up again towards their tips. This displays the brilliantly white, broad bands on the undersurface of the leaf in an attractive way. The cones are a good blue-purple and can be quite numerous on young trees and therefore close enough to the ground to be well seen. Given a reasonably damp acid or neutral soil, this tree will grow well at least for many years even in the drier eastern areas unsuited to most Silver firs.

LIMITATIONS: A relatively short-lived tree seldom surviving 80 years. In exposure or on thin alkaline soils the crown is soon thin and unsightly.

ORIGIN AND OCCURRENCE: Veitch's silver fir grows on Honshu, Japan and was introduced in 1879. It is reasonably frequent in large gardens, policies and collections in all areas except south-east England where it is scarce.

Araucaria araucana
Chile pine,
Monkey-puzzle

FEATURES: The Chile pine is a tree of character, but not an easy one to place. Young trees have open, conic crowns but soon become more dense and domed either broadly or narrowly. Forked or misshapen trees are all but unknown. The leaves are 3–4 cm long, triangular, and have a brown, spined tip. Male trees bear long-ovoid catkins 10 × 6 cm and females bear 15 cm globular cones. Root suckers are frequent. No specimen has yet exceeded 30 m although several are 28 m; big boles over 1 m in diameter are now common.

MERITS: In the right place, an interesting and often imposing tree. Single specimens when well-grown are majestic and a group on an eminence is a fine sight. Female trees bear massive globular golden-spined cones which cause comment. In the open, a specimen may be most impressive if it has healthy branches which bend to the ground but if the lower branches start to fail a good clean bole makes a splendid tree. This tree is exceptionally resistant to exposure and is rarely blown down. It will grow well on almost any soil, and is completely hardy everywhere.

LIMITATIONS: This tree is too unusual in form to be acceptable in the rural landscape, nor does it ornament town gardens. It drops a hard, spiny litter in quantity and when mature, a mass of bare, curved, slender shoots ideal as pipe-spills,

M

burning with a clear slow flame, but untidy on the ground. It also needs much room although how much cannot be foretold as the crowns vary enormously in their breadth. In many specimens, life-expectancy is no more than 110–120 years.

ORIGIN AND OCCURRENCE: The Chile pine is found high in the Andes both sides of the Chile-Argentina border. It was first brought here in 1795 but bulk imports first came in 1843 and after 1850. This is a very common tree even where it will not grow well – around towns and in exposed dry areas in the east. Fine specimens are frequent in the south, south-west, in Wales, Scotland and Ireland.

Cedrus atlantica
Atlas cedar

FEATURES: The Atlas cedar is almost invariably planted only in the blue-foliaged form var. *glauca*. Young trees have ascending branches but in old trees the heavy branches become level. The form *glauca* has a pale grey bark lightly fissured into small rectangular plates. The leaves on new shoots are solitary, spirally set, to 2.5 cm long; on older shoots they are in whorls of about 45 each on a short spur and are 1–2 cm long. Flowering is in September but well before this the males are prominent as erect light grey-green ovoids which expand to 4 cm, turn yellow shedding pollen in September, curve over dark-brown and are then shed. The female flower is in the centre of a whorl and needs searching for. It is 1 cm tall, domed, bright, fresh green. The cone is not ripe until the winter two years after the September in which the flower opened and is barrel-shaped, usually hollowed at the apex, 8 cm tall. During the two summers it is pale-green with lilac-edged scales.

MERITS: Few conifers can grow with the speed and make the huge specimen that this can, on dry sites and on chalk or limestone in eastern areas. The variety *glauca* is the form usually seen and this earns its popularity from the bright blue-grey or grey-white of the best forms. The crown is fairly regularly conical and, when planted small, growth is rapid and a sturdy tree

GLAUCA

is soon achieved. The coloured foliage is an excellent foil to the brightest gold conifers or will lighten an area of dark-green foliages. The tree is wind-firm and tolerant of a fair degree of exposure.

LIMITATIONS: Like the other cedars, the Atlas cedar requires space for a broad crown and full light after very few years. If planted as a big plant it will be slow in growth and remain spindly and frail for many years.

ORIGIN AND OCCURRENCE: The Atlas cedar grows in the Atlas Mountains in Algeria and Morocco and was introduced in 1841. The variety *glauca* was found in one valley in 1845 and introduced in that year. This form is common everywhere and is widely planted, whereas the deep-green coloured type is found in some older gardens and churchyards.

L

Cedrus deodara
Deodar

FEATURES: The Deodar is the only true cedar from beyond the Mediterranean region. The bole is straight and can be very long. The bark is dark-brown to blackish with ashen-grey, narrow, vertical plates. New shoots droop conspicuously and bear slender leaves 3–5 cm long. The leaves on spurs are equally long and all dark-green faintly lined grey, and in one common form not distinguished by a name, the spurs are remote and the leaves stout, held close together and dark, yellowish-green. Male flowers are erect 4 cm, opening to 7 cm in October when they are dark-purple before shedding pollen at the end of that month. Female flowers are less common and often restricted to branches without male flowers. They are at the tips of the spurs, 5–6 mm long, bright-green, usually tipped pink. The cone is barrel-shaped but bigger than in other cedars, to 14 cm tall. The tallest trees, still with spire-tops and growing, are 37 m and a few of the oldest have boles 1.8 m in diameter.

MERITS: A young, vigorous Deodar is exceptionally attractive with its pendulous shoots, often bluish-green or grey, and with a dense crown topped by a drooping leading shoot. On good sites, Deodars grow rapidly and their crowns are always conic to a narrow spire – or if they fork, as is far from rare – to two or more

L

narrow spires. Old trees can be very big with imposing boles and fine as single specimens able to fill a space needing a big tree with character. Deodars grow well in all parts north to beyond

Inverness-shire, given good, damp, deep soils and some shelter. It thrives in far hotter summers than ours, being common in towns in the southern USA.

LIMITATIONS: On thin, dry soils and in exposure in dry areas, the deodar rarely makes a good tree and is apt to dieback or to die fully when less than 100 years old. Even when it grows well it has a long middle-age period when it is rather twiggy in the crown and may be dull to look at. It is rather less windfirm than is *Cedrus atlantica*

and much less tolerant of drought and alkaline soils. As youth fades, the lower branches need removing or the mature tree may be spoiled by heavy, low limbs.

ORIGIN AND OCCURRENCE: The Deodar grows on the slopes of the western Himalayas, in Afghanistan and the Punjab, where trees have been noted nearly 70 m tall. It was introduced in 1831 and is common in gardens large and fairly small, in parks and churchyards, in town and country.

Cedrus libani
Cedar of Lebanon

FEATURES: The Cedar of Lebanon is characteristically a wide, spreading tree, but young trees are narrowly conic and somewhat sparse. Old trees have long level branches, often from multiple boles. Leaves on spurs are up to 3 cm long and spined. The female flower, is ovoid, bright pale-green tinged rosy-purple. The cones are 10 cm tall. Very few specimens of this tree exceed 35 m in height and clean boles are not often more than 2 m in diameter, but are known to 2.8 m

MERITS: Where landscaping requires a single tree of the largest size, very few can compete with the Cedar of Lebanon. Until nearing maturity it grows with great vigour, and it has character as well as well-founded associations with spacious lawns and mansions occupied by dynastic families in settled, mature landscapes. This is partly because it looks much older and more venerable than it is, due to the rapid growth. This cedar is as good on thin but not too dry alkaline soils in hot, dry areas as it is in deep soils in regions of heavy rainfall. Very young trees may rarely be damaged by severe late spring frosts but once about 10 m tall they are completely hardy. The colour of the foliage varies from deep-green to quite bright, grey-blue.

LIMITATIONS: This cedar requires more room than any other conifer and, unless required in a deliberate group should be planted at 50 m spacing. It casts a deep shade over a wide area.

It also is liable, when mature, to much damage from wet snow breaking the branches. Good drainage is essential for healthy growth. In recent years a leaf-cast of unknown cause has been making a few trees 50 years old or older largely deciduous. This weakens the tree but it may recover, partially at least.

ORIGIN AND OCCURRENCE: The Cedar of Lebanon is native to Mount Lebanon in Syria and in a slightly distinct form (var. *stenocoma*) in south-east Turkey. It was probably introduced in 1638 or 1639 but there is no unassailable evidence of the tree before 1664. It was reported that most young trees were killed in the exceptional winter of 1740, and although one tree is reputed to date from 1643, very few in general are older than plantings of 1780 and since. Big trees are common wherever there are large old gardens, around all old towns and in villages in England but the species is unusual north of Edinburgh.

Chamaecyparis lawsoniana
Lawson cypress

FEATURES: **The Lawson cypress is the most variable of all conifers and one of the most useful of all trees for amenity. The crown is conic or columnar with a conic apex from which the leading shoot droops in a wide arch and branch ends are also pendulous. The foliage has a scent, when crushed, of somewhat resinous parsley, and when held obliquely to the light, each leaf has a translucent spot. Growth is fairly rapid in height 0.6 m or occasionally 1 m in a year, but slows later, although the oldest trees, now 120 years old still maintain a leading shoot and have not**

yet stopped growing. A few exceed 37 m in height and the biggest boles are 1.4 m in diameter. Male flowers are usually profuse and a pink or dull crimson before shedding pollen towards April; female flowers are also profuse, slate-blue and ripen to bloomed green cones 7 mm across.

MERITS: This is arguably the most valuable purely decorative tree we have, in its highly various colours, habits and kinds of foliage. It is also completely hardy and tolerant of chalk or of acid peats and to a great extent, city air and sea winds and to some extent industrial pollution. It is also of enormous benefit to birdlife especially in towns. Without Lawson cypress in the parks, churchyards and front gardens, towns and city outskirts would have few, if any, breeding greenfinches, chaffinches, goldcrests or blackbirds. Without Lawson cypress in its bright golden, blue-grey and deep blue-green foliages, park and garden plantings would be impoverished in varied winter colour and summer background and shelter at all times. In short, this tree in one or more forms is an essential part in a high proportion of decorative plantings, and is sufficiently tough to thrive in almost any difficult conditions. (Some of the best cultivars are described briefly below.)

LIMITATIONS: The type tree if planted as lines, avenues or groves makes an exceedingly gloomy, dull feature. Land liable to even occasional flooding, especially in summer should be avoided or the trees may well die rapidly from *Phytophthora cinnamomi*. Good drainage is almost the only essential for the soil. In severe exposure or on thin soils in moderate exposure the crowns become thin and unsightly. Some sources of seed yield plants very liable to forking and for as long as possible the trees should have forks singled, also the lowest branches need removing or they will layer. Once so rooted the tips grow strongly vertical and the plant becomes a thicket.

ORIGIN AND OCCURRENCE: Lawson cypress is confined to the Oregon-California boundary where it ranged from near the sea at Crescent City, California, and Port Orford, Oregon to 2100 m in the Siskiyou Mountains inland. It is now nearly all above 1800 m in these mountains and in the Upper Sacramento Valley. It was discovered and introduced in 1854. It is now all but universal in cities, towns, suburbs and villages, in gardens, parks, policies and churchyards, in all parts of these islands.

CULTIVARS: **'Allumii'**. A narrowly conic tree from a bushy base with vertical plates of dull, grey-blue foliage. This is a valuable plant for formal planting.

'Columnaris'. This is a more recent form than 'Allumii', much narrower, quite columnar and brighter blue-grey. It is useful in even more formal plantings or as a spot tree where only moderate size is required.

'Ellwoodii'. Tightly columnar with narrowly conic apex or apices, this plant has grey-green adult somewhat congested foliage and is a good formal plant which is still growing steadily if slowly and is known to over 11 m tall.

'Fletcheri'. Similar to 'Ellwoodii' but of looser habit and juvenile foliage, bluer and darker. To 14 m so far.

'Green Spire'; 'Green Pillar'. Two very similar relatively recent forms, tightly erect from a stout central stem making a slim, conic crown of bright, pale-green foliage. Vastly superior to the old 'Erecta' (not recommended) and less liable to branches breaking out under wet snow.

'Lutea'. This has a conic rather pendulous crown of the brightest golden foliage. It is exceedingly valuable to brighten up dull corners or to contrast with grey-blue foliages. It has given rise to similar golden forms, ('Hillieri', 'Lanei', 'Winston Churchill') which are not pendulous and may have their lower foliage in

 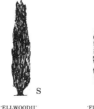    

'ALLUMII' 'COLUMNARIS' 'ELLWOODII' 'FLETCHERI' 'GREEN SPIRE' 'LUTEA'

vertical plates ('Winston Churchill') but are little if any brighter, although valuable for variety of form.

'**Pottenii**'. Has a bottle-shaped or spindle-shaped crown of feathery pale-green foliage. It is unusual and attractive until 40 years old and 12 m tall when it may have branches bent out and lose its shape.

'**Stewartii**'. A bright golden form differing from 'Lutea' and those mentioned with it, in its fern-like long sprays with the branchlets depressed, giving a most distinctive and attractive appearance. The interior foliage is bright green.

'**Triomphe de Boskoop**'. A sturdy, vigorous tree with a stout bole and an open, broadly columnar-conic crown, this has its outer sprays bright blue-grey. It is very useful where vigorous growth (to 24 m) is appreciated and as a foil to the golden forms.

'**Wisselii**'. This has an upright columnar crown with upswept tips to the branches forming turrets. It is very dark blue-green except in spring when covered in dull crimson male flowers. The foliage is in congested bunches and the tree is of surprising and continued vigour. Many trees exceed 20 m and one is 26 m tall and 1.1 m in diameter.

Chamaecyparis
nootkatensis
Nootka cypress

Every tree is a neat, regular cone whether broad or narrow. Its main uses are therefore for shelter where few trees will grow and as a distant feature where the regular crowns are conspicuous. Groups of five or more, spaced so that their bases almost touch (planting distance about 5 m) make quite a striking, large scale feature. Young trees on fairly loamy soils may grow rapidly and be fine narrow, pendulous plants.

FEATURES: The Nootka cypress is not an important tree for amenity but is useful in unusually severe conditions. The bark is orange-brown and stringy and the foliage heavy and thick; the branchlets lie each side of the shoot in fern-like sprays, and are deep-green. Male flowers are pale-yellow and prominent from late summer until shedding pollen in April. Female flowers are bluish-green and become globular cones bright grey-blue with a prominent hook on each scale. These fruit take two years to ripen. Growth is slow, after a more rapid start which may attain briefly well over 60 cm a year. It is, however, steady in growth and the pointed crowns on even the oldest trees show that they are still active; 25 m is quite commonly attained but only one is known above 30 m.

MERITS: The two chief merits of this cypress are its extreme toughness in the face of altitude, cold, and exposure on almost any reasonably drained soil, and its invariably shapely crown.

LIMITATIONS: This cypress is seldom the best tree purely for ornament, having dark, dull pendulous foliage, and is too sombre in numbers at close range. Near towns and industrial areas it becomes thin and lank as well. Old trees become liable to wind-throw.

ORIGIN AND OCCURRENCE: This cypress is native to the Pacific slope from mid-Alaska south to mid-Oregon. It was introduced in 1851. It is quite a frequent tree, in big Scottish gardens and policies and in churchyards, town parks and big gardens in England, less usually in town and city surburbs.

Chamaecyparis obtusa
Hinoki cypress

FEATURES: The Hinoki cypress is a pleasant, bright-green tree with the crown broadly columnar or conic, in either case obtusely pointed. The leaves are also obtuse, scale-like, bright-green with bright powdery blue-white on the underside towards the part overlain by the

next leaf. The biggest trees are now 22 m × 70 cm with an occasional specimen of 24–25 m.

MERITS: The Hinoki has bright, shining and attractive foliage, a welcome variety among duller greens. Big trees have fine chestnut-

---

coloured boles. It is a singularly healthy species.

LIMITATIONS: The type tree has a need for damp soils and humid air and is rare in the eastern parts of this country, thriving in the damp west (but see the cultivar). Growth is slow in height and the tree has a broad not very shapely crown.

ORIGIN AND OCCURRENCE: This tree is native to Japan and was introduced in 1861. It is frequent in the larger gardens in the west, infrequent in the south and rare in east.

CULTIVARS: **'Crippsii'** is apparently more adaptable than the type and grows well in drier areas, although never rapidly anywhere. Its

S

'CRIPPSII'

feature is its brilliant, golden foliage. Grown in full light it is as bright and rich a colour as any golden tree, but in some shade it is more green. It grows slowly and makes a broadly conic crown.

Chamaecyparis pisifera
Sawara cypress

FEATURES: The Sawara cypress itself is not a very attractive tree but it has yielded many good variants. The type tree has a strong tendency for low branches to layer and and grow up as a ring of trees. The foliage consists of small, sharply acuminate scale-leaves, bright-green above and with bright blue-white marking beneath. The cones are numerous and, as the name 'pisifera' implies, very like peas in size, crinkled appearance and colour. The biggest trees are 25 m × 80 cm.

MERITS: The cultivars include bright-coloured, tough trees useful in decorative plantings. The type has reasonable foliage and habit if well-grown and is a change from Lawson cypresses.

LIMITATIONS: This type of tree can be thin of crown and dull, although this is not always the case. It makes a sturdy tree only in favoured gardens in the southwest and west, rarely of any distinction.

ORIGIN AND OCCURRENCE: The Sawara cypress is a native of Japan and was introduced, with most of the cultivars, in 1861. The type is uncommon, mostly in big gardens in the south and west but several cultivars are common in smaller gardens, churchyards and town parks everywhere.

CULTIVARS: 'Aurea' is an attractive tree with good foliage, bright-gold new growth towards the tips of bright-green older foliage, fading to yellow-green.

'Filifera Aurea' is small-growing, ovoid and bushy or columnar and gaunt, with bright-yellow, slender pendulous shoots. It is often seen in tubs.

'Plumosa' is a broadly columnar tree to 20 m with dense, semi-juvenile foliage, the scale-leaves having spreading tips. It is common in parks and churchyards. 'Plumosa Aurea' is a little more frequent in the same places and has golden exterior foliage, bright when young but duller in old trees.

'Squarrosa' is a dense dark-blue tree to 20 m with fluffy fully juvenile foliage of free-standing linear leaves, fairly frequent in churchyards and large gardens. Although many specimens fork low in the crown they maintain a conic shape and unforked trees make fine specimens.

Cryptomeria japonica
Japanese red cedar

FEATURES: The Japanese red cedar resembles the Sierra redwood but has bright-green foliage. The leaves are four-sided and curve out at the base from the shoot then curve in towards their tips. Male flowers are prominent from late summer until pollen is shed in February, a dozen or so little ovoids clustered along the terminal 2 cm of every shoot. The female flowers are tiny, green rosettes ripening to globose, very spiny cones and often present in large numbers on trees only five or six years old. Growth can be, in early years, nearly 1 m a year but soon decreases and few trees exceed 30 m in height. Boles may be 70 cm diameter in 50 years and 1.4 m in a 100 except in the eastern half of the country where 1 m is rarely exceeded.

MERITS: Where growing well, which is usually in areas of high rainfall and cool summers, this is a vigorous tree with luxuriant bright-green foliage. It soon has a shapely bole with a rich red-brown stringy bark. The crown is a slender cone until maturity and a group or line makes a distinctive feature.

LIMITATIONS: Unless thriving this makes a poor specimen, thinly crowned, gaunt and yellowish. It needs plenty of moisture, so except in the humid west and far north, it needs damp hollows or good soils and shelter from drying winds. It deposits quantities of hard litter throughout the summer and needs plenty of room.

ORIGIN AND OCCURRENCE: The first seed was sent from China in 1845. The Chinese form has a loose crown of more open, slender foliage and many of the oldest trees of this form survive. The main population is on Honshu, Japan, and was sent in 1861 and is the common form. The tree is common in large gardens especially in the west.

CULTIVARS: 'Elegans' is a broad, bushy form, often leaning or on many stems which become splayed out. It has fully juvenile foliage which turns deep reddish-purple in the winter but resumes its bright blue-green colour in the spring.

'Lobbii' is a form sent from Japan in 1847 and locally common. It has its foliage in dense short bunches, and its more sparse crown is rather upswept at the tips. It is much less decorative than is the type.

L

**× *Cupressocyparis*
*leylandii***
Leyland cypress
(Nootka cypress ×
Monterey cypress)

FEATURES: The Leyland cypress is now planted in gardens in almost the same numbers as is the Lawson cypress. There are four main clones which differ in details (see below) but they share a columnar crown with a long conic, slightly bent apex and strongly upswept branches. Growth is remarkably uniform on a wide range of sites and soils, young trees adding 1 m a year and decreasing somewhat so that in 20 years they measure 15 m × 30 cm; in 40 years 25 m × 65 cm. One of the very few older trees was 32 m tall when 60 years old and they all seem well set to achieve 50 m or more. (The mean growth of many specimens is more easily given in Imperial measure: 2 feet a year in height; 2 inches a year in girth).

MERITS: The remarkable and sustained vigorous growth on almost any site or soil makes this a valuable and much planted tree. As a spot specimen it becomes a feature within a few years and will attain noble dimensions whilst keeping a shapely columnar or tall-ovoid crown. The four best clones provide a good variety of foliage forms and colours.

LIMITATIONS: In exposure, young plants making strong growth are apt to be lain over by the wind. Growth is poor and thin in shade and in soils which drain badly. It should always be borne in mind that unless prevented in those ways by the site or by constant clipping, any Leyland cypress will rapidly become a big tree casting heavy shade. Also this tree is so handy for making rapidly, big hedges or dense screens, that its use in these ways is now something of a cliché. Avenues are too dull and shady unless the final trees are spaced so that the gaps between the crowns are at least equal to the width of the crowns.

ORIGIN AND OCCURRENCE: The first six trees were raised from seed of a Nootka cypress at Leighton Hall, Welshpool in 1888. These were sent in 1892 to Haggerston Castle, Northumberland. The next two trees were also raised at Leighton Hall, from the seed of a Monterey cypress picked in 1911. In about 1940 seed was picked from a Monterey cypress at Ferndown, Dorset and two trees were raised at Stapehill Nursery. There is a slight mystery about these, for there is and was, no Nootka cypress visible in the vicinity of the parent tree yet in foliage these two are very close indeed to one of the Leighton trees of 1911, and the cones have the spiked scales of Nootka cypress. Trees older than of 1927 planting are confined to Leighton Hall, Haggerston Castle and the few gardens which received cuttings as 'unknown cypress', as at Bicton, Devon. In 1927, a few of the trees were propagated and some of that date are at Bedgebury, Kew, Wisley, Edinburgh and probably Wakehurst Place, Sussex and

Headfort, Co. Meath. After 1930 a few more were sent out (Westonbirt and Woburn) and in about 1935 the tree came on the market generally. It is now very common as a garden hedge in suburbia and as a screening tree or specimen in parks and gardens everywhere.

CULTIVARS: **'Haggerston Grey'** is the tree usually seen, accounting for over 90 per cent of recent plantings in the United Kingdom. It has its foliage in plumes and the minor sprays have lesser shoots at various angles. At some times of year there is a distinct grey in the foliage which is absent in the next clone.

'Leighton Green'. One of the two trees of 1911 seed, this is now strongly recommended and is the common form in Ireland, north and south. Its rich green foliage is in long pectinate sprays of thicker and broader minor shoots than in 'Haggerston Grey' and is much more attractive. It makes the same growth in height, but the heavier foliage causes it to have stronger branches and build up a bigger bole. Forms about 10 per cent of United Kingdom plantings.

'Naylor's Blue' is the other 1911 tree and was blown down in a small cyclone in 1954. It is slower in growth, more open in crown and varies with season from dull blue-green to bright blue-grey. It is a useful and handsome variant. Hardly yet in commerce.

L

115

'Stapehill 21'. This will require a new name to be more fully distinguishable from 'Stapehill 20' which is in the trade and occasionally encountered but has proved more susceptible to damage from drought and less healthy. 'Stapehill 21' is exceedingly vigorous, probably the most vigorous of all, and has been very healthy in trials. It will be strongly recommended for propagation. It has bright, green, hard, rough, braided foliage arranged in the flat, pectinate manner of 'Leighton Green' and scarcely distinguishable from it, but with an irregularity of outline of some minor sprays; gaps where a minor shoot is absent. 'Stapehill 20', which is sometimes seen in gardens has braided, roughened foliage, more sparse, yellower-green and carries much dead, brown foliage visible externally, in its open crown.

'Castlewellan Gold' was the first of several forms of golden or gold-variegated foliage. It has been available generally since 1972 and is a very vigorous and promising tree. The foliage is tipped pale-yellow, on plumose sprays. Raised from cones broken from a Golden Monterey cypress by the snows of 1962.

'Robinson's Gold' is a recent form with flattened pectinate sprays, bright-gold in spring sometimes fading nearly to green in late summer. It is of similar vigour to 'Castlewellan Gold' but of similar foliage to 'Leighton Green'. Found as a seedling in 1962 at Belvoir Castle, N. Ireland.

Cupressus glabra
Smooth Arizona cypress

FEATURES: The Smooth Arizona cypress is an exceptionally useful and attractive, tolerant tree. The minor shoots are short and at right-angles in the three dimensions, clad in pale grey-blue scale leaves, some with a white spot of resin. Cones are numerous, bunched and retained for many years, globular, 2 cm, dull-purple. A few of the oldest trees are now over 18 m tall and 50 cm in diameter of bole.

MERITS: Completely hardy, never known to have been damaged even by a winter like 1962-63, this attractive tree grows well on any soil from light sand to fairly heavy clay. It maintains a neat ovoid-conic crown of soft blue-grey foliage often enhanced by pale-yellow male flowers in quantity from late summer to April. Growth is usually moderate although some young trees add nearly a metre a year, and none is yet very big. The bark is interesting, purple with orange or grey blisters opening, becoming later very scaly, purple scales on pale-grey.

LIMITATIONS: There are no apparent disadvantages or difficulties at all with this tree.

ORIGIN AND OCCURRENCE: This tree was sent from Arizona in 1908 but was distinguished from the greener foliaged and stringy-barked *Cupressus arizonica* only as the variety *'bonita'* until it was accepted as a full species in about 1960. It is commonly seen in small gardens in the outskirts of towns and in big gardens mainly in southern England and eastern Ireland.

'PYRAMIDALIS'

CULTIVARS: The form '**Pyramidalis**' is superior as a specimen tree, having upswept foliage of thicker shoots distinctly brighter blue and copiously speckled white.

Cupressus lusitanica
Cedar of Goa

FEATURES: The Cedar of Goa is useful in mild areas as a variant on the Monterey or Lawson cypresses. The crowns of maturing trees are usually conic with a more open, less rigid apex than the Monterey cypress, and often leaning slightly. This sort of tree has a fine, straight, cylindrical bole but some are of poor, branchy form. The foliage loses the grey of the juvenile and becomes dark-green often with specks of white resin. The cones are small and in summer are bloomed blue-grey. The species has been 31 m tall but is rarely 25 m.

MERITS: Young trees are very vigorous, growing a metre or more in a season and attractive with greyish leaves and pink and purple shoots. Older trees vary and may be branchy and broad but many are narrow and shapely.

LIMITATIONS: A really severe winter may kill this tree, at any age, in any part of the country except the south-western peninsular. Winters of this severity have occurred only a few times in two hundred years but lesser ones may be fatal in eastern, exposed areas. In the west, generally, there is a fair chance that the tree can achieve a good size. It will not thrive on alkaline soils nor, for long, on dry sites. It is not very wind-firm.

ORIGIN AND OCCURRENCE: The Cedar of Goa is native to Mexico and was spread by Portuguese missionaries in the seventeenth century, hence the association with Goa (formerly a Portuguese settlement in India). It was introduced here in 1680 and before 1962 was present but infrequent in large gardens in the south. Since 1963 few survive except in Devon and Cornwall.

VARIETY AND CULTIVAR: Var. *benthami* has very different foliage, bright-green, in flat pectinate sprays and is somewhat less hardy. In Cornwall there are a few superbly shapely specimens 30 m tall with long cylindric boles.

'**Glauca**'. Possibly more hardy than the type, is a shapely tree with soft grey foliage.

Cupressus macrocarpa
Monterey cypress

FEATURES: The Monterey cypress can rapidly provide single specimens of great size and grandeur. Crowns are very dense whether the tree is columnar, ovoid or widely spreading like a Cedar of Lebanon. The bark is a pale, warm brown, shallowly ridged and stripping. Cones are numerous on old trees, clustered, globose and irregular, 3 cm across, dark purple-brown and held for many years. In the west early growth is exceedingly rapid, strong branches extending at a low angle with long feathery shoots, but in the east the tree may be neatly narrow – conic with regular ascending small branches, at first rather open. In most areas the trees have flat tops when reaching 25 m but in some shelter many attain 30 m and a few 35 m. Big boles are common and within 80 years of planting they can be 2 m in diameter and a few older trees are 2.5 m.

MERITS: In the south and west the growth is extremely rapid. Good trees, or any tree with judicious pruning in early years, can provide imposing boles of great size. The foliage is a bright, viridian green on most young trees although on old trees it is very dark. It is very tolerant of drought although the rapid growth occurs only on damp sites or in high rainfall areas, and it is tolerant for many years of thin soils over limestone and chalk.

LIMITATIONS: In some coastal areas there are already sufficient of these trees and lines make awkward shapeless features. Except in exposed areas of the Midlands, it grows rapidly into a very large and spreading tree needing a great deal of space and casting dense shade widely. It is not reliably wind-firm although single trees can withstand severe exposure. Big old trees are liable to shed big branches in gales or when laden with wet snow. In exposure in the east long periods of freezing winds can kill large areas of the crown which remain unsightly for many years, and sometimes the whole tree can be killed. The shape of maturing and mature trees can vary greatly. The tree is susceptible to the fungus *Seiridium (Coryneum) cardinale* and in some areas whole branches may die back from this cause in southern England, rapidly followed by death of the whole tree.

ORIGIN AND OCCURRENCE: This tree is found wild only on a few miles of low sandstone cliffs at Cypress Point and Point Lobos, Monterey, California. Seeds turned up in 1838 at Kew from an unknown source and after larger importings in 1846 and the next few years, planting was widespread. The tree is abundant in parts of the southwest; the dominant landscape tree in some coastal areas and is common throughout south and east England, particularly in parts of Essex and the Midlands. There are few in northern England and the Pennine region although it is again common in southern Scotland.

CULTIVARS: '**Lutea**' is a good tree against sea-winds and is marginally hardier than the type. It arose in 1892 and the oldest trees are 25 m tall and tend to have dense branching or multiple stems. Young trees are reasonably bright yellow but older trees can be dull.

'**Donard Gold**' is the oldest of several more recent selected golden seedlings which are brighter gold than 'Lutea'.

L

Cupressus torulosa
Himalayan cypress,
Bhutan cypress

FEATURES: The Bhutan cypress makes a shapely tree with slender pendulous foliage. The crown is conic, either narrow or broad, ovoid or columnar. The cones are globose, small and often prolific.

MERITS: Some good specimens of Bhutan cypress are in the region where the Monterey cypress is least successful, in Perthshire and Easter Ross. In Somerset it has grown to be very large (28 m tall and 1.4 m diameter) and although growing slowly in the Midlands, it makes a shapely tree there. The foliage is finely divided and a good light-green. It is highly tolerant of different soils except for chalk.

LIMITATIONS: This tree will not provide rapid growth and early effect, and in England, but not Scotland, it tends to be short-lived.

ORIGIN AND OCCURRENCE: This tree of the eastern Himalaya was introduced in 1826 and is widespread in collections and a few big gardens whilst nowhere less than rare.

Ginkgo biloba
Maidenhair tree

FEATURES: The Ginkgo is in a class by itself and there are important differences, botanical and apparent, between it and all other trees. The leathery leaf has a long petiole and fan-veined blade divided towards the tip into two lobes. Most trees in Britain are male but only a few bear the short yellow catkins which emerge in bunches with the leaves. The females, where known, are slender, erect trees (in contrast to their habit in Philadelphia and Washington where they spread hugely with serpentine branching) bearing minute, acorn-like flowers paired on long stalks. Growth is unpredictable, some young trees adding 60 cm in a year regularly for a few years, others spending alternate years, or two out of three, without making any extension growth on the main shoots or leader. Some trees have attained 20 m in 70 years. Many are 25 m tall and one is 28 m.

MERITS: This tree has character and great botanical interest as it is an entirely different sort of plant from any other; the only extant member of a once large tribe. It is exceedingly healthy, long-lived and tolerant of cities, towns, streets, drought and heat. It is one of the common street trees in every eastern American city from Montreal south to New Orleans, thriving in mean, crowded streets and in torrid downtown areas. In England it is frequently found in Cathedral closes and precincts and city parks and gardens. Quite early in spring it leafs out a splendid fresh green and in autumn it is a glowing gold. Many trees are shapely narrow spires. It thrives on chalk or limestone and in clay. It should be planted in gardens or near buildings as a fine specimen of interest.

LIMITATIONS: At high altitudes and north of Edinburgh the lack of heat restricts growth so much that it is not worth growing Ginkgo. Where not flourishing it makes a poor, gaunt plant of little merit. It is unhappy on most highly acid sands, or silts and unpredictable on some better soils where drainage is apt to be poor. In winter it can be stark, and poorly shaped specimens, which are frequent, are then unattractive. The female bears fruit in hot summers, only sparsely in Britain, but when these fall and the fleshy covering decays it gives rise to a strong and very rancid smell.

ORIGIN AND OCCURRENCE: Found wild only in a few woodlands preserved by monasteries in central China, the Ginkgo has been much planted in Japan for 800 years and was first seen by a westerner there in 1690. It was introduced to England in 1754. It is common in southern, eastern and Midland England, mainly in cities, towns, suburbs and the large gardens, especially near old mansions, and scarce in northern England, southern Scotland and rare as far north as Easter Ross, and in Ireland.

CULTIVARS: **'Fastigiata'** is a male upright form and very worthwhile but seldom seen here except as a small tree. It is frequent in some cities in the north-eastern USA, where it is known as 'Sentry Ginkgo'. It has a dense narrow crown – like a good Lombardy poplar.

M

Juniperus drupacea
Syrian juniper

FEATURES: This Juniper has the longest leaves of any, 2–3 cm long, sharply spined and a fresh, pale-green on the outer surface with two white bands on the inner. The tree is usually a slender column, acute at the apex or forked into two closely adjacent stems. Some old trees have retained and exaggerated this shape but some others have broadened and become ovoid in the crown.

MERITS: The Syrian juniper grows well on alkaline, neutral or acid soils, some of the best trees being on shallow soils over limestone. It is uniquely shapely among Junipers and makes the narrowest spire of any conifer grown in Britain. It is slow in growth but faster than other Junipers and can attain 18 m. The colour is an attractive one very unusual among conifers. Although a tree of markedly southern origin it seems very hardy and one tall specimen is as far north as Roxburghshire.

LIMITATIONS: This tree is slow to make a notable specimen and although growing well in some exposure it is rather liable to be blown down (and can continue to grow sometimes when it has). Its foliage is a little prickly to brush against.

ORIGIN AND OCCURRENCE: The Syrian Juniper ranges through Asia Minor to Greece. It was introduced in 1854. It is a scarce tree, found in rather few collections and occasionally in gardens south of the Midlands and in eastern Ireland.

Larix decidua
European larch

FEATURES: The European larch is a first class amenity tree with a wide range of valuable features. Extension growth begins in early May and continues sometimes until mid or late September, stopping earlier in shaded or less vigorous trees. Colour of shoot varies with origin from the stout pink of western alpine to the slender white of Polish trees but is usually yellow. The cone is ovoid-cylindric with scales incurved, straight or slightly outcurved at the tips and may be held on the tree for many years. Male flowers are disc-shaped, pale-yellow fringed crimson. In sheltered valleys and hillsides many trees grow to 35 m, especially in central Scotland and Argyll while a few exceed 40 m. Trees have grown 20 m in 20 years.

MERITS: In the right conditions, the exceedingly rapid growth makes a vigorous, luxuriantly foliaged plant and ensures a fair sized tree with a good bole within relatively few years. The early spring flowers, bright rosy-red, may pass unnoticed but the flush to bright-green is apparent and a group of larches makes a grand spring feature where other trees are wintry and unchanged. The good autumn colours, yellow and old gold are shown when most other deciduous trees have shed their leaves, in early November. This larch is particularly good for wildlife in general. Under its intermittent shade the oakwood pre-vernal flora may thrive - bluebells, sanicle, bugle, wood anemone and other plants, or on poorer upland soils, rich carpets of wood-sorrel, cinquefoil, heath bedstraw and fine grasses and mosses. These woods are good habitat for coal-tit, goldcrest,

L

bullfinch, redpoll, crossbill and wren, feeding grounds for great, blue, marsh and willow tits and tree-creepers and, when maturing, breeding places for birds of prey. The varied flora on the floor ensures good populations of butterflies and moths. Away from industrial or city air, this tree will thrive on light sandy soil and on chalk if there is a loamy top soil.

LIMITATIONS: Larches need to be thriving to be good amenity trees and the European larch will not succeed near industrial areas or in cities. It will not tolerate shade, bad drainage nor heavy clay. In winter it is rather twiggy and bare. Old trees shed quantities of dead shoots with old cones adhering. In moderately severe exposure, especially if other factors are not favourable, the tops bend over and the tree is short and poorly shaped.

ORIGIN AND OCCURRENCE: The native range is from the Savoy Alps to Vienna and, in distinguishable forms, in the Sudeten and Tatra Mountains and the plains of Poland. This larch was introduced in about 1620 but remained very rare for a hundred years. Planting in Scotland was widespread after 1750 and every hill farm now has some in its woods. In lowland areas it is less frequent and in urban areas it is rare and unhappy.

Larix × eurolepis
(*Larix decidua ×*
L. kaempferi)
Hybrid larch

FEATURES: The Hybrid larch is intermediate between its parents in most physical features, but will outgrow either on some sites. The main distinctions from the European larch are more scaly, less fissured bark, more dense crown; shoots orange or brown-pink, leaves longer with broader more conspicuous bands of grey beneath and taller, larger cone with the tips of the scales well curved outwards. A few trees are 30 m tall.

MERITS: Growth is even more rapid than in European larch, particularly in places where that tree is less thriving due to poor soil or industrial air. The Hybrid larch grows acceptably on shallow peats.

LIMITATIONS: See European larch (above). This hybrid is, however, more tolerant of urban conditions than is the European.

ORIGIN AND OCCURRENCE: This hybrid arose first from seed collected at Dunkeld in about 1895 but was known first from trees raised at Dunkeld in 1904. After 1910 it was planted in the middle Tay Valley on the Atholl Estates but elsewhere there were only a few specimen trees until about 1925 when some plantations were made by the Forestry Commission. Planting has been restricted by the small quantity of hybrid seed available but has been more widespread in the last 15 years. A number of stands of second and third generation Hybrid larch are known, raised from seed collected in older stands of Hybrid larch. The third generation tends to lack hybrid vigour, but there is usually an admixture of pure Japanese larch in the parent stand of hybrids and the second generation, raised from these, includes back-crosses of good vigour. Seed orchards of grafts from selected, superior trees of European and Japanese larches have been established to yield first generation seed.

Larix kaempferi
Japanese larch

FEATURES: This differs from the European larch in the same ways as does the Hybrid larch, but in greater degree, the Hybrid being fairly well intermediate. The shoots are orange-red or purple; the leaves broad and grey-green, well marked whitish-grey beneath; each shoot bears many more lateral shoots; the crown is broader and may have long, level, lower branches, and the cone is short and squat with the scales much rolled down.

MERITS: Similar generally to European larch except that, casting a more dense shade it is somewhat less encouraging to wildlife in general as a plantation tree although single trees attract the same birds. This larch builds up a stout bole much more rapidly.

LIMITATIONS: See European larch (above) but more vigorous on poor soils and in harder conditions generally.

ORIGIN AND OCCURRENCE: This larch is confined to central Honshu in Japan, at 1000 m to 3000 m. It was introduced in 1861 but was very rare until 1890. Large plantations were made between 1930 and 1940 in the western hills. Single trees are occasional in many urban areas and parks but do not thrive there.

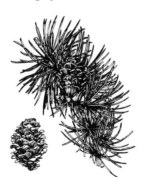

Metasequoia glyptostroboides
Dawn redwood

L

FEATURES: The Dawn redwood is still a sufficiently new discovery to be of added interest. The shoots and leaves are borne in opposite pairs and both shoots and leaves are shed in late autumn. New growth is often flushed lilac; strong growing shoots are pink. Cones occur in hot summers, globose or ovoid, green, on a long stalk. The biggest trees when 30 years old are up to 24 m tall and 65 cm in diameter.

MERITS: Rapid growth in early years is always valuable and this is very soon an elegant, narrowly conic tree, fresh green in April, pale-green much of the summer and giving late autumn pinks, russets and sometimes ruby-red. Given a damp site it thrives on any soil, in some shelter.

LIMITATIONS: In Scotland, growth is usually relatively slow and the plant is rarely well furnished as it needs a warm summer to grow well. It also needs moisture, and dry soils in any area are unsuitable. The winter aspect is gaunt, except in the best, spire-shaped trees. Once the tree is 10 m tall it needs shelter to continue rapid straight growth reliably, and is better if the roots have access to running or fresh standing water. It is sensitive to exposure and late frosts damage early shoots, although it flushes again and recovers fully.

ORIGIN AND OCCURRENCE: Discovered in 1941 in Hupeh and Szechuan, western China this tree became known more widely in 1945 and the first seed arrived in January 1948. Every major garden now has one or more and it is frequent in parks and smaller gardens. A remarkable feature

of this tree is that the original trees remeasured when 31 years planted show increases in diameter of bole that are still accelerating. Since 1976 many have expanded at 3 cm a year; one in New York State has added 5 cm a year in that period (now 1.25 m diameter).

Picea abies
Norway spruce

L

FEATURES: The Norway spruce is rather a dull tree as a specimen but can be useful for shelter or background. Mature trees can have the normal 'brush' crown of ascending upper branches or the more picturesque 'comb' crown with level branches and pendulous shoots. Few specimens seem to survive more than 200 years and since increase in girth becomes unusually feeble after the first 100 at most, there are no really big boles and 1.1 m diameter is rarely exceeded. There are a few trees 46 m tall in Scotland and Cornwall but 42 m is the tallest elsewhere.

MERITS: In most mountainous areas or western parts with a good rainfall this makes a thriving shapely tree growing quite rapidly to 30 m or so. It is moderately resistant to damage from late spring frost, high altitude or exposure. The glossy brown, long cones are pleasing.

LIMITATIONS: Unless flourishing, this becomes a thin, twiggy tree, with bare lower parts and thin, unhealthy upper parts. It is unhappy on thin soils; in sandy dry areas; near towns or industrial areas or in strong maritime exposure.

Unless on deep soils, it is unstable except as an open-grown, single tree. It is liable to be heavily infested with the pineapple galls of the Green spruce aphid.

ORIGIN AND OCCURRENCE: This species ranges across much of Europe in three main separable populations; centrally from southern France through the Alps, Hartz and Sudeten mountains to the Balkans; eastward in Poland and across Russia, and northward in Scandinavia. It was brought to England at least a short while before 1548, and in the period after 1780 it was extensively planted on estates and in forests, its popularity only waning when Sitka spruce came into general use after 1920. The Norway spruce is still planted on a large scale in areas too frosty or insufficiently maritime for the Sitka and is quite frequent in town parks and old gardens in or around towns.

Picea brewerana
Brewer spruce

FEATURES: The Brewer spruce is immediately prominent as a specimen tree. The crown shape varies from narrowly columnar to broadly conic, depending in part on the openness of the site. Cones are freely borne around the apices of trees 30 years or more old. They are long, irregularly shaped, tapering at both ends and very resinous. Seed in this country is viable from trees in a group but of low germination.

MERITS: This much-prized and sought-after tree has ascending upper branches from which hang lines of shoots making a curtain on each, to a depth of up to 2 m. The leaves are deep blackish blue-green above with well-silvered bands beneath giving a frosty tinge to the crown. Once growing well, after some 15 years, growth in height is moderate, about 30 cm a year but the bole increases rapidly and the plant soon becomes a sturdy tree. On a reasonably damp and sheltered site Brewer spruce is highly adaptable to climate and has made fine specimens in most counties from Morayshire to Devon and Kent. It is probably never damaged by frosts.

LIMITATIONS: This tree must be well-grown to show its great feature – the long, pendulous shoots – and it will not do this if it is at all crowded. Nor will it do so in exposure or on dry, thin soils, deep peats, or in shade. Unless well grown, a Brewer spruce is a sad, poor thing, dull and spindly. At its best it is so individual that no more than a few should be visible at a time. Growth is alarmingly slow for some ten years, during which it shows not a sign of the weeping habit. Partly for this reason and partly from periodic shortages of seed, many plants sold are grafts. These make one-sided growth for many years, when too low for a weeping tree to be graceful, and are doubtful prospects altogether. None of the good specimens known appears to be a graft. The leading shoot is apt to fail.

ORIGIN AND OCCURRENCE: Brewer spruce is confined to two small areas 1800 m up in the Siskiyou Mountains, one each side of the Oregon-California boundary. It was introduced in 1897 and the single original tree in Kew Gardens is neither large nor handsome. Seeds and plants were brought in by R. F. S. Balfour in 1908 and 1910 and many of the trees of these origins are fine specimens. Most major gardens in every country have a few Brewer spruces and several are now more than 16 m tall, but it is not yet a common tree.

Picea omorika
Serbian spruce

FEATURES: The Serbian spruce is, for some difficult sites, the most desirable amenity tree among the conifers. Crowns differ considerably although always distinctly narrow. The best trees have exceedingly slim columnar crowns densely foliaged with long uprising leaves which show the broad blue-white banded undersides. The next best have narrowly conic crowns, tapering evenly to the tip, and normal, shorter, less erect leaves. A small number are broader and less shapely. Cones are relatively frequent, small and fusiform, resinous and dull purple.

MERITS: The Serbian spruce has a long list of exceedingly valuable features. It can grow well on chalky or limestone soils and on very acid sands or peats, even deep peats in wet areas. It starts shoot-growth so late that it is rarely damaged by late frosts. It withstands urban atmospheres remarkably well for a spruce and is the best one for a town park, along with the much slower Blue Colorado spruce. It grows very rapidly on a good site, young trees making shoots of 60–100 cm, and has a slender, shapely crown which is highly attractive singly or in groups, in informal or formal plantings. The foliage of most trees is richly coloured and bright-red flowers are often borne when the tree is small enough for them to be seen easily.

LIMITATIONS: This is a short-lived tree on any but the best sites. It is a frequent experience to

L

see a Serbian spruce 19–20 m tall which has almost ceased growth and is thin in the crown and to find it a year or two later quite dead. It is highly susceptible to Honey Fungus. It should not be planted on very light or thin soils in dry places, nor in exposure unless with high rainfall.

ORIGIN AND OCCURRENCE: Found only in the upper reaches of the Drina Valley, Jugoslavia, this tree was discovered in 1875 and first sent here in 1889. It is to be seen in most collections, many large gardens everywhere and in small numbers in some more suburban areas and town parks. There are occasional small plantations.

Picea orientalis
Caucasian spruce

FEATURES: The Caucasian spruce is a neater, denser, small-coned version of the Norway spruce. It has the smallest leaves of any spruce, less than 1 cm long, pressed closely to orange-brown pubescent shoots. Young trees can grow nearly 1 m in a year and once well established, increase in girth is rapid, reaching 3 cm a year. The tallest trees, many of which are dying back, are 36 m tall and one is 1.2 m in diameter of bole. Male flowers are slender, shaped like a droplet and open late in May. Cones are frequently numerous but only high on trees above about 18 m tall. The crowns are dense and will remain well-furnished to the ground on trees growing in the open.

MERITS: On a reasonably deep, damp, non-limey soil in any part of these islands this makes a vigorous sturdy tree. The crown is narrowly conic with a long slender leader and the foliage dense and a good deep-green. It flushes too late to be damaged by spring frosts of normal lateness and severity.

LIMITATIONS: This tree is relatively short-lived except in Scotland. The few specimens 100 years old in England have been depleted by deaths and many others have died back at the tip. Growth slows very considerably in height after about 60 years and in girth somewhat later. Trees that are not in vigorous growth when young are twiggy with much bare crown and are no ornament. Thin soils, dry sites and chalk or severe exposure restrict growth.

L

ORIGIN AND OCCURRENCE: The Caucasian spruce is native to the central and eastern Caucasus Mountains and the hills to the southeast of them. It was introduced in 1848 and is widespread although in small numbers. Most large gardens have a few and it is occasional in small, even suburban gardens.

CULTIVARS: '**Aurea**' is spectacular in late May and early June when new shoots all over the crown are bright pale-yellow for a few weeks. At other times it is almost indistinguishable from the type but it should be planted in preference to it in decorative schemes.

Picea pungens
var. *glauca*
Blue Colorado spruce

FEATURES: This is a mixture of selected forms, raised from the part of the natural range of *Picea pungens* where the blue forms predominate. They are mostly sold as grafts and crown shape varies from elegantly conic to rather densely columnar. The leading shoot is stout, rarely more than 30 cm long and often slightly askew. The largest trees on good sites are now over 23 m tall when about 70 years old and about 50 cm in diameter of bole. Cones are clustered densely near the apex in some years at fair intervals, and are short, cylindric domes with hard, leathery, whitish or cream-brown ridged and toothed scales, very like those of Sitka spruce.

MERITS: On a variety of soils and sites apart from those mentioned below, this can grow into a shapely tree of great attraction with the blue foliage varying in intensity and whiteness with the cultivar chosen. It will rarely grow too big for quite small decorative plantings.

M

LIMITATIONS: On dry sites or in drying atmospheres without a damp soil and in towns this grows slowly and suffers badly from Green spruce aphid and Red spider mite. Slow growth prevents the development of a shapely crown in the forms which are not semi-dwarf. In an unhealthy state the lower crown becomes a mass of bare twigs. Any but the slightest shade should be avoided.

ORIGIN AND OCCURRENCE: The first variety *glauca* form was sent in 1877 from Pike's Peak, Colorado to Knaphill Nursery where it now stands 20 m tall. Selections of ten bluest forms from a large number where made in Holland in 1910 and together are known as 'Koster' (see below). This tree in many forms, but particularly as 'Koster', is planted in decorative plantings, churchyards, parks, gardens small and large everywhere, though less in northern Scotland than in England.

The forms referred to above, known as **'Koster'** (**'Kosteriana'**) are not separable but although varying somewhat, are all very blue and are tall-growing in time. **'Argentea'** is a whiter blue, a shapely, vigorous tree. **'Moerheim'** is smaller growing, more compact and dense but brighter blue-white than 'Koster'. **'Hoopsii'**, a recent introduction from America, is a striking ice-blue-white form of moderate vigour.

Picea sitchensis
Sitka spruce

FEATURES: The Sitka spruce has a use as an amenity tree limited to sites where growth is good and space is plentiful. This tree remains narrowly conic until it is often well over 40 m tall but the biggest trees are broadly columnar with long ascending branches arching out from the bole. Many 110 years old are 45–50 m tall and several are 2 m in diameter of bole. The leaves project widely from the sides of the shoot but lie flat along the top except in strong young shoots, and end in a stiff, sharp point. New shoots emerge from fat buds a bright fresh green, like brushes, until they expand. The female flowers may be red or green and are present only in some years, rarely on trees less than 20 m tall.

MERITS: Few trees can attain such great size in so short a time as the Sitka spruce near the west coast and in most of the Highlands of Scotland. It is remarkably resistant to exposure and tolerant of wet, acid soils. Young trees growing fast, often 1.3 to 1.5 m a year are an inspiring sight and older trees in their luxuriant green and silver-blue foliage make a nice contrast with prevailing deep greens.

LIMITATIONS: There is little scope for Sitka spruce in any plantings except those on the largest scale, for only where it grows with great rapidity into a monumental specimen is it an amenity. It grows poorly in areas of low rainfall unless it is in a damp site and even then it will become thin, slow and of little merit when it grows clear of surrounding shelter. On soils which are not water-receiving sites a rough guide is that rainfall should exceed 1000 mm. In some years the trees, even in areas very favourable to growth, may be partially defoliated by Green spruce aphid (*Elatobium*). Unless growing fast in full health this tree is not ornamental, and is unsuitable as a border to a path as the foliage is prickly.

ORIGIN AND OCCURRENCE: The Sitka spruce was one of the several important trees introduced from north-west America by David Douglas, this one in 1831. It has a remarkable range in latitude from Kodiak Island round the Alaskan coast through British Columbia, Washington and Oregon to Mendocino County, California, but a very narrow range in longitude, seldom being found 100 km from the Pacific Coast. There is no recognisable sub-specific change throughout this length but the reaction to growth factors in Britain vary in clinal fashion. Trees from Alaskan seed do not relish the short day-length here when it is warm enough to grow and once the days shorten further, after June 22nd, they stop what was in any case slow growth, hence making short leaders. Trees of Oregon origin on the contrary find longer days during the growing season than those to which they are accustomed and make rapid growth. Being quite unconcerned about the gradually shorter days after June they continue until September and make very long leaders. This is the predominant forest tree over huge areas of the west and north but is little seen in gardens except the largest in Scotland, Ireland and the south-west.

Pinus ayacahuite
Mexican white pine

M

FEATURES: The Mexican white pine is a vigorous tree when young and may develop a broad crown. The bark becomes craggy at the base and deep orange-brown. The branches are level, becoming long in the lower crown. The biggest trees are 26 m × 1 m.

MERITS: The fine needles, five in a bunch, have blue-white inner surfaces and tend to hang in a decorative curve. Old trees keep their shape well and maintain fairly dense crowns with a conic apex. The variably large cones, often very long and with prominently out-curved scales are a source of interest and are very freely borne. This is a useful tree of good growth and moderate size on a wide range of soils in the western parts.

LIMITATIONS: From the little evidence available it would seem unwise to grow this tree on chalk, limestone, thin or dry sandy soils. Unless growing well it can be thin in the crown and twiggy. It will not tolerate shade.

ORIGIN AND OCCURRENCE: The Mexican white pine comes from the mountains of Mexico and was introduced in 1840. It is uncommon at least, rare in most areas and confined to a few large gardens and collections in all parts.

Pinus cembra
Arolla pine,
Swiss stone pine

M

FEATURES: The Arolla is a five-needled pine with the slender leaves blue-white on the inner surfaces, but deep blue-green on the outer surfaces making a dark, usually dense, columnar crown with small level branches. A few of the oldest have bigger branches high in the crown, ascending.

MERITS: This can make a neat, attractive young tree and a fairly narrowly columnar, tidy older tree. It is exceedingly tough with regard to cold, altitude and late frosts. The cones when borne, are erect and deep-blue. It will make an unusual and effective group on a moderate scale. It does not fork or bend and is rarely misshapen.

LIMITATIONS: A tree of slow growth, seldom exceeding 20 m. It may not live long or well on soils with lime nor on dry soils. In exposure or shade it is thin and of no amenity value.

ORIGIN AND OCCURRENCE: This is the pine of the high Alps, used in avalanche control in snowfields. It was introduced in 1746 and is in collections and big gardens with conifers in all parts and is sometimes seen in parks and small gardens.

Pinus contorta
var. contorta
Shore pine, Beach pine

FEATURES: The Shore pine is valuable in amenity planting for shelter, unusual colour and vigorous growth on difficult sites. Young trees have a bushy base of upswept branches and a long, slender spire with a long, strong leader. The bark is usually pale-orange divided into darker squares, and the leaves either yellow-green or deep-green, closely pressed to the shoot. Flowers are freely borne within a few years of planting, the females bright rosy-red, the males in dense clusters, yellow variously tinged purple or brown.

MERITS: As a very vigorous grower to a sizeable tree this has its value partly for the ability to do this on the poorest soils and deep peats but partly for its interesting shape and colour. Old trees are often bright-green and have a dense, domed crown.

LIMITATIONS: This pine grows exceedingly rapidly from the first or second year and needs room and full light. In exposure it may be blown down or bent and it will not thrive on chalk.

ORIGIN AND OCCURRENCE: Shore pine ranges from Alaska to California, along the coast and to some 50 km inland. Along this border it is bounded by *P. contorta* var. *latifolia* north of the Columbia River and partially by *P. contorta* var. *murrayana* southwards in Oregon. *Pinus contorta latifolia* is not included in this list as it is neither so rapid in growth nor so attractive nor resistant at high altitudes, and has a poor crown, often much forked stem and shallowly scaly bark. Both forms were introduced in 1853–54 and were equally rare and confined to only a few collections until large-scale forestry planting began around 1950. The few old specimens more than 25 m (and one 34 m tall) are of var. *contorta*.

Pinus jeffreyi
Jeffrey's pine

L

FEATURES: Closely related to the Western yellow pine, Jeffrey's pine is, in cultivation, much more regularly shaped although in the wild it is less so. This three-needled pine has stout shoots bloomed blue-grey and big orange buds. It is sometimes regarded as a more southern and high altitude form of *Pinus ponderosa* but it hybridises artificially more readily with *P. coulteri*. There are several trees more than 28 m tall and one at Scone, Perthshire is 36 m tall; several over 1 m in diameter of bole.

MERITS: An exceptionally shapely tree, this retains a tall, regular and narrowly conic crown until it is a large tree a hundred years old after which upper branches grow out more strongly.

It rapidly achieves a stout, straight bole with black bark and light slightly upcurved branches bearing strikingly long, dull grey needles. Old trees bear numerous big cones which are rich purple during their first year. Excellent specimens occur from Sussex north to Morayshire.

LIMITATIONS: This fine tree will not thrive on alkaline soils; nor poorly drained soils and is suspect with regard to a short life except on good sites. Unless on a good site it will often be thin and looking starved.

ORIGIN AND OCCURRENCE: Jeffrey's pine occurs almost throughout California above 1800 m where it replaces *P. ponderosa*. At 2500 m in the San Bernardino Mountains there are splendid trees 408 years old with boles 1.8 m in diameter and on the granites of the Sierra Nevada trees over 60 m in height grow at 2000 m while there are some spectacular hill-top trees as at Single Tree Mountain, withstanding extreme exposure. Introduced in 1855 this tree is found in collections in all parts except near the west coast.

Pinus leucodermis
Bosnian pine

FEATURES: A two-needle pine closely related to the Black pine group (*Pinus nigra* varieties) this is unlike any of them in looking clean and fresh despite blackish foliage. The buds have white papery scales with red centres and the shoots have a pale bloom on them at first. Very few trees have been found which fork or are in any way misshapen, all the others being of regular, pleasing shape. The largest are now 24 m tall and over 70 cm diameter.

MERITS: The Bosnian pine grows steadily and at moderate speed on any soil on which it has so far been found. It is indifferent to whether it is on chalk and limestones or on peats or acid sands. It is completely hardy and tolerant of dry soils and some exposure. It is always neat, shapely and clean-looking, due to the smooth pale-grey bark,

finely fissured and paler with age and the regular, light ascending branches maintaining at all times a regular ovoid or conic crown. The foliage appears black, contrasting with the bark. Cones are soon borne in numbers and in their second year they are deep-blue or blue-black.

LIMITATIONS: It is hard to think of any good reason not to plant this splendid tree except where no conifers at all are acceptable, or only very big ones are needed.

ORIGIN AND OCCURRENCE: Found in the mountains of Jugoslavia and the Balkan Peninsular as a more shapely form of *Pinus heldreichii*, this was first planted in 1890 at Kew. Many collections have a tree or two, mostly in southern England but also in west Scotland, North Wales and Ireland.

Pinus muricata
Bishop pine

FEATURES: The Bishop pine is a tree with remarkable features of distribution and growth. The bark is rough with well-defined, deep vertical fissures, often parallel for considerable lengths of bole. The needles are in pairs set in regularly spaced whorls, male flowers replacing them for the basal part and often for more than half the length of the shoot. The female flowers are in whorls of three to six, around the shoot usually 10–30 cm below the tip and are large, pink and yellow. The cones are oblique-ovoid-conic, fiercely spined and tenaciously held on branch or bole. Some trees have branches bearing 60 or more whorls of cones.

MERITS: There are two distinct forms, northern and southern. Only the northern is recommended for amenity. In either form the Bishop pine will give, very rapidly, large trees on any well-drained soil, however poor, and trees of the utmost hardiness and resistance to sea-winds. The northern blue form grows the more rapidly into tall, narrowly conic trees with small branches bearing deep-blue or blue-grey foliage. For shelter from Atlantic winds it has no equal, especially on very poor, very acid soils. As a

specimen tree the blue form makes a handsome tree of exceedingly rapid growth. Leading shoots of more than 2 m are normal for a few years.

LIMITATIONS: This tree should be planted only where there is immediate room for a large tree casting a heavy shade. It is not a worthwhile tree on chalk unless that is at a little depth beneath more neutral soil. In the southern form it grows

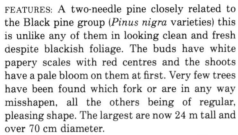

into a broad-headed domed tree with widely spreading low branches, in which form it is not really decorative. The superior blue northern form can suffer breakage and lose its good shape when young.

ORIGIN AND OCCURRENCE: The Bishop pine occurs in small, isolated groups along the coast of California and on off-shore islands down to Baja California (Mexico). These are small populations but the second most northerly, in Mendocino County extends for many miles inland and along the coast near the Noyo River and Fort Bragg. Fortunately this, like the most northerly at Big Lagoon is of the much superior blue form. The first introduction was of the southern form in 1846 and most of the big specimens in a few pineta in each country are of this form. The largest is 27 m × 1.3 m. The blue, northern form is found in Muckross Abbey grounds, Co. Kerry as a line of trees 27–30 m tall but not more than about 50 years old and similar but less blue and shapely trees are at Wakehurst Place, Sussex. There are a few small forest plots in Forestry Commission forests, dating from 1960–61. There is now great interest in this tree as a potential source of timber on poor soils and many larger plantings were made in 1974–75 and will be in the future.

Pinus nigra
var. *maritima*
Corsican pine

L

FEATURES: This two-needle pine has lax, slender needles unusual in this group, and a light crown casting little shade. Young trees in most places make shoots of 80 cm or more with much-twisted needles.

MERITS: The Corsican pine makes a shapely, columnar tree with light, level branching on a variety of difficult soils as well as on any well-drained soil. It grows well on thin soil over chalk, on heavy clays, light gravels, sands and thin peats. It withstands industrial pollution better than any other pine or most other conifers of any kind. It can grow to commanding stature commonly 35 m in any reasonably sheltered site and make an imposing big bole 1.4 m in diameter. It is long-lived and, except where unsuited climatically (see below) it is robustly healthy.

LIMITATIONS: In southern heathland areas this has little amenity value since there will be so many in plantations and gardens in the district. North of the Midlands, at high altitudes in Yorkshire and in parts of Scotland, the low summer temperatures render it liable to die-back diseases.

ORIGIN AND OCCURRENCE: A southern form of the Austrian pine, this is found in southern Italy and on Corsica. It was introduced to Kew in 1759. Some specimens were planted in early pineta and gardens before 1850 but it was uncommon until then. Since 1890 and especially after 1920 there has been large-scale use of Corsican pine in plantations on sandy heaths in the south and on clays and thin peats in general.

Pinus nigra
var. *nigra*
Austrian pine

FEATURES: In this form the bark is blackish-brown, crumbling into flakes from the faces and edges of deeply fissured plates. The foliage is dense and black, in whorls and even where there is a single straight bole this gives a different aspect from that of Corsican pine.

MERITS: The Austrian pine is nothing if not tough. It will grow in exposed places on pure chalk or hungry sands by the sea, and on the rubble of railway embankments, and is thus invaluable for shelter on very restricting sites. Single specimens may even have a kind of rugged grandeur. For a few years growth is more rapid and much more robust than that of the Corsican pine.

LIMITATIONS: This tree always seems to be sooty, dusty and generally unkempt and should be used only where nothing else will grow. Some specimens have straight boles and narrow crowns, but this is unpredictable; many fork or go over at the top and others are vastly bushy. It is a dull, dark tree.

ORIGINS AND OCCURRENCE: This tree occurs in the eastern Alps, in northern Italy and south to the Balkan Mountains. It was introduced by Lawsons of Edinburgh as late as 1840. It is the common pine of railway embankments, and perimeter shelter belts to Victorian gardens near towns, also in shelter belts near the coast and on chalk.

Pinus peuce
Macedonian pine

FEATURES: The Macedonian pine is an exceedingly valuable conifer for amenity planting on difficult sites. Since the needles are five in a bundle, they are slender, lax at the ends of shoots but clothing closely the leader and strong shoots.

The biggest trees are the few known of about 100 years in age and are 28 m tall and 1 m in diameter, but one at Stourhead is 35 × 1.17 m.

MERITS: This pine has a remarkable facility for growing at the same reasonable but steady rate in almost any soil on almost any site in any region of these islands. It is immune to White pine blister-rust and remains in good health when trees around are dying from poor drainage. It survives more industrial pollution than most conifers although it may look a little thin when doing so. It grows equally at 600 m and at sea-level, on chalk and limestone or acid peats. It has a neat columnar crown with conic apex and is densely clothed in rich green and blue-white needles. The bark may be purple or pale-grey, finely fissured, and the tree bears numerous cones from quite an early age. Late frosts have not been known to damage this species.

LIMITATIONS: None, where any medium to large

conifer is acceptable. Difficulties may arise in pronouncing the name to foreigners. A finely executed 'pay-ootzay' for an Italian may be met with 'oh, you mean "poicher"'. A Dane calls it 'poker' and some Englishmen, alas, 'puce', or 'pukey'. 'Pewchay' seems generally the safest course.

ORIGIN AND OCCURRENCE: This tree is native to a restricted area of mountains in southern Bulgaria and northern Greece and was introduced in 1864. It is not common but is present, often singly, in collections and many big gardens. There are few forest plots mainly at high altitude or on difficult sites.

M

Pinus pinaster
Maritime pine

FEATURES: The Maritime pine is now a little known tree, but it can grow into a good specimen of character. Some cones are retained on the branches in the crown for many years. Young trees may attain 10 m height in ten or twelve years. Many specimens are about 30 m tall and one is 38 m.

MERITS: The Maritime pine will grow exceedingly fast on the poorest, driest sands and in considerable exposure. The leaves are the longest and stoutest of all the two-needle pines and a contrast, with their pale colour, to those of the more usual pines. Mature trees hold lofty domes high on good boles with rich purple-red bark fissured into small shiny plates. Cones are freely borne and some are shed whilst often still unopened, when they are substantial, shiny brown objects which may be prized for ornaments. Vigorous shoots on small young trees are stained red.

LIMITATIONS: Growth will be poor unless the soil is light and well-drained and there is maximum light. Even specimens fully in the open become bare of lower crown by the time they are 20–30 years old, and give no low shelter or screening, and by this age they have little attraction as focal points or at close quarters. Grown in groups, there is a tendency for all the boles to be swept near the base, in the same direction. There may be difficulty in transplanting.

ORIGIN AND OCCURRENCE: The Maritime pine is a tree of the western Mediterranean area and was introduced some time before 1500. Although occasional specimens are seen there, it is rare in Scotland and frequent only locally in southern England, where it has been used in plantations in Dorset and behind sand-dunes in several areas.

L

Pinus ponderosa
Western yellow pine

FEATURES: The Western yellow pine is an excellent tree for amenity on many sites. The needles are borne in threes and are deep-green 15–24 cm long, in dense bunches but lax. Male flower are abundant, large purple ovoids clustered tightly along the basal half of the annual shoot, shedding pollen in mid-June. The

cones vary in size, usually 10–15 cm long and are ovoid-conic with each scale bearing a downward pointing spine.

MERITS: A healthy, big Western yellow pine is a handsome and imposing tree. It has a shapely crown, sometimes still acute at the top, and a long fine bole with pink flaky bark in long plates.

The foliage is bold and dense or hanging in star-like whorls on pendent shoots. As a young tree it is also a good plant. It grows well in a wide range of the better soils and sites, in Kent or Wiltshire, Powys or Perthshire.

LIMITATIONS: To grow well and show the fine crown, this needs plenty of room at all times. It does not thrive on chalky soils, and on soils a metre deep over limestone it tends to become unhealthy and may die when less than a 100 years old. It is not suitable in exposed places in Britain as it is then not reliably wind-firm although growing in some considerable exposure in California. It grows best on fairly good, deep soils, mildly acid and well-drained.

ORIGIN AND OCCURRENCE: This pine has an extensive range in the Rocky Mountains, from southern British Columbia to Mexico. It is at its best in the Siskiyou Mountains where there are many trees well over 60 m (200 ft) tall, and it covers wide areas of mountains below 1800 m altitude, with exceptionally shapely trees 50 m tall along miles of the Merced Canyon in the Sierra Nevada. It was one of the first trees introduced by David Douglas on his journey in Oregon and California in 1827. A few trees from

this seed survive and are extremely fine and big specimens. It is a species found in conifer collections, especially those in the policies of Scottish castles; widespread but nowhere frequent.

L

Pinus radiata
Monterey or Insignis pine

L

FEATURES: The Monterey pine is one of the most remarkable trees in the world. In San Francisco, with irrigation it can grow 16 m in five years and in New Zealand it has grown 60 m in 43 years. The needles, in bundles of three are slender and about 10 cm long. Male flowers, at the base of the new shoot, may shed pollen by March or before, since the cycle of shoot-growth is ill-defined. In mild winters in the far south-west, growth pauses only briefly and can be well advanced by February, while in other parts it may be continuous from March to October, or divided into two periods separated by bud-setting and brief dormancy in July. In exposed coastal areas shelter-belts commonly grow to 20–23 m before height culminates. In less exposed districts 25–30 m is frequent while one individual in a sheltered wood is 44 m tall.

MERITS: An exceptionally vigorous tree on a variety of soils in the west or near the coast in most parts, this tree can be 20 m tall in less than 20 years and 30 m in 40 years. Young trees growing fast are a rich, bright-green and of good, narrow shape with long leading shoots. Old trees make picturesque rugged specimens of great size in a relatively short time. This tree is of great value in providing rapidly good, dense shelter against strong sea-winds.

LIMITATIONS: In some inland areas of the eastern half of England and in the Midlands the Monterey pine is insufficiently thriving to be attractive. On thin soils over limestone or chalk it may grow fast for 30 or 40 years then suffer from chlorosis and soon die. The occasional really severe winter with freezing easterly winds can scorch the foliage badly. Big trees show a tendency to drop heavy, cone-encrusted branches especially in wet snow. Transplanting can be difficult, and growth declines strongly with increasing altitude.

ORIGIN AND OCCURRENCE: The Monterey pine is now native only to two small areas on the coast of California. Around Monterey it occupies 2300 ha of undulating land just inland of the cliffs near Carmel and a narrow stretch of low hills and canyons north of Monterey to Santa Cruz. Further south there are scattered woods around Cambria. In the hills a few trees attain 27 m but throughout the woods the size limit set by the fatal onslaught of dwarf mistletoe is about 20 m × 50 cm. Introduced by Douglas in 1833 this tree revels in the more moist summers of western Britain. It is locally abundant, quite dominating the landscape in some small valleys or in gardens on the coast, in the southwest and common in most parts of the west north to Ayrshire and locally Argyll to Wester Ross and infrequent east to Kent (locally common as in Cranbrook-Hawkhurst districts) but almost rare from Surrey to the Midlands and East Anglia.

Pinus sylvestris
Scots pine

L

FEATURES: The Scots pine is a familiar tree everywhere, very easy to raise and establish. The short 5–8 cm needles are twisted and appear whitish-blue from the numerous close lines of pure white stomata on each surface. Female flowers, red, at the tips of strong shoots are borne by young trees after about six years and male flowers, whorled at the base of weak shoots seldom appear until the tree is about 20 years old.

MERITS: As an accommodating pine for a wide spectrum of soils and situations, the Scots pine ranks high. Early growth is rapid on any well-drained soil from the poorest sands and shallow peats to thin loam over chalk, and from sea-level to a considerable altitude, depending on local topography. The foliage is bluer than that of any other two-needle pine and a different shade from the blues in three- or five-needled pines. The bark of young trees is orange-red and flaky, variously fissured dark-grey. On old trees it may be craggy and almost black at the base or prettily divided into cinnamon or orange-coloured plates, but the main branches are in any case dark-red. Old trees can make imposing and picturesque rather rugged specimens, the red bark in the upper parts showing well from a distance. This tree makes attractive groves in suitable areas, if planted fairly closely and thinned regularly or planted more than 6 m apart and left to develop crowns from low branches, or alternatively pruned to give clean boles.

LIMITATIONS: In many parts, from the Hampshire, Surrey and Berkshire heaths to Northumberland or to the hills of east Devon, Scots pine proliferates without help. Young trees soon grow out of the pleasantly vigorous well-furnished stage and during their middle years they tend to be rather thin of crown and have little character. Good growth is not sustained on chalky soils or in industrial atmospheres.

ORIGIN AND OCCURRENCE: This tree has the widest range of any pine and is native from Spain to eastern Siberia, north to Scandinavia and Scotland and south to the Crimea and Asia Minor. Native Scottish stands are found from the Black Wood of Rannoch in north-eastern Perthshire to Ben Eighe in Wester Ross. It was introduced to north Hampshire and Surrey in about 1660 and to the New Forest in 1777. Until the large scale arrival of north-western American conifers of much faster growth, Scots pine with Norway spruce and European larch, was the standard tree of upland forestry on small and large estates. On southern heaths it was partially replaced by Corsican pine after about 1930 and now competing with that and the Monterey and Bishop pines, it will find little place in southern forestry but will probably remain the favoured tree in large areas of Northumberland, Morayshire and Nairnshire.

Pinus wallichiana
Bhutan pine

FEATURES: The Bhutan pine has its needles in fives, very slender, to 20 cm, and blue-white on the inner surfaces. They are retained only two or three years and when shed they expose the smooth shiny grey bark of young branches. The stout shoot is at first bloomed pale lilac, a ready distinction from the shorter-needled *Pinus strobus* with which it is often confused. Old trees, very heavily branched and usually dying back have attained 32–34 m in height and 1.2 m in diameter.

MERITS: Young trees are very vigorous and very handsome, with their long, pendent bluish grey-green needles. The best trees are 20 m tall in little over 20 years and may be 27 m in 40 years. Early production of cones, within 12 to 15 years of planting is an advantage as the large, long cones in twos or threes are an attractive feature on the tree and, dry and open, of interest when shed, lying beneath it. Any reasonably moist, deep mineral soil provided it is not alkaline gives good early growth in all parts of these islands. It is immune to Blister-rust.

LIMITATIONS: To be at all decorative this tree needs at least moderate shelter from strong winds, and a deep neutral or acid soil. It needs plenty of room, and should have no overhead shade whatever. It makes a broad, branchy tree with age and seldom survives much more than 100 years without becoming obviously senile, dropping branches and dying back extensively. At best it is a short-term tree.

ORIGIN AND OCCURRENCE: This tree is native to the western Himalayas and was introduced in 1823. It is frequent in large gardens and in collections but also, unexpectedly, in some town parks and gardens where it seldom thrives for long.

Podocarpus andinus
Plum-fruited yew

FEATURES: This unusual plant could well be used as more than just an occasional specimen. The bark is very smooth and nearly black. The flowers, male and female on separate trees, are borne on bright blue-green erect pedicels, the males being bright-yellow. Fruit are sporadic on the females, some plants bearing many pale apple-green fleshy ovoids.

MERITS: This plant, whether bushy or of tree form, has excellent foliage, dense and fresh green slender leaves marked with blue-grey bands beneath. It stands clipping well and makes a first class and exceedingly unusual hedge. It looks well as a background to a shrubbery or as a small tree amongst others.

LIMITATIONS: No specimens have been found north of North Wales so although this appears to be absolutely hardy in the south there is a strong indication that it does not flourish in the north. It can be relatively short-lived, many trees of about 80 years of age having died. It is not suitable as a single specimen tree unless the transplant is particularly well shaped, for mature trees vary from many stemmed bushes to tall narrow trees. Growth is never rapid.

ORIGIN AND OCCURRENCE: Introduced from southern Chile in 1860, the Plum-fruited yew is uncommon in the larger gardens of the south, the west and in Ireland.

Pseudotsuga menziesii
Douglas fir

FEATURES: The Douglas fir is a very common and rather variable tree. The bark varies in old trees from dull purple, shallowly fissured, through dark-grey with deep, corky, buff fissures to dark-brown, very corky with crevices and protuberances. The crown is narrowly conic while height is being made, which can, in very favourable conditions still occur when the tree is over 50 m tall, then becomes irregular and broad with heavy branching. The leaves are slender and soft and sweetly aromatic when crushed. The cones are small, 6–8 cm, cylindric or fusiform and have protruding three-pronged bracts. Many of the older specimen trees are 1.5–1.6 m in diameter and a few of the biggest are 2 m.

MERITS: The Douglas fir is a vigorous young tree on any reasonably good soil, making a good background planting or ultimately a very big specimen tree. At numerous localities from the New Forest to Inverness-shire but mainly in the west, it has grown more stands and individuals generally over 45 m tall than any other tree. It will rapidly attain imposing dimensions as a single specimen or as a grove, to 30 m in 40 years or less. The foliage becomes more dense as the tree ages and can be luxuriant, usually deep-green.

LIMITATIONS: For decorative growth this tree needs full light in a site sheltered from strong winds, and a deep mineral soil. In areas receiving less rain than about 800 mm it should be on a receiving site, and it will not thrive on alkaline soils. Old trees are unsuitable in much frequented places as they may drop big branches heavy with dense foliage. Young trees are better where the foliage is not brushed against by passers-by since they are frequently infested with *Adelges* which is sticky and woolly. In a frost hollow the leading shoot usually escapes damage by opening later but side-shoots are easily burned and result in a bushy-based tree. In anything more than moderate exposure the tops of tall trees shatter or die-back readily.

ORIGIN AND OCCURRENCE: This tree has an enormous range from northern British Columbia almost throughout the Rocky Mountains to Mexico. Across this range it is divided into three geographical forms, the typical form being the Coastal from Vancouver Island to northern California. In the rain-forest of the southern Olympic Peninsular there is a stand with most trees around 85–90 m tall and 2.5 m in diameter, clear of branches for 50–60 m. David Douglas sent the first seed from near Portland, Oregon in 1827 and all the plantings until about 1850 were derived from this seed or seedlings from the trees raised. The tree is very common in plantations in western and northern areas, also in large gardens everywhere and in some smaller gardens.

VARIETY: Var. *glauca* is the form growing in the eastern Rocky Mountains, through Montana to Colorado, Arizona and Mexico. It was not introduced until after 1875 from British Columbia. Of slower growth than the Coastal green form and in places liable to a needle-cast disease, this tree can be an attractive light blue-grey with long, upstanding leaves. The bark is at first smooth and light-grey, becoming dark leaden grey with some narrow fissures. It has attained 25 m and is usually of good shape.

L

Sequoia sempervirens
Coast redwood

FEATURES: The Coast redwood is rather a sombre tree but is enlivened by the red bark and is an interesting plant. The crown which starts as a slender cone becomes broadly columnar, acute at the apex until clearing local shelter then becoming flat-topped. This is one of the few conifers which will coppice even when very large trees are felled. In sheltered places or where the summers are cool and wet there are trees over 40 m tall and many are now around 2 m in diameter.

MERITS: Young trees with favourable local conditions, even where climatically unsuitable for a big specimen, make interesting upright plants of great vigour often growing 1.3 m a year. In the right regions, generally anywhere except the Midlands, East Anglia and the east coast, this makes a superb solitary specimen on the largest scale and no tree makes a better shady grove. At a final spacing of only about 6 m, preferably irregularly 5–8 m, they can grow into trees 35 m tall with rich deep-red clean boles. Young trees can grow in deeper shade than most trees but should have clear headroom fairly early as they will soon grow into the shading trees.

LIMITATIONS: A tree at home where sea-fogs shroud the crown nearly every day in the summer, the Coast redwood will make a good, tall specimen only where the summers are cool and the air moist. In the eastern and Midland counties or near towns the growth stagnates after 20–30 years and the foliage will be browned by cold winds. The soil should be slightly acid, deep and damp in a sheltered hollow preferably, as it is a poor tree on alkaline soils, and on dry or exposed sites.

ORIGIN AND OCCURRENCE: The natural range runs in a narrow belt 10 to 15 miles across but 550 miles long from just in Oregon to south of Lucia, California. In Del Norte and Humboldt counties in northern California this forms the tallest woods in the world where all the dominant trees are 90 m or more in height. The tallest tree

L

known is 112 m, seven miles from Orick along Redwood Creek. South of the Golden Gate, where it is much drier, the trees are smaller but 50 miles south there is a small area catching some sea-fog, Big Basin, with some trees nearly 100 m tall and 5 m in diameter. Early collectors came to California overland (San Francisco and the Bay were not discovered from the sea owing to the daily fogs) and although this species had been found by Portuguese missionaries and taken to Portugal in about 1770, and was seen by

Archibald Menzies in 1792, it was not brought by collectors until 1850. The first trees in Britain came from seed sent from Leningrad in 1843 as the Russians, with a colony at Fort Ross until 1840 had seed, and were growing trees in the Crimea. Several of these first trees survive but the tree became common in big gardens and policies only after 1855. It is now quite frequent in some churchyards and larger town gardens and parks but the big trees are in collections and big estates.

*Sequoiadendron
giganteum*
Sierra redwood,
Giant sequoia,
Wellingtonia

FEATURES: The Sierra redwood is well-known as the Wellingtonia, but that name is used only in Britain. A large proportion of the trees have narrowly conic crowns but there is some variation; a few are broad with big twisting branches and the rare tree is forked. The bole tapers hugely for the first 1–2 m and above this there is a greatly decreased tapering in most trees but some are almost cylindric. The foliage is hard cords of scale leaves with points curving out then forwards and may be deep-green or pale blue-grey. Height growth in young trees after a slow start can attain 1 m a year but not more and over a period an average of 60 m a year is quite good. Growth of the bole is always rapid and may be at a rate equalled only by one *Metasequoia* (see p. 122). Almost every tree 100 years old is 2 m in diameter (an average increase in girth of 6 cm a

L

year) and a few are 2.6 m in less than 120 years. Among younger trees one cutting planted 23 years has a bole 68 cm in diameter and one seedling 55 years old is 158 cm through (at 1.5 m).

MERITS: Within 100 years of its introduction the Sierra redwood became probably the largest tree in every county from Cornwall to Caithness. This is a mark of both its adaptability and its enormous powers of growth. Any mineral soil (but not peat) except chalk, if not too poorly drained, suits it well. It never blows down and is exceptionally healthy and long-lived. Honey fungus (*Armillaria mellea*) causes a few deaths. As a tree for a single specimen of the largest size it is rivalled only by the Cedar of Lebanon, and as a tree for close groves to make imposing boles it is unequalled except by the Coast redwood. This species seems never to be damaged by frost.

LIMITATIONS: This extraordinarily adaptable tree will grow almost anywhere, but on chalk or thin soils in dry, exposed areas, it remains thin and small. Anywhere it is worth growing it will need plenty of space as it will soon become a huge tree and it is miserable and thin in any but the very lightest shade. Tall trees are constantly at hazard from lightning in the south although seldom suffering more than dieback at the tip. It is susceptible to smoky air and useless in cities although it is one of the very best trees for chemical smogs and is planted for this reason in the hills behind Los Angeles.

ORIGIN AND OCCURRENCE: Confined after the Ice Ages to small groves scattered along the western flanks of the southern part of the Sierra Nevada, in California this species was discovered in 1851. Some of the trees are nearly 3500 years old and 7 m in diameter. There have been trees 90 m tall and several are now 75–80 m. There were two introductions in 1853 both in quantity, and numerous trees, avenues and groups survive in all parts of Britain from these imports. The tree is found on all big estates, in large gardens, in many churchyards and town parks and can be seen in almost any lowland landscape, towering above surrounding trees. In Scotland several are now 50 m tall.

Taxodium distichum
Swamp cypress

L

FEATURES: The Swamp cypress is a tree of considerable character. The unique pneumatophores ('knees') often arise in waterside or swamp plantings and occasionally on normal soils. The leaves are alternately set on shoots also alternate, 80–100 on each, 10 × 2 mm and thin. The shoots, about 10 cm long are shed with the leaves. Male catkins are frequent on large trees, prominent at the tips of shoots in the winter, expanding to shed pollen in April. Cones are less commonly seen, globular, 3 cm across on a short stalk. Old trees are often 25 m tall but only on good, damp and sheltered sites do they much exceed 30 m and sometimes reach 35 m.

MERITS: Apart from the well-known ability to grow splendidly in swampy, ill-drained or often flooded land this is a useful tree to add a light, feathery, bright fresh green foliage to a scene. No tree is better for prolonging the season of autumn colour, many Swamp cypresses being in full rusty-orange foliage well into December. A tree of but moderate vigour, seldom making a shoot more than 50 cm long, this is nonetheless capable of becoming a very large specimen and is completely free of diseases, whilst it has recently been said (*The Trees Around Us,* Phillips and Barber) 'that no dying nor dead tree has been seen here'. Although exceedingly rarely seen as a

group this is a first class tree to make a grove, and the lack of such use makes it more desirable and offsets the somewhat hackneyed, but still worthwhile plantings beside water or on islands. It is an excellent tree in cities and towns.

LIMITATIONS: This species grows so slowly and poorly in the cool summers of the north that no worthwhile tree is found much north of the Midlands, where there are many, except one or two in Perthshire and Wigtownshire. A dry, sandy soil is obviously unsuitable although ordinarily well-drained soils give good results, and exposure is limiting. Crown form is variable and some confused and untidy specimens make a poor showing when bare in the winter. The season in leaf is somewhat short despite the tree not shedding foliage until late November or December, for it is hardly noticeably in leaf until mid-June.

ORIGIN AND OCCURRENCE: This tree is extremely numerous along the coastal flats, inlets and bayous from Delaware, especially in Virginia, through South Carolina and Georgia and beside the Mississippi and on its flood-plain north to near St. Louis. It also ranges down the Gulf Coast west of New Orleans into Mexico. It was introduced in 1640. Two trees may date from that time and still survive (it is very long-lived) but few were planted until after 1750. It is common in parks and gardens in the southern half of England, scarce elsewhere. Many good trees are in London suburbs and parks.

Taxus baccata
Yew

FEATURES: Yews are either male or female trees and flower early in February. Growth is steady but slow, scarcely exceeding 25 cm a year, and culminates early, often at 10–12 m although in sheltered hollows, churchyards or in woods some grow to 18–20 m and even to 27 m. In diameter, growth can be that of a normal, slow tree, about 0.8 cm a year for about 100 years but by then, or sometimes much before, it declines to 0.5 cm for a long period and then declines gradually further to less than 1 mm a year. Trees with boles measurable by tape at 1.5 m are not common among the old open-grown churchyard trees but there are a number and many of these are over 2.5 m in diameter and must be in the region of 1500 years old while some bigger boles may be nearer 3000 years old.

MERITS: The yew is the toughest, most indestructible and longest lived tree we have. It will grow on any soil except acid peats or ill-drained areas and thrives on chalk and limestone. It withstands any frosts, great exposure and, although not unaffected by it, industrial pollution of moderate intensity. It makes the classic hedge for topiary and for backing a herbaceous border or framing a prospect or statue. Female trees are pleasantly sprinkled with bright red berries in autumn although birds may soon eat them. It is good cover for birds and background to decorative plantings. This is valuable for shrubs which flower early with pink or white flowers which need a dark background to be seen well. The yew withstands much shade and can grow quite tall in deciduous woods. It also withstands any degree of cutting back, shaping or clipping.

LIMITATIONS: Unless a dark, mysterious, unexplored area is deliberately planned to contrast with wide sunny prospects, to reveal sudden statuary or to enhance the setting of a cave, folly or temple, the planting of yews must be done with a great restraint. They spread widely and often more rapidly than they increase in height, casting a deep shade under which no plant can grow except ivy trailing in from outside. The time scale needed for a specimen to show a large, handsome bole is somewhat beyond that acceptable in most designs as it will be of little real note in the first 300 years.

ORIGIN AND OCCURRENCE: This yew is native to all of the British Isles and much of Europe and northern Asia. It is found more or less wild and in pure woods in a few combes in the southern chalklands, and scattered through old oak and beechwoods. It is a common roadside tree in chalk areas and is in almost every churchyard in the land. The massive and ancient churchyard yews show a distinct zoning being very common from Kent to Devon, north through Somerset, Wiltshire, Gloucestershire, Herefordshire, Gwent, Powys, and again in Clwyd whilst there are occasional outliers like the two in Middlesex and one in Derbyshire. In Scotland they are smaller and are concentrated in the Lothians and Perthshire.

CULTIVARS: An excellent form '**Adpressa**' arose in Chester nurseries in 1838. A female; it makes a neat but very broad, domed tree to 10 m distinct in rather pendulous small shoots lined with tiny elliptic leaves. A golden form is smaller and an exceptionally desirable plant.

'**Fastigiata**', the Irish yew, is a sombre, slow plant, growing in the far west of England and

Scotland to 16 m tall, more squat and broader in the east, and universal in churchyards. In garden design it is used in formal gardens, often clipped or shaped but its best use seems to be that in Cornish gardens where it may have been purposely planted as a dark, upright foil to the rounded humps of brilliant flowering rhododendrons. A female plant, this was found on a hillside in County Fermanagh, Northern Ireland in 1780.

'**Dovastoniana**' is a strange form of great character, spreading widely. The central stem bears level branches which extend by long arched shoots every year, and are hung with

'DOVASTONIANA'

curtains of dark foliage. It was bought from a peddler at the door by a Mr. Dovaston in West Felton, Shropshire in 1777, and is now 17 × 1·18 m. Grafts from this are occasional in parks and gardens.

Thuja occidentalis
White cedar

FEATURES: The type tree is rarely worth growing, but the two cultivars given are splendid trees.

MERITS: A young tree is often a shapely ovoid of a pleasing light-green, bearing its sprays of foliage in slightly twisted vertical planes. In areas of bad drainage and periodic flooding this will grow as well as anywhere. Some older trees bear cones in great abundance which, being yellow in the summer, turn the tree into a golden one. One tree is 20 m × 70 cm but few achieve 15 m × 40 cm.

LIMITATIONS: Slow growth, a short life and a sad, drooping appearance with age limit the uses to sites too wet to grow most other conifers.

ORIGIN AND OCCURRENCE: This tree grows in cold, wet areas in eastern Canada and the north-eastern USA. There is some evidence that it was introduced as early as 1536, the first conifer from America. It would still be the first if the later and better attested date of 1596 be accepted. It is fairly common in gardens, often as a hedge but usually a small undistinguished tree, probably acquired in error for *Thuja plicata* (q.v.).

CULTIVARS: As a robust and handsome tree '**Lutea**' is much superior to the type. The new shoots are bright golden-yellow, greening considerably by the second year.

'**Spiralis**' is a highly desirable, neat and pretty tree of such narrow form that it can be grown almost anywhere. It has attractive fronds of

foliage, bright-green in short, dense flattened sprays held spirally on erect shoots and makes a slender, pointed column growing at little more than 25 cm a year.

Thuja orientalis
Chinese thuja

S

FEATURES: A slow growing plant, the Chinese thuja is sometimes seen as a gaunt tree with upswept branches bare towards their bases and the foliage held in vertical plates. It is mostly a tree of provincial towns in the Midlands and is scarce in other parts. It apparently requires hotter summers than can be experienced here to grow well, and the type tree is not recommended.

CULTIVAR: 'Elegantissima' is seen as a highly attractive ovoid tree to 10 m tall in gardens between mid-Wales and Kent and is tolerant of a wide range of conditions. In early life it is highly suitable as a courtyard or patio tree, able to grow in a tub or in a gap in pavings. In spring it is tipped bright-yellow and this pales variously in different specimens or is slightly bronzed in winter.

ORIGIN AND OCCURRENCE: The type tree was sent from northern China in 1752 and is seen as a tree of poor shape in town gardens and parks, but rarely in collections, in southern England. 'Elegantissima' was selected in 1860 and is in collections and in some cottage gardens also in southern England.

Thuja plicata
Western red cedar

FEATURES: This tree is generally of conic, moderately dense crown, shining green of a brighter shade than in most of the cypress group, and has purple-brown bark which peels in strips. It is of rapid growth in cool humid regions where young trees may grow 1 m a year but become slow above 30 m in height and it has rarely attained more than 37 m.

MERITS: The bright, highly fragrant foliage is less oppressive when used as a screen or background than is the darker green of some other trees. Young trees growing fast have an open, rather elegant, appearance and soon make fine specimens. This red cedar will grow well on most soils which do not dry too rapidly, even on chalk if there is a thin clay layer on the surface, and on clays too heavy for most conifers. It will thrive for many years in any part of the country although it will make a big first class specimen only in the north and west or only on particularly favourable sites elsewhere. It will survive some aerial pollution but will not make a good tree in big towns. It can grow rather slowly in considerable shade.

LIMITATIONS: On soils which dry rapidly and in highly exposed areas the red cedar is not a good tree. Unless well suited to the site the tree is thin in the crown and very uninteresting visually.

ORIGIN AND OCCURRENCE: The Western red cedar grows from south-west Alaska southwards to North California and inland to Idaho. It was introduced in 1854 and is everywhere common, as a hedge, shelter-tree, specimen tree or as a forest crop.

CULTIVARS: The Golden-barred thuja, 'Zebrina' has been planted since soon after 1900 and is in

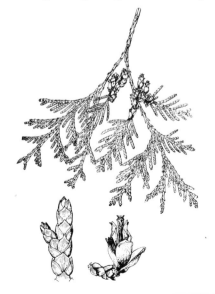

L

M

'ZEBRINA'

many gardens, major and very minor. It is a splendid tree of generally golden appearance, a broad, regularly conic crown and steady growth. In towns it seems more healthy and well furnished than the type tree. The plants vary in the intensity of the yellow colour and the proportion of this colour in the bands across the sprays of foliage. A few 'Zebrina' are more than 20 m tall and it seems probable that the tree is capable of growing to well over 30 m tall.

'Semperaurescens' is a narrow, shapely form more like the type in growth and form but greenish-yellow varying with the season. It is an unusual colour and is very rare.

Thujopsis dolabrata
Hiba

FEATURES: This tree occurs in two distinct forms. One has relatively light foliage and is multistemmed, often 10 or 20 subequal slender stems forming a broad conic bush. The other form has heavy, pendulous foliage and a few stout, upcurving branches from a single bole. This second form is much the less usual and is mainly seen in Cornwall, Devon and Dorset.

MERITS: The best feature of the Hiba is the bright, glossy green foliage of large hard flat scale-leaves. The underside of this foliage is boldly marked in bright white. In the tree-form the bark is bright orange-brown or rufous and stringy. Growth is everywhere slow and the plant can be safely regarded as a large shrub and a good background. It is hardy everywhere and will grow on any normal soil which is neither too chalky nor too peaty. It is a pleasant, almost pretty but not a striking nor exciting tree.

LIMITATIONS: The Hiba will be slow to make a worthwhile single specimen tree. The best growth is in damp soils in sheltered hollows in the far west or southwest, and there the tree-form will grow to 20 m in rather over 100 years. It is unsuited to exposed sites or to thin soils which dry out rapidly. The life-span is now seen to be very limited and many of the once fine trees have died, even in Dorset where they grew well.

ORIGIN AND OCCURRENCE: The Hiba is confined as a native to Japan. The first plants were brought to England in 1853 and the first seed followed in 1861. It is quite common in the larger gardens everywhere but particularly in the west and near the coast.

Tsuga canadensis
Eastern hemlock

M

FEATURES: The Eastern hemlock makes a broad-crowned, irregularly shaped tree in this country, usually on a short bole and with low, heavy branches. In its native range especially in North Carolina and Tennessee it is a slender spire with light branching. The foliage differs from all other hemlocks in there being a line of leaves twisted to lie underside uppermost along the line of the shoot. The white bands on the underside make a small-scale pattern in a spray of foliage.

MERITS: The main use of the Eastern hemlock in decorative planting is as a tough and tolerant background or shelter plant of moderate size. The foliage is pleasant and the tree withstands a fair degree of exposure.

LIMITATIONS: This tree can be required as a specimen tree only where the Western hemlock is unsuited, for the Eastern is a poor tree by comparison. It can be spreading, requiring much room and it casts a dense shade.

ORIGIN AND OCCURRENCE: The natural range is from eastern Canada and the Lake States to the southern end of the Allegheny Mountains in North Alabama. Introduced in 1736 this was the only hemlock known for the next 120 years so it was planted quite widely, but with the greatly superior Western hemlock available after 1860 it fell from favour. Old trees are in many big, old established gardens. Younger trees are infrequent but may be seen in roadside gardens in semi-rural areas.

Tsuga caroliniana
Carolina hemlock

FEATURES: A small tree, tending to have a bushy crown but usually only a single bole, the Carolina hemlock is notable in gardens in eastern States for its dense, rich, shiny, green foliage. In Britain the foliage has to be distinguished from the even more dense Western hemlock and in comparison it is brighter, but more noticeably, the leaves are slender and have a spiky appearance.

MERITS: This little tree is a very good foliage plant and the foliage is a change from and brighter than that of the Western hemlock. It seems to thrive in any sheltered site and normal soil.

LIMITATIONS: A small tree of rather slow growth at best, any other limitations are not yet apparent.

ORIGIN AND OCCURRENCE: The Carolina hemlock is found scattered amongst Eastern hemlock, Red maple, many oak and hickory species in high rocky valleys in the Allegheny Mountains from south-west Virginia to north-east Tennessee. It was introduced in 1886 and is rare here, seen only in a few collections.

Tsuga heterophylla
Western hemlock

L

FEATURES: The Western hemlock is an elegant, shapely tree at all times, growing a slender conic crown with a spire-like apex tipped by a long drooping leading shoot and with ascending regular branches from which hang dense masses of small foliage. The hanging branchlets are often crowded with small, 3 cm ovoid cones which have matured from little rich plum-purple female flowers.

MERITS: The Western hemlock is among the few really first class conifers for single specimen trees of great stature combined with character. It will grow on suitable sites with great vigour, often making shoots of 1.3 m in a year and is an attractive tree whilst doing so. It makes this vigorous growth on a surprisingly wide range of soils from apparently dry, very acid open sands to relatively heavy clays and in moderate shade like that beneath well-thinned larch or oak. It is a very healthy tree and can evidently have a long life as most of the oldest trees, now 110 years old are still growing strongly. Individual trees withstand high winds remarkably well and make exceedingly shapely narrowly conic specimens. The Western hemlock can be clipped closely to make a dense very attractive and serviceable hedge.

LIMITATIONS: Near cities or industrial complexes, or on exposed high, dry ridges the Western hemlock is unable to thrive. Trees failing for these reasons are thin and unsightly. The shade cast by healthy trees is too heavy for anything to grow beneath them. Neutral or acid soils are much preferred and on chalk growth may be checked after a rapid start.

ORIGIN AND OCCURRENCE: The Western hemlock is found at low and moderate elevations from south-west Alaska along the coast of British Columbia, Washington, Oregon and northern California and inland in southern British Columbia and Washington. Occasionally trees to 70 m tall are found. It was introduced in 1851 but the oldest trees now known in Britain were planted from 1861 onwards. It is a common tree in big gardens, policies and in plantations in the north and west but less common near the east coast of England and in East Anglia. It is much used in forestry for underplanting and eventually replacing inferior oak and larch woods. In Scotland several are now 50 m tall.

Tsuga mertensiana
Mountain hemlock

FEATURES: The Mountain hemlock is an eccentric hemlock in foliage and in cones. It is the only one with the leaves uniformly coloured on all sides and not flattened with an upper surface differing from the lower, and with the leaves radiating from the shoot equally in all directions. The cone is more like that of a spruce than a hemlock and is cylindric and 7 cm long.

MERITS: The Mountain hemlock makes a very distinct tree with a long, slender conic crown, often tapering into a fine spire, small branches and hanging masses of grey blue-grey foliage. It is exceedingly hardy and although the best trees are in central and northern Scotland it makes a good tree in all parts of the country in the right conditions. It takes up little space and is an attractive tree usually of moderate growth.

LIMITATIONS: This hemlock becomes too thin in the foliage to be attractive in dry and exposed sites. It requires a good damp loam or sand in areas with warm summers but is less demanding in cool, humid areas. It is quite unsuited to the vicinity of towns. It can be slow to grow in height and even on the most favourable sites growth rate increases slowly for many years but after 30 or 40 years it can be reasonably rapid.

ORIGIN AND OCCURRENCE: The Mountain hemlock is native from south-west Alaska at low altitudes and southwards at increasing altitudes to the Olympic Mountains of Washington at 2300 m and along the Cascades at similar heights in Oregon and at increasing altitude along the Sierra Nevada in California to 3000 m altitude. It was introduced in 1854. The best trees are now 110 years old in Perthshire and exceed 30 m in height, and are still growing well. It is occasionally seen in roadside gardens in semi-rural areas like parts of south-west Surrey.

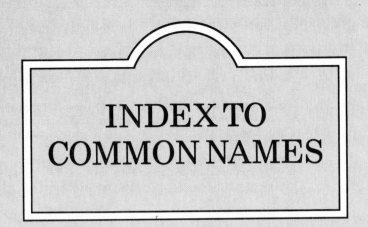

INDEX TO
COMMON NAMES

A

Acacia
  False 86
Alder
  'Aurea' 34
  Caucasian 34
  Common 33
  Grey 34
  Italian 33
  Oregon 34
  'Pendula' 34
  'Ramulis-Coccineis' 34
  Red 34
Almond 73
Apple
  'Golden Hornet' 61
  'John Downie' 60
  Pillar 60
Ash
  Caucasian 50
  Common 49
  'Diversifolia' 49
  Flowering 50
  'Jaspidea' 49
  Manna 50
  Narrow-leaved 49
  'Raywood' 50
  White 49

B

Bay 55
Bean Tree
  'Aurea' 41
  Indian 41
Beech 47
  'Asplenifolia' 48
  'Dawyck' 48
  Dombey's Southern 61
  'Pendula' 48
  'Purpurea' 48
  Rauli 63
  Roble 61
  'Zlatia' 48
Birch
  Black 36
  Canoe 36
  'Dalecarlica' 37
  Downy 37
  Himalayan 38
  Jacquemont's 34
  Maximowicz's 36
  Monarch 36
  Paper-bark 36
  River 36
  Silver 37
  Yellow 35
  'Youngii' 37

Bitter-nut 39
Box 38
Buck-eye
  Yellow 31
  Bull Bay 58

C

Catalpa
  Hybrid 41
Cedar
  Atlas 108
  Deodar 109
  'Elegans' 114
  'Glauca' 116
  Japanese Red 114
  'Lobbii' 114
  'Lutea' 138
  of Goa 116
  of Lebanon 109
  'Semperaurescens' 140
  'Spiralis' 138
  Western Red 139
  White 138
  'Zebrina' 139
Cherry
  'Accolade' 74
  'Amanogawa' 75
  'Autumnalis' 77
  Bird 73
  'Colorata' 73
  'Fugenzo' 76
  'Hokusai' 76
  'Horinji' 76
  Japanese 75
  'Kanzan' 76
  'Kiku-shidare' 76
  'Kursar' 74
  'Longipes' 76
  Manchurian 73
  'Okiku' 76
  'Pandora' 78
  'Pendula' 77
  'Pink Perfection' 76
  'Plena' 73
  Sargent 74
  'Shimidsu' 76
  'Shirofugen' 76
  'Shirotae' 76
  'Shosar' 74
  'Tai-haku' 77
  Tibetan 74
  'Ukon' 77
  'Watereri' 74
  Weeping rosebud 77
  Winter-flowering 77
  Wild 72
  Yoshino 78

Chestnut
  'Baumannii' 31
  'Briotii' 31
  Common 31
  Horse 30–32
  Indian 32
  Japanese 32
  Red 30
  Sweet 40
  'Sydney Pearce 32
Crab
  'Aldenhamensis' 60
  'Eleyi' 60
  Hupeh 60
  Japanese 59
  'Lemoinei' 60
  'Profusion' 60
  Purple hybrids 59
Cypress
  'Allumii'' 110
  'Aurea' 114
  Bhutan 118
  'Castlewellan Gold' 116
  'Columnaris' 110
  'Crippsii' 113
  'Donard Gold' 117
  'Ellwoodii' 110
  'Filifera Aurea' 114
  'Fletcheri' 110
  'Green Pillar' 110
  'Green Spire' 110
  'Haggerston Grey' 115
  Himalayan 118
  Hinoki 112
  Lawson 109
  'Leighton Green' 115
  Leyland 115
  'Lutea' 110, 117
  Monterey 117
  'Naylor's Blue' 115
  Nootka 112
  'Plumosa' 114
  'Plumosa Aurea' 114
  'Pottenii' 111
  'Pyramidalis' 116
  'Robinson's Gold' 116
  Sawara 114
  Smooth Arizona 116
  'Squarrosa' 114
  'Stapehill 21' 116
  'Stewartii' 111
  Swamp 136
  'Triomphe de Boskoop' 111
  'Wisselii' 111

D

Dawn Redwood 122
Deodar 109
Dove-tree 45

E

Elm
  Camperdown 98
  Caucasian 99
  Chinese 99
  Cornish 97
  Golden Wych 98
  Huntingdon 98
  Jersey 97
  'Lutescens' 98
  Mountain 98
  Siberian 99
  Smooth-leaved 96
  'Vegeta' 98
  Wheatley 97
  Wych 98
Euodia 46

F

False Acacia 86
Fir
  Algerian 105
  Caucasian 104
  Douglas 134
  Grand 103
  Grecian 102
  Low's 103
  Nikko 104
  Noble 105
  Santa Lucia 102
  Silver 102
  Veitch's Silver 106
  'Violacea' 103
  White 103
Foxglove Tree 64

G

Gean 72
Golden Rain Tree 54
Gum
  Cider 46
  Shining 46
  Snow 46

H

Hawthorn 44
Hazel
  Turkish 43
Heaven, Tree of 33
Hemlock
  Carolina 141
  Eastern 141
  Mountain 142
  Western 142

Hiba 141
Hickory
  Shagbark 40
Holly
  'Bacciflava' 53
  'Camellifolia' 52
  Common 52
  'Ferox' 53
  'Golden King' 52
  'Handsworth New Silver' 53
  'Hendersonii' 52
  Highclere 52
  'Hodginsii' 52
  'Perry's Weeping' 53
Honey-locust 50
  'Inermis' 50
  'Sunburst' 50
Hornbeam 38
  'Fastigiata' 39
Horse-chestnut
  'Baumannii' 31
  'Briotii' 31
  Common 31
  Indian 32
  Japanese 32
  Red 30
  'Sydney Pearce' 32

J

Judas Tree 43
Juniper
  Syrian 120

K

Katsura Tree 42
Keaki 100

L

Larch
  European 120
  Hybrid 121
  Japanese 121
Laurel
  Poets' 55
Lime
  Broadleaf 95
  Caucasian 93
  Mongolian 94
  Red-twigged 95
  'Rubra' 95
  Silver 96
  Silver pendent 94
  Small-leaved 93
Locust Tree 86
  'Frisia' 87

M

Magnolia
  Bull Bay 58
  Campbell's 57
  'Charles Raffill' 57
  'Diva' 59
  'Exmouth' 58
  'Goliath' 58
  Southern 58
  Yulan Lily 58
  Willow-leaved 58
Maidenhair Tree 118
  'Fastigiata' 118
Maple
  'Auratum' 26
  'Drummondii' 27
  Field 24
  'George Forrest' 25
  Hers's 25
  'Laciniatum' 29
  Lobel's 25
  Nikko 27
  Norway 27
  Oregon 26
  Père David's 25
  Red 29
  'Schwedleri' 27
  Silver 29
  Sugar 30
  Van Volxem's 30
  Variegated ash-leafed 26
  'Variegatum' 26
Mazzard 72
Mimosa 24
Mockernut 40
Monkey-puzzle 106

O

Oak
  Caucasian 83
  Chestnut-leaved 80
  Common 84
  'Concordia' 85
  Cypress 85
  Durmast 83
  English 84
  Exeter 82
  'Fastigiata' 85
  Golden 85
  Holm 82
  Hungarian 81
  Japanese Chestnut 79
  Lucombe 82
  Mirbeck's 80
  Pin 83
  Red 86
  Sawtooth 79
  Scarlet 81

Oak *continued*
  Sessile 83
  'Splendens' 81
  Turkey 81
  Willow 84

P

Pear
  Bradford 79
  'Chanticleer' 79
  Willow-leafed 79
Pine
  Arolla 127
  Austrian 129
  Beach 127
  Bhutan 133
  Bishop 128
  Bosnian 128
  Chile 106
  Corsican 129
  Insignis 132
  Jeffrey's 127
  Macedonian 129
  Maritime 130
  Mexican White 126
  Monterey 132
  Scots 132
  Shore 127
  Swiss Stone 127
  Western Yellow 130
Plane
  London 65
  Oriental 67
  'Suttneri' 67
Poplar
  'Aurora' 68
  'Balsam Spire' 72
  Black 70
  Black Cottonwood 72
  'Eugenei' 69
  'Fritzi Pauley' 72
  'Gigantea' 71
  Grey 68
  Hybrid balsam 72
  'Italica' 71
  'Italica Foemina' 71
  Lombardy 71
  Manchester 70
  'Plantierensis' 71
  'Richardii' 68
  'Robusta' 69
  'Scott Pauley' 72
  'Serotina' 69
  'Serotina Aurea' 70
  'TT 32' 72
  'Vereecken' 71
  Western balsam 72
  White 67

Privet
  Chinese 55

R

Rauli 63
Redwood
  Coast 134
  Dawn 122
  Sierra 135
Robinia 86
  'Frisia' 87
Roble Beech 61
Rowan 90
  'Beissneri' 90
  Cashmere 90
  Chinese Scarlet 91
  'Embley' 91
  Hupeh 92
  'Joseph Rock' 92
  Sargent 92
  'Xanthocarpa' 90

S

Sallow 88
Sequoia
  Giant 135
Southern Beech
  Dombey's 61
Spruce
  'Argentea' 126
  'Aurea' 125
  Blue Colorado 125
  Brewer 123
  Caucasian 125
  'Hoopsii' 126
  'Koster' 126
  'Kosteriana' 126
  'Moerheim' 126
  Norway 122
  Serbian 124
  Sitka 126
Sweet-gum 55
  Chinese 55
Sycamore 28
  'Worleei' 28

T

Thorn
  Broad-leaved Cockspur 44
  Carrière's 44
  Cockspur 43
  Grignon 44
  Hybrid Cockspur 44
  Midland 44
  'Paul's Scarlet' 44
Thuja
  Chinese 139
  'Elegantissima' 139

Thuja *continued*
  Golden-barred 139
  'Lutea' 138
  'Semperaurescens' 140
  'Spiralis' 138
  'Zebrina' 139
Tree of Heaven 33
True Service Tree 91
Tulip Tree 56
  'Aureomarginatum' 57
  Chinese 56
  'Fastigiatum' 57
Tupelo 64

W

Walnut
  Black 54
  Common 54
Wellingtonia 135
Whitebeam 89
  'Chrysophylla' 90
  'Decaisneana' 90
  Himalayan 91
  'John Mitchell' 91
  'Lutescens' 90
  'Majestica' 90
  Swedish 92
  'Wilfrid Fox' 93
Wild Service Tree 93
Willow
  Bay 89
  'Chermesina' 87
  'Coerulea' 87
  Coral-bark 87
  Corkscrew 88
  Crack 88
  Cricket-bat 87
  Pussy 88
  'Tortuosa' 88
  'Tristis' 87
  Violet 88
  Weeping 87
  White 87
Wing-nut
  Caucasian 78
  Hybrid 78

Y

Yew
  'Adpressa' 137
  Common 137
  'Dovastoniana' 138
  'Fastigiata' 138
  Plum-fruited 133
Yulan Lily 58

Z

Zelkova
  Caucasian 99
  Chinese 100